UNIVERSITY OF WALES ✔ KU-730-791
PRIFYSGOL CYMRU ABERTAWE
LIBRARY/LLYFRGELL

Classmark HQ 1599 WI 09 1994

Location Miners' Library

1004329694

..med-
..orarian,

OUR SISTERS' LAND

The Changing Identities of
Women in Wales

Edited by

JANE AARON, TERESA REES,
SANDRA BETTS and MOIRA VINCENTELLI

CARDIFF
UNIVERSITY OF WALES PRESS
1994

© The Contributors, 1994

All rights reserved. No part of this book may be reproduced, stored in a retrieval system, or transmitted, in any form or by any means, electronic, mechanical, photocopying, recording or otherwise, without clearance from the University of Wales Press, 6 Gwennyth Street, Cardiff CF2 4YD.

British Library Cataloguing-in-Publication Data

A catalogue record for this book is available from the British Library

ISBN 0-7083-1247-0

Published with the financial support of the Arts Council of Wales

Printed in Wales by Dinefwr Press, Llandybïe, Dyfed

LIBRARY
SWANSEA

CONTENTS

PART ONE

ILLUSTRATIONS

A section of photographs by Mary Giles will be found between pages 180 and 181.

TABLES AND FIGURES

Tables

Figures

EDITORS AND CONTRIBUTORS

JANE AARON is a senior lecturer in English at the University College of Wales, Aberystwyth, where she teaches courses on Welsh writing in English, women's writing and critical theory. She is the author of *A Double Singleness: Gender and the Writings of Charles and Mary Lamb* (Clarendon Press 1991), and co-editor of the volume *Out of the Margins: Women's Studies in the 1990s* (Falmer Press 1991). She is currently working on a Welsh-language book on nineteenth-century Welsh women's writing.

SHAN ASHTON is a bilingual lecturer (Welsh/English) in Sociology at University College of North Wales, Bangor. Her teaching areas include women, family and economy; feminist theory; women's studies and rural sociology. She has research interests in rural sociology and women, work and the family. She is also a Ph.D. candidate researching the internal relations of farm households.

SANDRA BETTS is a lecturer in Sociology at the University College of North Wales, Bangor. She has research interests in the sociology of childhood, and gender and society. She is currently undertaking research on social interaction in the multi-cultural classroom.

NICKIE CHARLES is a lecturer in Sociology at University College Swansea. She is author of *Gender Divisions and Social Change* (Harvester, 1993) and co-author of *Women, Food and Families* (Manchester University Press, 1988). She is currently researching gender issues in social policy development.

GILLIAN CLARKE's published poetry collections include *Snow on the Mountain* (Christopher Davies, 1971), The Sundial (Gomer Press, 1978), *Letter from a Far Country* (Carcanet, 1982), *Selected Poems* (Carcanet, 1985) *Letting in the Rumour* (Carcanet, 1989) and *The King of Britain's Daughter* (Carcanet, 1993). The last two won Poetry Book Society Recommendations. She has been a broadcaster, freelance writer and lecturer on creative writing since the 1960s, and was editor of the *Anglo-Welsh Review* from 1974 to 1984.

RONI CRWYDREN spent her childhood years in Pembrokeshire, first on a smallholding in the Gwaun Valley, then at Porthgain between Fishguard and St David's. After working in England and travelling to Australia and through South East Asia, she returned home to Wales where, amongst other activities, she set up and ran a whole-food shop.

PATRICIA DANIEL has taught in schools and colleges in various parts of the world, including Nicaragua. Most recently she taught on the postgraduate Certificate of Education course at University College of North Wales, Bangor where she worked on equal opportunities projects. She has contributed to national conferences on teacher education and gender issues.

CHARLOTTE AULL DAVIES is a lecturer in the Department of Sociology and Anthropology at University College of Swansea, and is the author of *Welsh Nationalism in the Twentieth Century* (Praegar, 1989).

MENNA ELFYN's volumes of poetry include *Mwyara* (Gwasg Gomer, 1976), *Stafelloedd Aros* (Gwasg Gomer, 1977) which won the Arts Council Prize at the National Eisteddfod for the best verse collections; *Tro'r Haul Arno* (Gwasg Gomer, 1982) *Mynd Lawr i'r Nefoedd* (Gwasg Gomer, 1986); and an edition of her selected poems *Aderyn Bach Mewn Llaw* (Gwasg Gomer, 1990). She has also edited two collections of contemporary Welsh-language women's poetry, *Hel Dail Gwyrdd* (Gwasg Gomer, 1985) and *O'r Iawn Ryw* (Honno, 1992). Her play on the life of Simone Weil, commissioned by the television company Dalier Sylw, toured Wales in 1992.

PAM GARLAND was a mature student when she did her first degree in sociology and social policy. Her intellectual interest in women's issues was further developed through voluntary involvement in women's support groups and through her work with social services. She is currently a lecturer in Women's Studies and a Ph.D. candidate at University College of North Wales, Bangor. Her research interests include women and deviance and women and ageing.

DELYTH GEORGE has recently given up her editorial post at Cyngor

Llyfrau Cymraeg, the Welsh Books Council, and established herself as a freelance writer, editor and translator. Her Welsh-language publications include a book on the Welsh novelist Islwyn Ffowc Elis in the *Llên y Llenor* series, and articles on contemporary women's fiction and on feminist critiques of male writers.

MARY GILES is a freelance documentary photographer particularly interested in women's issues and the representation of women. She works with Argraff, a design and photography co-operative based in Cardiff.

MARY LLOYD JONES was brought up in a rural Welsh community and trained in Fine Art in Cardiff. She has worked as teacher and resident artist in schools and colleges, and between 1985 and 1989 was the Visual Arts Development Officer for Dyfed, but she now pursues her art full-time. For many years she used textiles as her medium, but now identifies herself as a painter in oils and water-colour. She has exhibited regularly since 1966, in Wales, Britain and abroad.

ENID MORGAN is Director of Mission for the Church in Wales, and was at the time of writing cleric-in-charge of four rural parishes in the Aberystwyth area: she was one of the first women to be ordained deacon. The editor of *Y Llan* for seven years, her recent Welsh-language publications include articles on feminist theology.

ELIZABETH J. MUIR is the founder and managing director of the European marketing and training consultancy, the Alternative Marketing Department Limited, with offices in Cardiff and Athens. She is a board member of a number of public authorities and consultant to the European Commission. Having completed an M.Sc. Econ. in Women's Studies at the University of Wales College of Cardiff, she is now studying for a doctorate looking at the roles of successful women entrepreneurs in the European Union.

JANE PILCHER teaches at the Department of Sociology at the University of Leicester, having recently been awarded her doctorate from the University of Wales College of Cardiff. She is the co-author of numerous publications on girls' occupational choices.

TERESA REES is Reader at the School for Advanced Urban Studies, University of Bristol and a consultant to the European Commission on women and training. She was until 1992 at the University of Wales College of Cardiff, where she taught on the M.Sc. Econ. in Women's Studies. Recent publications include *Women and the Labour Market* (Routledge 1992).

GWYNETH ROBERTS was awarded a doctorate from the University College of Wales, Aberystwyth, in 1992 for her thesis on Raymond Williams. She has published articles on Williams's work and is currently teaching cultural studies on an access course at Coleg Ceredigion.

JANE SALISBURY, formerly a Sociology teacher at St David's Sixth Form College, Cardiff and a tutorial fellow at the School of Social and Administrative Studies, University of Wales College of Cardiff, is currently a lecturer in the School of Education at the same institution. She has published papers on classroom ethnography and the teaching of adults and is currently editing a book on qualitative studies in education, with Sara Delamont. Her research interests include classroom ethnography and the sociology of work and the professions and these are reflected in her doctoral research on the occupational socialization of teachers.

ANGHARAD TOMOS, ex-chair of Cymdeithas yr Iaith Gymraeg, has been a leading campaigner within the Welsh language movement since the 1970s. She is also well known as a novelist, and as a writer for children. Her first novel, *Hen Fyd Hurt* (Urdd Gobaith Cymru, 1982), won the fiction prize in the Urdd National Eisteddfod, and was followed by a novel based on her experiences of imprisonment, *Yma o Hyd* (Y Lolfa, 1985) which won the Welsh Academy prize. Her series of books for children, *Cyfres Rwdlan*, won the Tir Na N'Og prize, and her latest novel, *Si Hei Lwli* (Y Lolfa, 1991), was awarded the Prose Medal in the National Eisteddfod and shortlisted for the Welsh Book of the Year Award. In 1992 the theatre company Hwyl a Fflag toured Wales with her play *Tanddaearol*. She is currently working on film.

MOIRA VINCENTELLI is a lecturer in Art History and curator of the ceramics collection at the University of Wales, Aberystwyth. She writes on ceramics and textiles and is currently preparing a book on women and ceramics.

G. CLARE WENGER holds a personal chair in Social Gerontology at University College of North Wales, Bangor. She is co-director of the Centre for Social Policy Research and Development and has published widely. She is on the editorial board of the international *Journal of Cross-Cultural Gerontology* (USA).

PREFACE

At a time when minority identities have become an important focus of debate, the particularities of women's experience in one minority culture may have resonances and significance for other such cultures. All minorities are marginalized but together they can effect change.

When, in 1991, the University of Wales's Women's Studies Colloquium chose as the theme for its proceedings 'Women in Wales', the need for more published material on the subject was strongly felt, and a few of us began planning this book there and then. The Colloquium has been meeting annually since the early 1980s; as a group, we are now affiliated with the Women's Studies Network (UK). In the first years, nearly every member was a lone figure in her department: our annual gathering was a vital source of support and confidence-building at a time when Women's Studies was little understood. More than ten years on, the subject has a much higher academic profile; Women's Studies features not only as an optional course within other disciplines but as an independent, interdisciplinary subject, standing on its own feet. The pioneering M.Sc. Econ. in Women's Studies at Cardiff has now been joined by one in Swansea: Bangor, also, will shortly be offering a taught Women's Studies postgraduate degree. At Aberystwyth, two undergraduate Part One courses in Women's Studies are being taught, one through the medium of Welsh and one in English, and a joint honours degree course is planned. At Wales's other university, the University of Glamorgan, students can already take a BA degree in the subject, while Trinity College, Carmarthen, offers an MA in Women's Writing and Feminist Theory. Optional courses concerned with the study of Welsh women in particular feature on all these new schemes, yet the amount of resource material in print at the students' disposal is still minimal. The growth of Women's Studies has largely been the result of student demand, and the academy, in Wales at any rate, is still catching up.

This book is the product of that process of growth and expansion. Its four editors worked throughout very much as a team, though Sandra Betts was largely responsible for editing the first section, Teresa Rees the second, Jane Aaron the third, and Moira Vincentelli and Jane Aaron the fourth: Moira also took responsibility for the book's illustrations. But it would not have existed, of course, without the energies and goodwill of its contributors, and we would like to thank them all very warmly. We are also grateful for the support and funding we received from the David Hughes Parry Fund and its officers at the University of Wales, Aberystwyth, and to Ned Thomas, Richard Houdmont and Liz Powell of the University of Wales Press for their support and assistance

We dedicate the book to all those staff and students who have helped to develop Women's Studies as a subject, and to all who have shared the struggle to change attitudes and improve opportunities for women in Wales. We hope it will be a useful resource for future students and general readers, and will help to stimulate further debate around women's lives and experience in Wales.

INTRODUCTION

Identities in transition

JANE AARON AND TERESA REES

In the visitors' centre of the Cardiff Bay Development Corporation a short film, showing on twelve adjacent screens, presents a new image for Cardiff's Docklands. Many of the familiar stereotypes of Welshness are on display: the red jerseys hurtling down the pitch to the roar of the crowd, the massed choir resplendent in dinner jackets. The current transformation of the locality is indicated by shots of heavy earthmoving equipment, of half-built post-modernist edifices clad in scaffolding, of men with instruments and hard hats surveying the landscape. To the pulsating tones of up-beat music, the future is portrayed as airy offices, equipped with all the latest technological aids, and leafy suburbs bathed in bright sunlight. An affluent new image is constructed for Cardiff, marrying the familiar and the distinctively Welsh with a designer dream scenario.

It is not only the existing multi-ethnic community of Butetown and the Docks which is absent from this image-making: women also, as a group, are strangely invisible, except for a few office models posing at computer keyboards. Women's voices are not heard on the sound-track. Their versions of Wales, and of what it is to be Welsh, are missing. Nothing, it would appear, has changed since Deirdre Beddoe, examining the representation of women in the mid-1980s, found that 'Welsh women are culturally invisible' (Beddoe 1986, 227). The majority of images of Wales and the Welsh have always been largely representative of male views of a masculine Wales; women's perspectives have hitherto had little place in orthodox accounts of Welsh life. The turmoil of the nine-teenth century seems to have left Welsh women with only two lasting – indeed, painfully persistent – images of themselves: the

Welsh-costumed figure in her tall black hat and shawl, smiling for the tourist trade; and the Welsh 'Mam', the staunch mother who gives her all to her hard-beset family, a figure immortalized on celluloid in the Hollywood version of *How Green Was My Valley*. Some of us may have very different pictures in our minds of the contemporary Welsh woman: we may visualize women marching from Cardiff to Greenham to set up the first 'benders' outside the US airbase; women on picket lines during the miners' strike of 1984–5; activists in the Welsh language movement in prison in England due to the lack of gaols for women in Wales; Welsh Women's Aid establishing refuges throughout Wales; Valleys' Initiative women establishing their own co-operatives, and bringing new life to depressed areas in south Wales; business women in Cardiff side-stepping the exclusionist old boys' networks by setting up women's business clubs. And yet the vitality of change in Welsh women's lives which such images denote still seems to lack general credence; 'macho' Wales is still the norm in terms of public representation.

But despite the tenacity of old images and stereotypes, gender relations in Wales are changing: transformations in the family, in the workplace, in culture and in politics, are all contributing to a new mesh of social processes, and to resultant shifts in the construction of individual identities. Which is not to say, of course, that Welsh female experience is homogenous: women in Wales experience both commonalities in their sense of identity and also dramatic differences, influenced by determinants such as ethnicity, language, class, age and locality. How do we now see ourselves? How are we coping with the changes? Does the family remain the *raison d'être* of Welsh women, as the 'Mam' image implied? What impact, if any, is the feminist movement having on identities in a state of transition? To what extent is there still a distinctive 'Welshness' about female experience in contemporary Wales? Hitherto, very little published material has addressed itself to such questions as these.

According to a Welsh proverb, 'nid byd, byd heb wybodaeth', a world without knowledge is no world. If to live without self-knowledge is not to live, then the world of the Welsh woman, doubly under-represented as it is within the dominant English and male-orientated culture, can hardly yet be said to exist. Recently, however, one or two publications have appeared with the aim of

beginning to fill the huge gaps in our know[ledge]
Women in Wales: A Documentary of our Recent H[istory],
Luana Dee and Katell Keineg in 1987, and the collecti[on of histori]-
cal essays, *Our Mothers' Land: Chapters in Welsh [Women's]
History 1830–1939*, edited by Angela V. John in 1991. But [*Women*]
in Wales, which was intended as an annual publication, neve[r got]
beyond its first issue, and limited itself largely to reports on [cul]-
tural and political developments relating to women in south Wales.
And *Our Mothers' Land*, for all the wealth of information it provides on women in nineteenth-century and early twentieth-century
Wales, stops, of course, in 1939.

This present collection of commissioned essays aims to fill up
some of the gaps in our knowledge by providing an up-to-date
account of many of the shifts and changes in the contemporary
Welsh woman's world: as such, it could be seen as a sister volume
to *Our Mothers' Land*, as its title suggests. The various contributors explore diverse aspects of women's lives within a nation
characterized by marked social and cultural 'internal difference'
(Thomas 1992). Different chapters focus on the situation of
women in north and in south Wales, in the rural west and the
urban east, in English-speaking Wales and in Welsh-language
culture, in the business world and in agriculture, in politics and in
religious institutions, as well as investigating female experience at
a variety of temporal stages, from schooldays to old age.

In order to present, in so far as one volume may, the diversity of
current Welsh women's experience, the book combines two apparently very disparate types of discourse: the academic report and
the personal experiential account. The first fourteen essays in the
book present the findings of current research into many aspects of
change in the public and private spheres of Welsh women's lives.
Grouped into three sections they deal with changes relating to i)
home life and the community, ii) work and education, and iii) cultural and political representation. In the final section of the book,
seven women, chosen to represent a variety of different outlooks
within both the English- and Welsh-speaking cultures of Wales,
reflect upon their own personal experience of late-twentieth-
century Welsh life, and upon the determinants and choices which
helped to form their own sense of identity.

In the next few pages, we introduce the book's main themes,
chapter by chapter. To those not familiar with the interdisciplinary

mixture of sociological and cul-
ay seem surprising, but within
, long since been accepted that it
conventional – but arbitrary –
that a full picture of women's
no single volume can hope to
ations of a nation's social, cul-
ct women, particularly not a
les, and we are very aware of
we are grieved not to be in a
on Welsh women's current
to film and television culture, on Black
women's experience within the very long standing Black communities of Cardiff, and on women working within the Welsh Labour
movement. Articles were commissioned, or solicited, on each of
these topics originally, but of course it is often very difficult for
hard-pressed activists and working mothers to meet the demand of
publication deadlines. Rather than delay the production of the
volume, we thought it best to go ahead with what we had. A book
of this kind, for all its limitations, is certainly needed; we hope it
will prove useful as a starting point for further work on the
subject, and look forward to its successors.

1. Private lives: home and community

The ideology of the family has a particular resonance in Wales: it
is underpinned by the Nonconformist movement and has been
fuelled by rates of female economic activity that are low compared
with the rest of Britain. And yet, the traditional white nuclear
family with a male breadwinner, woman at home, and two dependent children, describes remarkably few households in Wales
today. Figures from the 1991 Census show a considerable increase
in elderly people (mostly women) living on their own, and a wide
diversity of family and household formations. Cohabitation is
more frequent. 'Reconstituted' families with step-children, multi-
family households, and single-sex couple households have all
increased. The ethnic origin of people in Wales is more diverse.
The number of single-parent families has increased, and many of
the heads of those families are women in their teens or early twenties. Nevertheless, despite the fact that the nuclear family as a

household form does not describe most people's living arrangements in contemporary Wales, the ideology of the family continues to inform social welfare support, housing policy, what the state will provide in terms of community care, and what is expected to be taken care of by the family.

'The personal is the political' became a slogan of the women's movement, indicating the significance of gender relations and gender divisions in the family for women's experiences in wider society. Feminists in Britain have drawn attention to the fact that (until recently at least), while the rape of a stranger was a criminal offence, rape within marriage was perfectly legal, and crimes of violence within the home were largely ignored by the police as they were 'only domestic' (Dobash and Dobash 1992). The long-term repercussions of the women's movement are at last beginning to affect the ways in which the family as a system is understood and analysed. Uneven patterns of domestic division of labour in the home are being measured and charted, and the extent to which 'community care' policies depend upon unpaid work being undertaken by women is being documented.

The first section of this book explores issues in the home and community in relation to Wales. It begins with a chapter which sets out statistically and in discussion the changing nature of family life in Wales, providing a backcloth to the other contributions. Stereotypical images are challenged by Census and other data. This is followed by Jane Pilcher's examination of accounts by three generations of women living in south-east Wales of how domestic chores should be and, in their experience, are allocated between men and women. Distinct generational differences are found between the grandmothers in their sixties, their daughters in their forties, and, in turn, *their* grown up daughters, now in their late teens and early twenties. Different sets of vocabularies, rooted in the contrasted socio-historical period of their upbringing, are used by each generation to describe their contrasting sets of expectations about who should do the dishes.

The following chapter by Nickie Charles discusses the hidden problem of domestic violence, originally associated with Erin Pizzey and inner-city England, but now found to be as much a feature of rural Wales. It is not a problem confined to a particular class, ethnic group, or spatial area. However, its identification as an 'urban' phenomenon, associated with urban poverty and homelessness, has led to difficulties in securing funding for refuges in rural Wales. The voices of women in rural Wales suffering from violent abuse are rarely heard.

The final chapter in this section, by Clare Wenger, gives graphic biographies of five elderly women living in rural Wales. Elderly people are projected to comprise over half the population by the end of the century, and yet we know relatively little about the determinants of quality of life in old age. Chosen because they represent different categories or degrees of independence, or of levels of support from the state, or from individual friends and relatives, the cameos illustrate highly contrasted experiences of life in old age in rural Wales. They show that elderly women are more likely than men to strive to maintain independence and autonomy, and a sense of themselves as not entirely dependent upon the family or community. At every age, therefore, female identities cannot be conceived of as wholly absorbed into familial structures, even though state welfare systems may treat women as if such was the case.

2. Public lives: education, training and work

The ideology of the family affects public lives as much as it does private lives. It affects who has what kind of education, and training, who works in which industry and which occupations, and who can claim unemployment benefit. Schoolgirls making option and career choices in school are informed by their likely future roles in the home. Expectations that women will become wives and mothers inform employers' recruitment and work organization practices, irrespective of the intentions of individual women (Collinson et al. 1990).

The first chapter in this section spells out the 'political arithmetic' of women and paid work in Wales. It illustrates the progress that will need to be made to fulfil the hopes of initiatives to increase fair play for women in work, both quantitatively and qualitatively. At present, women in Wales are less likely to be in work, less likely to be in a top job, and they receive less pay than women anywhere else in Britain. The labour force in Wales is highly segregated by gender. Nevertheless, demographic changes, and increased emphasis on high-level skills in the workplace, may mean that there will be more emphasis in the future on training women, and developing their potential.

Certainly, increasing participation in paid work by women, and the growth of credentialism, have led many women in Wales back to the classroom. Chapters by Pam Garland and Jane Salisbury explore the experiences of women returning to education, respectively as mature age students on degree courses in north Wales, and as unqualified further education lecturers seeking credentials mid-career at university in south Wales. Both sets of students talk movingly about their growth in confidence, the reactions of others to them, and their changing self-perception and sense of identity brought about through the return to learning.

Women's contribution to paid work is under-recorded, in particular in agriculture, tourism, and family businesses. The European Commission has recently enacted legislation to ensure that wives of self-employed workers who contribute to their partners' businesses become eligible for pensions and other entitlements currently denied them. This should ensure a greater recognition of the unsung labours of such women. In a highly revealing chapter, Shan Ashton gives us an insight into the busy lives of the wives of north Wales hill farmers. They are revealed to be a highly diverse group, but they all combine an extraordinary range of family, work and community activities. Some of the difficulties they face, for example as business partners in their own right who are not recognized as such by banks, are echoed in Elizabeth Muir's contribution to the last section of this book, where she, as the first woman member of the Wales Confederation of British Industry, describes the problem of the 'face not fitting'.

For women already in the labour market, these chapters show signs of a slow change in the recognition of their contribution and potential by employers, by the state, and by themselves. But what of future generations? Are schools more aware of the need to widen choices? Are girls who are at present making option choices ensuring that they gain entry to a wider range of occupations and industries than their mothers' generation? A recent study of 500 south Wales schoolgirls found that, with the exception of middle-class girls moving in greater numbers into the professions (accountancy, medicine, law), on the whole girls' option choices, and hence their higher education, training and occupational opportunities, remain remarkably similar to those of previous generations (Rees 1992). However, there are some initiatives in Wales designed to challenge these patterns, and increase awareness of gender stereotyping in schools. Patricia Daniel explores some of these initiatives in north Wales. She looks at Genderwatch, an Equal Opportunities Commission project translated into Welsh in Clwyd, and targeted at children, and at a project designed to increase gender awareness in trainee teachers. She argues that the inclusion of Welsh in the National Curriculum will mean more women will be able to become teachers and stay in Wales, rather than having to move to England to get work, commuting 'home' at weekends.

In all these chapters, Welsh women are shown to be, to a greater or lesser extent, in the process of change. Mature women, mostly with families, are going back to the classroom again as apprehensive students. 'Farmers' wives', currently struggling to juggle their different roles and identities, will shortly be recognized as workers in their own right. Working-class women, who strayed into further education, are now seeking to become 'proper' lecturers. Special initiatives designed to challenge sex-role stereotyping in schools may influence images and identities of women in Wales in the future. In both the private and the public sphere, a growing diversity of patterns of women's lives and identities challenges popular images of women in Wales; at the same time, structures which perpetuate gender divisions at home and work remain stable. The growing disparity between images and experiences confuses and confounds women's sense of identity.

3. Representing women: culture and politics

The two sections which make up the second part of this book deal with the cultural and political manifestations of the contemporary Welsh woman's changing life. The revolutionary decade of the 1960s had long-term repercussions for Welsh women on two different counts, those of gender and nationality. The feminist movement of the late 1960s changed their lives, while the movement to protect the Welsh language from what looked like imminent extinction, which began its campaigns in 1963, affected many. It also brought with it a related, and more widely diffused, new awareness of what it was to belong to a minority culture, an awareness that had significance for the English-speaking as well as

Welsh-speaking people of Wales. The essays which follow in this book are generally concerned with either the one or the other of these effects as they relate to women; some are concerned with both, and with the tensions which can exist between them. For within self-protective Welsh communities, whether Welsh or English speaking, feminism is frequently viewed with suspicion, as an alien Anglo-American movement.

The essay which opens this second part of the book argues, however, that the 'traditional' concepts of gender difference within Welsh culture are themselves largely the result of alien 'outside' influences, that is, that they are in part a consequence of the colonizing intervention of Victorian England, with its extremely rigid ideology of gender – as well as class – difference. But it suggests that this persistent influence is, at last, in the process of being eroded by the manifest strength of women's current contribution to the cultural and political life of Wales. The second chapter in this section, Delyth George's essay on the 'strains of transition' in Welsh-language fiction by women, traces the difficult stages of this emancipatory development. After an introductory account of the dearth of female voices in pre-twentieth-century Welsh literature, it analyses the changes in the way female roles and sexual relations are depicted in the work of contemporary writers. It concentrates in particular on two representative novelists, Eigra Lewis Roberts and Jane Edwards, whose writing careers span the wide divide, in feminist terms, between the repressive 1950s and early 1960s and the present day. Gwyneth Roberts's essay which follows provides, as it were, the other side of the coin to Delyth George's account, through its investigation of the representation of women in the English-language fiction of one of Wales's most influential male writers, Raymond Williams. She argues that, for all his left-wing political alignments – or, indeed, because of them – Williams, in his fiction, shows ambivalence about the effect of feminist ideas upon his image of the Welsh working-class community. Heavily male-dominated, but dependent for its well-being upon the co-operation of its marginalized women, that community has traditionally, for the most part, resisted female emancipation, and Williams's fiction tends to endorse its reactionary repressiveness: in his novels women who attempt to win some freedom for themselves are punished for their hubris. Read together, these three essays serve to illustrate the particular difficulties facing women in their struggle to develop an autonomous identity within the two linguistic cultures of Wales.

But of course it is not only through language that a sense of identity is nourished or impeded. Moira Vincentelli's chapter traces the significance of the tradition of collecting and displaying china in Wales, and explores its relevance to contemporary Welsh women's idea of themselves. The dresser, that bastion of the Welsh interior – the female sphere – features in this essay as an 'altar' upon which women preserve handed-down artefacts, which act as an anchor not only for their own history and personal memories, but that of their mothers and grandmothers as well. Its persistent, indeed growing, significance as marker of a female tradition of 'Welshness' serves to illustrate how visual and material culture can contribute to the sources of identity, even in the face of its double repression, as Welsh and as female, within the dominant linguistic culture.

Finally, in this section, Charlotte Aull Davies examines the history of women's participation in the one specifically Welsh political party, Plaid Cymru. Given that she shows how alien it was – before the women's movement began to make its influence felt – for women to fill any role in party politics beyond that of tea-making or fund-raising, her essay can stand as representative of women's general relation to political power, in parties other than the one with which she is chiefly concerned. But she also discusses the changing image of women within nationalist ideology *per se*, and shows how the 'mother of the nation' syndrome, in which women were valued primarily for their reproductive functions, has given way to a greater appreciation of the significance of women's contribution as individuals in their own right.

4. Personal voices: the politics of identity

The seven 'voices' which make up this last quarter of the book in effect speak for themselves, but the way in which this section relates to the preceding one needs, perhaps, some words of intro-duction. The third section included researched essays on women's representation in, and involvement with, literature, visual culture, and politics in Wales; in this final section the testimonies of indi-vidual women who are practitioners or activists within those fields, or in related areas, balance and enhance, through their direct relation to experience, the more abstract material of section three.

Angharad Tomos, the first 'voice' in this section, could have served our purposes in a dual capacity, for, as a long-term activist within Cymdeithas yr Iaith Gymraeg, the Welsh Language Society, and a renowned writer, she is a significant figure within both the literary and the political camps of Welsh-language culture. In one memorable week in the summer of 1991, she was arrested for her political activities on the Monday and awarded the Eisteddfod's Prose Medal for the best novel of the year on the Wednesday. The many references to her fiction in the first two essays of section three are testimony to her contribution to women's writing in Wales, but she devotes her own entry to portrayals of many of her fellow women activists within the language movement: no one else could have written on women in Cymdeithas yr Iaith without commenting at much greater length on the role of Angharad Tomos. Through its accounts of what it can mean for individual women when their sense of identity becomes bound up with a grass-roots protest movement, her chapter brings home to us the life-changing effect of political activism, and thus enhances the material on women's role in politics provided in the third section of this book.

The next 'voice' describes the way in which her own sense of identity has been formed in relation to another area of influence, one which has not previously received much attention in this volume, but which has historically been of enormous significance to women in Wales, and still continues to be so for many – that is, religion. Enid Morgan, who is Director of Mission for the Church in Wales, and was previously Deacon-in-Charge of four parishes in Dyfed, reflects on the manner in which her faith has shaped her identity, and discusses the sometimes difficult relation between her commitment to the institution of the Church and her sympathies with progressive change in women's status. This essay was written before the General Synod of the Church of England voted to permit women to become priests, and before the Church in Wales, in April 1994, decided by a narrow margin against such a development. Seven clergy votes prevented the ordination of more than fifty Welsh women deacons, and frustrated the wishes of its lay members, the bishops and the archbishop, who voted by a wide majority for the change. It is but to be hoped that this anomaly will soon be rectified.

Mary Lloyd Jones, our next 'voice', is an internationally-known landscape painter, who has exhibited widely in Germany and North America as well throughout the UK. Brought up in rural mid-Wales, in a cottage without mains water or electricity, she associates her sense of identity as an artist with that childhood immersion in a particular natural locality. Like Moira Vincentelli she also stresses the importance for women of establishing links with the visual culture of the past; in her case, discovering the tradition of women's textile arts in Wales provided her with the foundations from which to develop, 'safe in the knowledge that my work was linked with that of previous generations'.

Both the next two 'voices' are poets who have deliberately set out to explore female experience, and both have been widely recognized as influential and innovative writers. Indeed, both are recipients of the somewhat dubious honour of literary canonization: Menna Elfyn's poetry collections have featured on 'A' Level syllabuses, and Gillian Clarke is one of the few women listed in the Minister of Education's recent prescriptions of suitable writers for inclusion in the National Curriculum. Each writes in a different language, however – Menna Elfyn in Welsh and Gillian Clarke in English. Their personal accounts of what they experience as the sources of their identity as poets and as Welsh women serve to enhance the researched material on the changing representation of women in the two cultures of Wales provided in the third section of this book.

Neither of the literatures of the dragon's two tongues were of much assistance to our next 'voice', however, as she sought for positive images to which she could relate as both Welsh and lesbian. Incest is said to be the 'last taboo': two Welsh-language novels dealing sympathetically with sibling incest were published within one week of one another in 1992, but no Welsh text, in either language, has as yet been centrally concerned to put forward a sympathetic representation of lesbianism. In an age when lesbian detective novels are popular best-sellers – to homosexual and heterosexual readers alike – in Anglo-American culture, the complete absence of such material in Wales does seem signally repressive. Roni Crwydren's courageous account of her wanderings in search of a community in which she could bring together the two divided aspects of her identity may, in the Welsh context, prove of particular value to readers similarly positioned, as well as enlightening to others.

Finally, the last of our 'voices' bears most interestingly on material discussed in the second section of this book rather than the third. Elizabeth J. Muir describes her experience as one of the pioneers at present breaking new ground for Welsh women within the business world: her contribution adds to our 'inside' knowledge of factors analysed in essays such as Teresa Rees's 'Women and Paid Work in Wales'. It serves as a grim reminder of how heavily the dice are still loaded against women when it comes to 'real' power – that is, in our capitalist economy, to financial power – whatever changes may be taking place on a cultural and social level. And yet it also testifies to the fact that changes are being made, at however slow a pace, in the business world too.

5. Our Sisters' Land

A common theme to emerge throughout this book as a whole is the importance of the support which women give to each other as they negotiate change. It is women friends and relatives who, in the absence of any other adequate state or professional system, provide the childcare needed when a mother retrains or re-enters the workforce. It is women who provide refuges for wives escaping from domestic violence. It is largely female carers who help elderly women to continue to live full lives in their own homes. It is female mentors who serve as necessary role models for subsequent generations of women writers breaking new ground in terms of the representation of women in Welsh culture. It is the example and inspiration of other women which activates many a political campaigner, whether within the Welsh language movement or within sexual politics, at Greenham or on a picket-line.

Such supportive sisterliness has, of course, always been a key factor in feminist social change; nor is it surprising that a co-operative spirit should be particularly evident when the influence of feminist ideas is felt in close-knit communities, such as those of Wales. At the same time it is also true, however, that a close community which experiences itself as beleaguered, whether it be for cultural or economic reasons, can also be a closed community, self-defensively resistant to anything it may perceive as an alien, new-fangled influence. But change is always possible. During the first decades of this century, it was another radical political movement which was frequently represented within both Welsh- and English-speaking

Welsh culture as a threat from the outside, brought into Wales by 'outsider' English demagogues. Socialism then, like feminism today, was regarded askance by traditional Nonconformist Welsh culture as a socially divisive development (see Thomas 1992, 15 and 18). But by now, of course, the labour movement has become practically synonymous with 'Welshness' in many of the most populated areas of Wales. Who knows what changes may have occurred with regard to the women's movement in Wales in fifty years' time?

Whatever the future may hold, changes are today taking place in Welsh women's lives and in their sense of identity. This book aims to set some of those changes on record, in the hope that to increase our awareness of them may be to strengthen and speed their development, and militate against the possibility of any future erosions of women's hard-won emancipation.

References

Beddoe, Deirdre (1986). 'Images of Welsh Women', in Tony Curtis (ed.), *Wales: The Imagined Nation* (Bridgend, Poetry Wales Press), 227–38.

Collinson, D., Knights, D. and Collinson, M. (1990). *Managing to Discriminate* (London, Routledge).

Dobash, R. E. and Dobash, R. (1992). *Women, Violence and Social Change* (London, Routledge).

Rees, Teresa (1992). *Women and the Labour Market* (London, Routledge).

Thomas, M. Wynn (1992). *Internal Difference: Literature in Twentieth-Century Wales* (Cardiff, University of Wales Press).

PART ONE

I. *Private Lives: Home and Community*

1

The changing family in Wales

SANDRA BETTS

> Within the space almost of a single generation there have been rev-
> olutionary changes in the roles and attitudes of women. To a large
> extent these changes have been the product of more than fifty years
> of radical change in the vital statistics of birth, marriage and death.
> Time and again our investigations of family behaviour in contem-
> porary Swansea have returned to this basic point of the recent
> liberation of women from the wheel of prolonged childbearing – an
> emancipation which is only just beginning, with the present
> 'daughters of the revolution', to exert its full effect.

These were the words of Rosser and Harris (1965, 171) in their
work on the *Family and Social Change* in a south Wales town.
Nearly thirty years on it is appropriate to ask how the 'daughters
[and indeed the granddaughters] of the revolution' have fared in
the context of the family in Wales. In 1965 Rosser and Harris spoke
of 'a dramatic story of demographic change'. The main themes of
this story related to the increasing popularity of marriage, especially among the young; a concentration of childbearing in the
early years of marriage; an extension of the length of marriages
and an increase in life expectancy. This chapter will continue the
story by exploring the main dimensions of family change in Wales
over the last thirty years. It will show that the structure and composition of family life in Wales has continued to undergo radical
change and that this has had a particular impact on the lives and
identities of women. Many traditional features of family life have
been challenged. In Wales, as in the rest of the United Kingdom,
our understanding of the family has been fundamentally questioned. Significant shifts in patterns of marriage, cohabitation,

divorce, childbearing and ageing have produced a diversity of family forms, structures and experiences many of which bear little resemblance to the family of the 1960s. These shifts have become more marked with the passage of time and show every sign of continuing to produce substantial change in the demography of families in Wales. In the following section the main trends are examined.

Family trends

Marriage and cohabitation

Since the 1960s, significant changes have occurred in patterns of marriage and cohabitation in Wales. Whilst the number of marriages has remained fairly constant, at around 19,000 per year, the proportion of the population getting married has substantially declined: from 19.5 per thousand population aged fifteen and over in 1961, to 15.8 per thousand in 1990 (Welsh Office 1992). Although this might suggest that the institution of marriage is no longer as popular as it was, this is not necessarily the case for all sections of the population. A more detailed analysis of the figures reveals important variations between groups. There has been a marked fall in the number of single people getting married, but a significant increase in the number of people who remarry after divorce. Marriage of single females has fallen by almost a quarter (from nearly 18,000 in 1961, to 13,594 in 1990), but marriage of divorced females has risen more than five times (from 752 in 1961, to 4,346 in 1990). The pattern for single and divorced males is similar (Welsh Office 1992). Increasingly remarriage is becoming a more significant proportion of total marriages. In 1990 approximately 26 per cent of all marriages in Wales were remarriages (Central Statistical Office 1991). This is somewhat lower than the figure for England and Wales as a whole where as early as 1987, the proportion of remarriages as a percentage of all new marriages was 36 per cent (OPCS 1987).

Changes have also occurred with respect to age and marriage. People in Wales today are older when they get married than was the case in the 1960s and early 1970s. In 1971, the average age of marriage for men was 26.6 years; by 1990 it was 30.3 years. The average age for women in 1971 was 24.3 years, in 1990 it was 27.8 years (Welsh Office 1992). During this period teenage marriages have declined significantly. In 1990, only 444 males and 1,416 females married in Wales under the age of twenty. This contrasts sharply with the figures for 1971 which record 2,291 males and 6,540 females marrying whilst in their teens (Welsh Office 1992). The numbers of those marrying over the age of forty-five years has remained relatively constant. Whilst these age trends reflect those occurring in the UK as a whole, it is nevertheless the case that couples still tend to marry younger in Wales than in the rest of the UK and that the rate of teenage marriage remains higher in Wales than elsewhere in Britain.

The fall in the rate of marriage in the last thirty years has been accompanied by an increase in the rate of cohabitation. Whilst the trend towards cohabitation is observable in Wales as it is in the rest of the UK, it is nevertheless the case that Wales has the lowest percentage of cohabiting couples of any part of Britain. In 1986–7, 7 per cent of men and 8 per cent of women in Wales were cohabiting compared with 13 per cent of men and 14 per cent of women in Great Britain as a whole (Haskey and Kiernan 1989). The incidence of pre-marital cohabitation is higher for second marriages (when either one or both partners have been married previously) – this is true in Wales as in the rest of the UK. More recently, the 1991 Census recorded 45,980 cohabiting couple families in Wales. These families account for 5.8 per cent of all families in the Principality. The majority of cohabiting couple unions (57.9 per cent) have no children, 38.4 per cent have dependent children and 3.7 per cent have non-dependent children only. Nearly 30,000 dependent children (0–18 years) live in cohabiting couple families. This constitutes almost 5 per cent of all dependent children living in Wales.

Divorce
Another significant change in patterns of family life over the last thirty years is to be found in the increased incidence of divorce. Changes in the law have meant that divorce has become progressively easier to obtain and over the last thirty years divorce rates have increased sixfold, from a rate of 2.1 per thousand marriages in 1961 to a rate of 12.7 per thousand marriages in 1987 (OPCS 1987). These figures refer to England and Wales combined and whilst it is the case that the incidence of divorce is rising in Wales, it is also apparent that the Principality has a lower divorce rate

than that of England and Wales as a whole. According to 1991 Census data, the rate for Wales is 10.8 per thousand marriages. Figures on divorce petitions filed in the 1980s reveal a steady increase in the number of petitions filed in Wales. There has been an increase of 13.9 per cent from 9,070 petitions filed in 1981 to 10,333 in 1991. The proportion of petitions filed by wives has remained relatively constant, at around 75 per cent of all petitions filed.

Childbearing and parenting
One of the major roles of the family has been to produce, nurture and socialize the next generation. A feature of the 1980s has been the increased separation of marriage and childbearing, but still the majority of children, although a declining proportion, are born to women in their first marriage. Statistics show a decline in the birthrate in Wales since the early 1960s and a relative stability during the 1980s and early 1990s. In 1961 the birthrate per 1,000 women aged between fifteen and forty-four years was 89.3, in 1991 it was 64.3 (Welsh Office 1992). Wales continues to have a higher birthrate than England, but the difference is now much reduced.

In Wales, as in other parts of Britain, the trend is towards the postponement of parenthood. Since the late 1960s couples have been delaying starting their families. In 1971, 37 per cent of babies were born to mothers aged between twenty and twenty-four years. By 1990 this figure had fallen to 28.2 per cent. In 1971, 13.1 per cent of women giving birth were aged between thirty and thirty-four years, by 1990 this figure had risen to 19.5 per cent (Welsh Office 1992). More children are now born outside of marriage. Figures for England and Wales as a whole show that the 'extra marital birth ratio', that is, the proportion of all live births that occur outside marriage, has more than doubled in recent years, from 12 per cent in 1980 to 25 per cent in 1988. In Wales, the figure was 21 per cent in 1986. Spatial variations are apparent in the Principality with the rate being highest in the predominantly urban areas of Mid Glamorgan, South Glamorgan and Gwent. At the same time, birth has become significantly safer for both mothers and babies. The number of stillbirths as a proportion of all births has fallen from 22 per 1000 in 1961, to 5 per 1000 in 1990. The proportion of infant deaths has also fallen, from 24 per 1000 in 1961 to 7 per 1000 in 1991 (Welsh Office 1992).

Lone parenting

The traditional white nuclear family image of husband, wife and children living together in one household, is today challenged by a variety of alternative images, one of which is the lone-parent family in which a conjugal bond has either been severed or has never been initiated. Recent evidence suggests that lone parenting is becoming a more significant feature of family life in Wales. In 1989 it was estimated that one-parent households made up 9.4 per cent of all households in Wales. This pattern showed some variation within the Principality, ranging from 8.1 per cent in Powys to 10.7 per cent in South Glamorgan (Table 1.1).

More recent evidence comes from the 1991 Census. Data derived from the Census ten-per-cent sample shows that lone-parent households continue to make up 9.4 per cent of all households in Wales. However the distinction made in this Census between households and families allows further analysis to be undertaken. Thus whilst lone-parent families constitute 9.4 per cent of all households in Wales, they make up 13 per cent of all families in the Principality. It is estimated that 100,920 dependent children live in lone-parent families. This constitutes 16.3 per cent of all dependent children in Wales. Some 93 per cent of lone parents with dependent children are female and the majority of these, 64.7 per cent, are economically inactive. Only 12.2 per cent of female lone parents are in full-time employment. A further 16.2 per cent have part-time jobs and 1.6 per cent are self employed.

Table 1.1 Lone-parent households as a percentage of all households 1989

Lone-parent households	%
Wales	9.4
Clwyd	8.5
Dyfed	8.5
Gwent	10.0
Gwynedd	9.5
Mid Glamorgan	9.6
Powys	8.1
South Glamorgan	10.7
West Glamorgan	9.2

Source: Central Statistical Office (1991)

The remainder are classified as having other forms of economic activity (5.16 per cent) or as being 'economically active students' (0.14 per cent).

Reconstituted families

Being a member of a lone-parent family is frequently not permanent. Many lone parents marry or remarry as do a substantial proportion of divorced people. In 1986, 25.8 per cent of men who married in Wales were remarrying as were 24.6 per cent of women. This was a somewhat lower proportion than for the UK as a whole, where the equivalent percentages were 26.3 per cent for men and 25.2 per cent for women (Haskey and Kiernan 1989). A significant proportion of divorced and separated people choose to cohabit permanently or as a precursor to remarriage. In 1986–7 this applied to 35 per cent of divorced and separated men in Wales and 21 per cent of women. In this respect both men and women in Wales were more likely to cohabit than those in Britain as a whole, where 30 per cent of men and 20 per cent of women cohabited after divorce or separation (Haskey and Kiernan 1989).

Household composition

The evidence discussed so far shows that significant changes have occurred in patterns of marriage, cohabitation, divorce, childbearing and lone parenting in Wales over the last thirty years. These changes have produced a picture of family diversity which can be further illustrated and brought together by an examination of household composition. Household living arrangements are amongst the more significant aspects of everyday life and provide important clues to demographic change. Table 1.2 illustrates the direction of change.

These figures show that a decline is occurring in the proportion of married-couple households and an increase in one-person and other household types. The proportion of lone-parent households has remained relatively constant. As the table indicates, not all households contain families, many are composed of single persons. However, according to 1991 Census data, households with families make up 72.5 per cent of all households in Wales. Of these, 79.7 per cent are married-couple families; 13 per cent are lone-parent families; 5.8 per cent are cohabiting-couple families and 1.5 per cent are households with two or more families. Whilst

Table 1.2 Household composition: Wales (thousands)
1985 and 1991

Household type	1985		1991	
	No.	*%*	*No.*	*%*
Married couple	645	62	632	58
Lone parent	95	9	103	9
One person	243	23	270	25
Other	57	6	85	8
All households	1040	100	1090	100

Source: Welsh Office (1989) and OPCS (1991) Census Local Base
Statistics 10%

the married-couple family continues to predominate the scene in Wales it is clearly the case that other family forms are becoming more significant features of family demography.

In the same way as not all households contain families, it is also the case that not all families contain children, although by definition all lone-parent families do. But given the prevailing ideology of family life as involving a heterosexual married couple and their dependent children it is important to investigate the family situation of children in Wales today. Over 62,000 dependent children (0–18 years) live in families in Wales. The majority of these live in married-couple families, but a growing minority live in lone-parent or cohabiting-couple families (Table 1.3). Whilst traditional nuclear family life remains the experience of the majority of children in Wales, it is nevertheless the case that more than one-fifth of dependent children live in alternative family forms.

The picture with respect to families and non-dependent children is equally interesting. Some 15.8 per cent of married-couple families and 3.7 per cent of cohabiting-couple families have non-dependent children only, but amongst lone-parent families the figure is 42.6 per cent. Exactly why this figure should be so high for lone-parent families is not clear. It may be that more non-dependent children remain in the lone-parent family setting because of their contribution to the household economy.

Table 1.3 Dependent children (0–18 years) by family type:
Wales 1991

Type of family	No. of children	%
Married couple	473,480	76.2
Lone parent	100,920	16.3
Cohabiting couple	29,940	4.8
Shared household families	16,580	2.7
Total	620,920	100.0

Source: OPCS (1991)

Ageing and the family

The ageing of the population in the last thirty years is another factor which has had a major impact on the structure of the family in Wales. Between 1961 and 1991 the number of people aged sixty-five and over in Wales increased from 317,800 to 494,700, from 11.9 per cent to 17.2 per cent of the population (Welsh Office 1992, Census data 1991). Within this overall change, there has been a greater increase in the proportion of the population which is over the age of seventy-five. Between 1961 and 1991 it has almost doubled, from 108,200 to 210,100. Two-thirds of this age group are women (Welsh Office 1992).

The increase in the proportion of the elderly in the population has had a major impact on health and welfare services. As people grow older and become more dependent their needs for health care and social support also grow (see Clare Wenger's chapter in this volume). In 1989, 22 per cent of persons over the age of sixty-five years consulted their general practitioner and 63 per cent reported long-standing illness. According to these measures, levels of illness amongst the elderly in Wales are higher than in Great Britain as a whole, where only 19 per cent of those over the age of sixty-four consulted their general practitioner and 61 per cent reported long-term illness (OPCS 1991).

Significant changes have occurred with respect to the provision of accommodation for the elderly. Between 1986 and 1989 the number of persons over the age of sixty-four in residential accommodation in Wales rose from 11,992 to 13,653, an increase of 13.9 per cent. In 1986 the majority of these elderly persons was resident in homes staffed by local authorities. Relatively few lived in registered private homes and even fewer were resident in registered voluntary homes. By 1989 the pattern had changed. The proportion of the elderly living in local-authority staffed homes and voluntary homes had marginally declined while the proportion living in private homes had increased by almost 50 per cent (Central Statistical Office 1991).

Not all elderly persons need residential accommodation. Over the last twenty years there has been a growing emphasis on care in the community and an increase in provision of support services to enable elderly persons to remain in their own homes. Day care places in Wales have increased from 795 in 1974 to 2,251 in 1988–9, an increase of 183.1 per cent. There has also been an increase in other home-based services. Between 1974 and 1988–9 the provision of home helps increased by 101.5 per cent, the number of elderly people who received chiropody services increased by 61.5 per cent and there has been a 33.3 per cent increase in the number of those who receive meals on wheels (Welsh Office 1991). However, services vary a great deal throughout Wales. Using the indices of home helps, chiropody services and meals on wheels and comparing provision by county with the average for Wales as a whole, the level of support given to members of the population over the age of sixty-five is highest in Mid Glamorgan, Powys and Gwent; it is relatively low in Dyfed, Gwynedd, South Glamorgan and West Glamorgan, and lowest of all in Clwyd (Welsh Office 1991).

Ethnic diversity

Another important aspect of the demographic picture of Wales is that of ethnic diversity. Ethnicity is an issue of far greater concern today than it was in the 1960s. Ethnic origin is now a standard item of information recorded by both official and unofficial surveys of the population. The 1991 Census data show that the overwhelming majority of the population in Wales is white and born in the UK. Ninety-eight per cent of the population fall into both of these categories. Other groups thus form a very small proportion of the total population of the Principality. The largest of these is the Irish, representing 0.73 per cent of the population. Indians and Pakistanis taken together represent 0.4 per cent and the Chinese 0.16 per cent. Other groups are significantly smaller. Ethnic diversity in Wales exists, but is not as great as many may have been led to believe. It is, however, a far more prominent feature in some areas of Wales than in others. The black community in Cardiff docklands, for example, is one of the oldest established black communities in Britain and continues to grow. It should also be noted that whilst the majority of the population is white and of UK origin, this obscures the very real distinction between the Welsh and the English as much as it obscures the existence of other groups such as the Italian and Ukrainian communities in the south Wales valleys.

Most of the available data on ethnic diversity relates to population and to households. There is a relative lack of information concerning the family composition of ethnic groups in Wales. What evidence there is suggests that Asian women have higher fertility rates and that there is a higher incidence of lone parenting within the Afro-Caribbean community (Welsh Office 1991). Much valuable work remains to be done in this area to provide a fuller picture of family life in Wales.

Discussion and conclusion

The structure and composition of family life in Wales continues to change and a revised version of the story told by Rosser and Harris in the mid-1960s is now needed. Many of the patterns observable at that time have been reversed and new variants of family life have come to the fore. There has been a decrease in the popularity of marriage; a decline in the number of youthful marriages; a significant trend toward later family-building patterns and a sharp increase in the rate of divorce. During the same period cohabitation, the severance of marriage and childbearing, lone parenting, remarriage and reconstituted families have become important features of family demography. These features found no place in the picture of the 1960s. The change in the age distribution of the population is the only trend which appears to have continued.

The situation in Wales today is one of growing family diversity and an increasingly differentiated process of family formation. The traditional nuclear family (married couple and dependent children), although still the most prominent form, is, for increasing numbers of individuals, only one of several possible family types that they may experience during their lives. Whilst in many respects the changes that have occurred in the family in Wales reflect those occurring in England and in the UK as a whole, there are some variations. People in Wales tend to marry at younger ages than in England. Wales has a higher rate of teenage marriage. Cohabitation prior to first marriage occurs less often in Wales, but is more likely prior to remarriage. Divorce rates, whilst rising, remain lower than those in England. Remarriage is less popular. The elderly in Wales report higher levels of illness. In the light of this picture of change it is important to consider its impact on family life and family experiences.

The effects of family change
Changes in family structure and composition have a particular effect upon women. The family is conventionally considered to be central to the lives of women. Women and children have historically been defined in terms of their relationship to the kinship system whilst men have typically been described in terms of their place in the occupational system. Women's identity has historically been seen to be forged in the context of the family and domesticity. But for many women in Wales today, experience of family life may bear little resemblance to that of their mothers and grandmothers. Marriage, home-making and motherhood are no longer the sole or secure occupations of women that they may once have been. Women today are more likely to remain single. They are more likely to cohabit prior to or instead of marriage. Those who do marry tend to do so at a later stage in life than did their mothers and grandmothers. The same is true for childbearing whether this occurs within or outside of marriage. Women today are more likely to experience marital breakdown and some period of lone parenting during the course of their adult lives. They are also more likely to participate in the labour market and to combine this with motherhood and home-making (see section II of this volume).

These trends suggest that change is occurring in the roles, attitudes and identities of women in Wales. Traditional domestic identities are no longer as central to the lives of women. Feminine identity is no longer grounded solely in the domestic and private sphere. A greater degree of independence characterizes the lives of younger women in Wales today. This can be seen not only through women's increased participation in the public arenas of life, but also through the changes that have occurred in the private domain of the family. Women have sought and achieved a degree of independence from men, they have refused to be tied to traditional domestic roles and, much more than previously, they have 'volunteered' into the family and its associated caring responsibilities. At the same time, other changes have occurred which have challenged the very basis of traditional family life and familial ideology. Lesbianism constitutes a challenge to 'straight' society and demonstrates that there is a viable alternative to heterosexuality and its values. Lesbianism can be seen as one response to the oppression of women in society and as a denial of the alleged primacy of men in women's orientations. A potential source of knowledge and power for all women, lesbianism is viewed by male-dominated societies as a threat. It is met by silence, taboo, pressure or coercion and as a consequence little accurate knowledge or appreciation of gay and lesbian relationships exists. Nevertheless, lesbianism is an important aspect of the changing identity of women in Wales and one which demonstrates centrally the issue of women's independence from men (see Roni Crwydren's 'voice' in this volume).

In the following chapters of this section the theme of changing identity is explored through different examples of family and community life. In each case women can be seen making important statements about identity involving the issue of independence. In 'Who should do the dishes?', Jane Pilcher shows that there are clear differences in the ways in which different generations of Welsh women talk about men's participation in housework. Older women attach importance to traditional gender roles and identities and are resistant to the idea of any significant male participation in housework. Their identities are firmly grounded in the domestic sphere. Younger women are not at all concerned to defend housework as an exclusive or even primary female activity. For these women identity is not rooted in the domestic sphere. They assert their independence by seeing themselves as more than just housekeepers and are emphatic in their claims that domestic work should not be solely the responsibility of women. Significant as this finding may be, Pilcher also points out that such assertions and claims are not always easily put into practice. The actual domestic division of labour within households may often vary from the ideal and the majority of household and caring tasks continue to be carried out by women.

Nickie Charles provides further evidence of women seeking to establish and support independent identities. The refuge movement in Wales has focused attention on the issue of domestic violence. The family is not always a haven of emotional support and affection. For many women it is a place of terror and violence. Since the early 1970s Welsh Women's Aid has sought to provide support for women and children seeking to escape violence in the family. The chapter explores the development of Welsh Women's Aid, focusing on issues of provision and funding throughout the Principality. Increasingly women are refusing to put up with violence from male partners. They are asserting their rights as independent individuals by leaving such situations and, as importantly, are being empowered to do so by the efforts and support of other women.

Clare Wenger's chapter focuses on the question of family relationships in old age and illustrates the life-styles associated with different support networks found to exist amongst elderly women in rural Wales. Despite the variations in support networks, the themes which dominate the life histories of the women whose stories are told are those of autonomy and independence. As Wenger says, the common message in the women's presentation of self is 'I am competent, I am capable, I want to stand on my own two feet'. The extent to which elderly women are able to act out this identity frequently depends on the structure and nature of their support network. Whilst old age threatens them with dependence, these elderly women seek to maintain independence.

The shape of the family in Wales has altered quite significantly in the last thirty years and at the same time a transformation has taken place in the position and roles of women. The traditional nuclear family, although still clearly 'alive' in the Principality, is now challenged by alternative family forms. The diversity of family and household formations that exist today mean that women will have differing experiences of 'private life'. The chapters in this section do not attempt to provide a complete picture of family life in Wales, but rather to illustrate how some women negotiate identity within their domestic and family contexts. As with any selection, many issues are left unaddressed, but the topics discussed, namely housework, violence against women, and old age, are ones which are at the centre of sociological, feminist and policy debates over the ever-changing family. In feminist terms these chapters highlight the fact that, whilst the 'daughters of the revolution' have indeed made some advances along the road to liberation and emancipation, there is still far to go. Familial ideology (assumptions about families and what goes on inside them) remains strong in Wales as elsewhere in the Western world and the dependent, domestic, caring role of women is not one which is easily challenged.

Note

The author would like to acknowledge the help and assistance given by the statistics division at the Welsh Office in providing data from the 1991 Census which at the time of going to press was unpublished.

References

Haskey, J. (1988). 'Trends in marriage and divorce and cohort analysis of the proportion of marriages ending in divorce', *Population Trends* No. 54 (London, HMSO).

Haskey, J. and Kiernan, K. E. (1989). 'Cohabitation in Great Britain – characteristics and estimated numbers of cohabiting partners', *Population Trends* No. 58 (London, HMSO).

Central Statistical Office (1991). *Regional Trends* No. 26 (London, HMSO).

Office of Population Censuses and Surveys (1987). *Marriage and Divorce* (London, HMSO).

Rosser, C. and Harris, C. (1965). *The Family and Social Change* (London, Routledge and Kegan Paul).

Welsh Office (1989). *Digest of Welsh Statistics* No. 35 (Cardiff, Welsh Office).

Welsh Office (1992). *Digest of Welsh Statistics* No. 38 (Cardiff, Welsh Office).

Welsh Office (1991). *Welsh Social Trends* No. 8 (Cardiff, Welsh Office).

2

Who should do the dishes?
Three generations of Welsh women talking about men and housework

JANE PILCHER

The myth of the Welsh Mam (Beddoe 1988) serves to underline the fact that, historically, the principal identity of women in Wales has been located within the home. Feminine identities firmly grounded in the domestic sphere have been especially important for earlier generations of Welsh women. This has been partly due to the lack of female employment opportunities associated with the overwhelming dominance of heavy industry in south Wales (Beddoe 1988; Crook 1982). There is an extensive body of research evidence documenting the segregated division of labour which predominated in the first half of this century. The evidence shows that men primarily held responsibility for the financial provision of households, and women for the management and performance of tasks necessary for the day-to-day running of the household. (See Pahl 1984; Morris 1990; Thompson 1975; Lummis 1982; Roberts 1984; Mogey 1956; Dennis, Henriques and Slaughter 1969; Zweig 1952. For evidence on Wales, see Crook 1982; Red Flannel Films 1988; Brennan, Cooney and Pollins 1954.)

For much of the twentieth century, women have had low rates of participation in the formal labour market, but the end of the 1950s, and in particular the 1960s, saw an unprecedented rise in the proportion of married women in paid employment. Studies began to suggest that patterns of the domestic division of labour were undergoing change (Bott 1971; Young and Willmott 1975; Gavron 1983; and, on Wales, Rosser and Harris 1965). Such research indicated that 'jointness' and equality had become, or would shortly become, the predominant pattern. However, a considerable amount of research evidence has since been ranged against such optimistic conclusions about the extent and significance of changes in conjugal relationships and the domestic division of labour (Oakley 1974; Edgell 1980; and, on Wales, Leonard 1980). More recent research evidence continues to point to the prevalence of gender role segregation in the domestic division of labour, despite women's increased participation in the paid labour market. Evidence on Wales is provided by studies by Callender (1987), Hutson and Jenkins (1989), and Morris (1985) (but see also Brannen and Moss 1991; Mansfield and Collard 1988; Martin and Roberts 1984; Pahl 1984). The general picture that emerges from this review of the evidence is summarized by Winckler (1987a). She writes that, although there have been substantial and significant shifts in women's roles within contemporary Wales, these do not amount to a transformation of women's position from past times:

> rather, they suggest an increasing heterogeneity and complexity . . . within the fundamental and enduring constraints of the sexual division of labour.
>
> (Winckler 1987a, 53)

This chapter examines accounts of men and housework given by three generations of Welsh women. It shows that the varied ways in which each generation talked about men and housework are related to their differing expectations, which in turn arise from their contrasting socialization experiences of norms surrounding men's participation in housework, and women's participation in paid employment. Through an examination of the women's accounts, it is suggested that, for younger generations of Welsh women, feminine identities are less bound up with notions of exclusive female domestic roles than is the case for older women.

The study

The data form part of a wider study of differences between generations of women in their accounts of feminist issues (Pilcher 1992). In keeping with this wider study, this chapter draws upon the sociological theory of generations developed by Mannheim in the first half of this century (Mannheim 1952). Mannheim proposed that the socio-historical circumstances in which people are born and grow up 'set the framework for [their] existence and development, affecting their life chances, their view of the world, their aspirations and their prospects' (Rosow 1978, 69).

Generational location points to 'certain definite modes of behaviour, feeling and thought' (Mannheim 1952, 291), and the formative experiences during the time of youth are highlighted by Mannheim as the key period in which social generations are formed. Thus it is possible to make sense of differences between the three generations of women in their accounts of men and housework by placing what they had to say, and how they said it, in terms of their likely formative socio-historical experiences. In the analysis of the women's accounts, particular attention is paid to the *vocabularies* with which such accounts were constructed, and to issues of identity thereby conveyed.

The participants in the study were families of women (mother, daughter and adult granddaughter) who had lived in Wales for at least two generations. Individual interviews were held with fifty-seven women in 1989–90. The women, all living in the south Wales area, represented three broad age groupings. The women of the oldest generation had a mean average age of seventy-four, those of the middle generation were on average aged forty-six, and those of the youngest generation, twenty-two.

Much of the data examined in this chapter focuses on responses to the interview question 'Do you agree with men taking responsibility for housework?'. Comparative data on how domestic work responsibilities should be organized between men and women are provided by Mansfield and Collard (1988), who identified four types of accounts. The 'traditional' view was that women should be responsible for the housework, only having the right to help from husbands when incapacitated, for example, through illness. The 'neo-traditional' view (found by Mansfield and Collard to be the most popular) was that women should be mainly responsible for the housework, but with the right to regular help from their husbands. The 'equitable' view was that the workload should be shared equitably according to what each partner is best at, a position which leads to traditional roles being maintained. Finally, the 'egalitarian' view was that spouses should share everything equally (Mansfield and Collard 1988, 129–31). In the study reported here, the three generations of women gave similar accounts, and thus Mansfield and Collard's categorizations are used to organize the data. Data are presented by generation, beginning with the accounts of the oldest generation of women. Quotations from the women are accompanied by a pseudonym and by an abbreviated

reference indicating their generation (thus G1 for the oldest generation, G2 for the middle and G3 for the youngest).

Oldest generation

Many of the accounts given by the oldest generation were found to
be resistant to the idea of men having a substantial degree of
responsibility for housework. They emphasized the limits of male
participation in housework and stressed the particular *circumstances* under which the domestic work of men should take place.
Accounts constructed with a traditional gender role vocabulary
were prominent, characterized by references to help given under
special conditions when the husband could (temporarily) step in:

> *JP: Would you agree with men doing all the housework?*
> Not doing all the housework. No. But . . . if you are ill and that, the
> hubby always more or less takes over . . . and does it for you.
>
> Irene Harvey G1

> Should the wife be ill or take a job, then I think they should share
> it.
>
> Nancy Caswell G1

> *JP: Do you agree with men doing housework?*
> Well, if they have to. I agree with helping.
>
> Sarah Mitchell G1

For Hetty Morgan (G1), a determining factor was the type of job
in which a man was employed. In her qualified agreement to men's
having responsibility for domestic work she was concerned to
stress the limits to male involvement:

> *JP: Do you think that men should do housework?*
> Well, yes I do . . . If they haven't got too hard a job . . . Not too
> much, you know, just little things. So as you can depend on them,
> like, if anything goes wrong.
>
> Hetty Morgan G1

Like those who mentioned circumstances in which women were
incapacitated through illness, Hetty Morgan was suggesting that
men should act as 'back-up' help should things 'go wrong'. Such
accounts can be recognized as comprising a vocabulary of traditional gender roles. Another respondent also used traditional

gender role vocabulary to convey her hostility to the participation and involvement of men in housework:

> *JP: Would you say that attitudes to men doing housework have changed very much?*
> I think so, yes. I don't think it is for the best at all. I still think a woman's place is in the home and the man to go out and earn the money.
>
> Alice Nicholl G1

Alice Nicholl's use of the word 'still' indicates that she was aware that such views may not be widely held in contemporary society.

Accounts which can be recognized as being comprised of a neo-traditional gender role vocabulary contained references to the relative employment status of a male and female partner. Several women made mention of the employment status of the wife.

> *JP: Do you agree with men taking responsibility for housework?*
> Yes, if they feel like it. If their wives are working, they should, I think, do a little bit as well.
>
> Agnes Baker G1

> Well, I don't see it hurts them at all . . . They can't expect a woman to go out and work and come home and do the household chores as well.
>
> Rose Jessop G1

For Agnes Baker (quoted above), a further factor on which men's domestic involvement was seen to be conditional was the disposition of men toward housework: 'if they feel like it'.

Several of the oldest generation of women made mention of the employment status and hours of work of the male partner as a factor that should determine their involvement in housework. Lillian Thomas (G1) replied 'Oh, indeed, certainly I do' to the question asking whether she agreed with men having responsibility for housework. She then qualified her agreement in relation to the relative employment status of the male and female partner:

> It's hardly fair to expect men, if they are out in a job, working all day, that the wife considers he should come home and do house-work . . . But, if she was out working as well. It should be on a fifty–fifty basis then, I would assume.
>
> Lillian Thomas G1

This account was the only clear example of a woman of the oldest generation employing an egalitarian vocabulary, although others also used the term 'sharings' in their accounts.

Most of the oldest generation agreed with the idea of men undertaking housework in certain circumstances, but, as noted above, they tended to qualify this agreement by making reference to the limits of a man's participation. Irene Harvey (G1), in an earlier quotation, did not agree with men doing all the housework, whilst Agnes Baker (G1) said men should 'do a little bit'. Hetty Morgan (G1) similarly spoke in terms of restricted help, with men not doing 'too much' but 'just little things'. Restricted domestic activities were also mentioned by Ivy Keating (G1):

JP: Do you agree with men taking responsibility for housework?
Yes, I do. I think they should do a bit of it, myself.

Thus, the oldest generation's accounts of men and housework referred to a supportive male role. However, this support was highly qualified both in terms of the extent of men's domestic involvement, i.e. limited, and in terms of specifying circumstances in which it should take place, i.e. illness of the woman, and relative working status of the male and female partner.

Middle generation

Although making reference to the relative employment status of partners in much the same terms as did the oldest generation, some of the middle generation expressed their support for the participation of men in housework in a less qualified and more emphatic manner.

JP: Do you agree with men taking responsibility for housework?
If they are both out to work . . . Certainly, why not. They should.
Janice Caswell G2

Yes, definitely [laughs]. Well, if women are going out to work, I do.
Carol Mitchell G2

Other women were emphatic in their support for men's doing housework in a general sense, in that they did not specifically relate it to employment status, or to any other set of circumstances:

JP: Do you agree with men taking responsibility for housework?
Oh certainly I do. Especially today, why not?

Vera Mitchell G2

Oh I do. Yes, yeah. Definitely.

Shirley Owens G2

Oh yes, yes . . . I feel now that any man should be prepared to take 50 per cent responsibility in the running of the household.

Pauline Evans G2

Yes, of course I do. I don't think it's nothing demeaning.

Angharad Baker G2

Pauline Evans's comment about 'going halves' in terms of responsibility was echoed by several other women. For example, Brenda Jessop (G2) specified the conditions under which men's participation in housework was acceptable to her:

Well, I think, if the woman is working and the man, they should do half each, you know. Help with the housework. But if the woman is not working and the man is, I think the woman should do the housework and the cooking.

Similarly, Rosemary Thomas (G2) agreed with men having responsibility for housework 'in an equal situation', that is, when both partners work full time. Susan Griffiths (G2) also felt that couples should 'share' the housework when both work full time, as did Janet Morgan (G2): 'if you are a working housewife, then I think it's good to share. I believe in sharing.' These accounts, in stressing equality and sharing, can be recognized as using a vocabulary of egalitarianism. The tendency for the women of the middle generation to give accounts characterized by a greater egalitarianism is underlined by their conscious distancing of themselves from the view that men doing housework is 'wrong':

I have never thought it wrong (for men to do housework), never . . . I have never been one of these mothers to say, 'Oh no, love, I'll do that'.

Joan Lestor G2

When I was younger, I wouldn't have felt it was wrong for men to do housework . . . now I'm more confirmed in that idea.

Cynthia Daniels G2

Although, in the above quotation, Joan Lestor seemed unconditionally supportive of men's doing housework, she did express some doubts that men would perform household tasks to an acceptable standard, saying that she doubted that her own husband would do housework 'as well as me'. This can be recognized as an equitable vocabulary, stressing the competencies of spouses as a factor in who should do household tasks.

As with the oldest generation, some of the women of the middle generation were resistant to the idea of men having responsibility for housework. One woman used a vocabulary of traditional gender roles when she spoke in terms of men acting as 'back-up' domestic help in circumstances where the woman was indisposed:

> I think they should you know, if you are ill or something, [so] that the house is kept tidy.
>
> Miriam Powell G2

Others made use of a vocabulary of traditional gender roles and associated female domesticity:

> *JP: Do you agree with men having responsibility for housework?*
> Deep down, no. I would rather be home . . .
>
> Gwen Keating G2

> *JP: Do you think ideas about men doing housework have changed from when you were first married?*
> They have changed, yes. But I suppose really, I still think that, you know, that it's a woman's place to do it.
>
> Valerie Harvey G2

Valerie Harvey's use of the word 'still', as in the case of a similar phrase used by Alice Nicholl (G1), indicates an awareness that such a viewpoint may not be widely held in contemporary society.

Compared to the accounts of the oldest generation, the middle generation's support for the idea of men having responsibility for housework was less qualified and more emphatic. Several women of the middle generation made an attempt to distance themselves consciously from any idea that men doing housework was 'wrong'. Nevertheless, some women from the middle generation group did express hostility to the idea of men being involved with housework, with one of these making explicit reference to traditional gender role ideology.

Youngest generation: anticipating the future

Unlike the oldest and middle generations, most of the youngest generation had not had any experience of living independently with a male partner. Eleven unmarried or non-cohabiting women were living in their parental home at the time of the interviews. They spoke of their expectations of the future with regard to the ways in which domestic work, in households in which they lived with a male partner, would be organized. None of these women anticipated that they would have complete responsibility for the domestic work of the household, but one woman expected that her future spouse should 'help' rather than share domestic responsibilities:

> I'm not going to do all the work myself. I think that they [men] should help.
>
> Mandy Mitchell G3

This example can be recognized as a vocabulary of neo-traditional gender roles. For the other women of the youngest generation, however, the expected domestic arrangement between themselves and a future male partner was expressed in terms of 'sharing':

> I would prefer to say 'Oh no, you get it this time', or 'you make the tea' . . . Fair's fair, isn't it. You know, especially . . . if you haven't got any children in the beginning and we both go out to work. You know, share and share alike then, isn't it.
>
> Wendy Caswell G3

In another example of a woman employing an egalitarian vocabulary of sharing, a conscious comparison was made to the domestic situation which operated in her parents' household:

> I don't think I'd like to be like my Mum and Dad, with her doing all the housework all the time. I wouldn't put up with it . . . If I was married, it would be shared. We'd both do the housework and we would both have jobs . . .
>
> Ruth Richards G3

Ruth Richards's adamant declaration that she 'wouldn't put up with' an inequitable domestic arrangement was a prominent feature of these women's accounts of their anticipated domestic situations. For example, Hayley Baker (G3) explained her expectations for a future household:

> I think you should come to some agreement on sharing things. Like I wouldn't expect to come home from work and prepare a meal. I just wouldn't do it. I think the person I lived with would have to understand that as well.

A similar vocabulary was employed by Eryl Thomas (G3) who declared that, in a future domestic relationship with a partner, 'if he wouldn't do it [the housework], I wouldn't do it either', even if that meant the work did not get done, so that the 'dishes would just pile up'. These accounts of anticipated domestic arrangements are recognizably emphatic in tone, and this vocabulary is further evident in the following examples:

> When I get married it will have to be fifty–fifty. Or we will have to get somebody in to do it.
>
> Lindsay Farrall G3

> When I set up home . . . if he thinks I am cooking for him every night, he has got another think coming, you know. We will share the household chores.
>
> Isabel Ascote G3

> *JP: Would you expect your husband to share the housework?*
> Oh yeah. Too right [laughs].
>
> Elaine Griffiths G3

The emphatic and insistent tone characteristic of these accounts of anticipated domestic responsibilities suggests an underlying set of principles related to ideas of fairness and equality and hence have a 'taken-for-granted' quality about them.

The accounts given by these single women of the youngest generation were prospective in nature. These women had not faced the issue of arranging domestic responsibilities between themselves and a partner in practice. The value of the accounts lies in revealing the ways in which the young women thought domestic work *should* be organized between men and women, given an ideal situation.

Youngest generation: men and housework

The egalitarianism which characterized the anticipated futures of the single women in the youngest generation group was also apparent in the general accounts of the organization of domestic responsibilities provided by the whole of the youngest generation group (single, married and cohabiting). Many of them replied briefly and succinctly to the question concerning men and housework, saying 'Oh yes, definitely' (Karen Lestor; Rhian Keating; Lindsay Farrall) and 'Yes, totally, totally' (Wendy Caswell; Rebecca Daniels). Such short affirmations indicate that, for this generation of women, the participation of men in housework was regarded as something that should happen, in a taken-for-granted way. This interpretation is given support by the response of one woman to the question of whether men should have responsibility for housework:

> *JP: Do you agree with men having responsibility for housework?*
> Oh yes [laughing].
> *JP: Why are you laughing?*
> Well, I mean, why shouldn't they?
> *JP: Well, not everyone agrees with men doing housework . . . ?*
> That's ridiculous.
>
> Eryl Thomas G3

Other women of the youngest generation gave expanded accounts and made reference to the relative employment status of each partner:

> *JP: Do you agree with men doing housework?*
> I think it should be done between them really. It's fair that way. If they both work, they should share the housework. I don't see why the wife should come home and cook all the meals and that. It's not fair.
>
> Sharon Owens G3

Whilst this account can be recognized as being constructed with a vocabulary of egalitarianism, others employed a vocabulary of 'helping' rather than of 'sharing':

> I don't see why they shouldn't stop and help . . . [But] if they are in work all day, I don't say they got to do it.
>
> Denise Nicholl G3

Yeah . . . If they [women] are in work, then the men have got to help.

Bethan Parry G3

These accounts can be recognized as being constructed with a neo-traditional gender role vocabulary. In fact, only one woman made explicit reference to the principle of equality between men and women in her reply about men and housework:

JP: Do you agree with men taking responsibility for housework?
Yeah. I think it's, you know, all equal these days, isn't it.

Elaine Griffiths G3

Although not explicitly making reference to any egalitarian ideology, Isabel Ascote (G3) (after having described her father's occasional vacuum-cleaning as a 'token' activity) explained her view that there is more to the issue of the domestic division of labour than 'who does what around the house': 'It is more of an attitude than who actually ends up doing the washing up and everything.' Isabel Ascote, quoted earlier, had described the 'attitude' that she anticipated taking in a future domestic relationship, saying 'if he thinks I am cooking every night, he has got another think coming'.

One woman of the middle generation suggested that men would not be as competent at housework as women, and this equitable vocabulary also featured in the accounts of the youngest generation. Karen Lestor (G3) replied 'Oh yes, definitely' to the question asking whether she agreed with men's having responsibility for housework, but then went on to tell a 'horror story' about her husband's effort at clothes washing which had led to clothes being ruined. Similarly, Wendy Caswell (G3) explained that she did not completely believe in men having responsibility for housework because she had 'looked after' her father and her brother, in terms of preparing meals for them and ironing their clothes. She said that her brother would even be unable to put up an ironing board. She further went on to stress the general incompetence of men: 'It all boils down to the fact that they make more mess, anyway.'

A prominent feature of the accounts of the women of the youngest generation was, then, their brief and succinct affirmation of support for the participation of men in housework. Their replies were much less conditional than those of the two older generations. It would appear that, for the youngest generation, the idea of men's having responsibility for housework was non-problematical and taken for granted.

Conclusions

The data examined in this chapter have been concerned with the ways in which three generations of women talked about the participation of men in housework. The oldest generation's talk was found to be highly conditional, in terms of specifying the extent and circumstances of men's participation. They were found mainly to employ traditional and neo-traditional gender role vocabularies. They appeared resistant to the substantial involvement of men in the domestic sphere and held low expectations in this respect. Overall, the accounts of the oldest generation seemed consistently to imply that the domestic sphere should properly be, where possible, the sphere of the woman. In contrast, the middle generation's accounts contained fewer conditions and qualifications, and several of the women distanced themselves from a view that men undertaking housework was 'wrong'. The women were found mainly to employ an egalitarian vocabulary. Some women of the middle generation did make reference to normative gender roles as they explained their disagreement with the involvement of men in housework, but on the whole the accounts of the middle generation were considerably more accepting of the idea of men's involvement in domestic work than were those of the oldest generation. The accounts of the youngest generation, particularly when they spoke of their anticipated domestic arrangements, were emphatically supportive of the involvement of men in housework. For these women, the issue of men's undertaking housework was unproblematical, and frequently, it was men's *not* doing housework that was an issue. Overall, the youngest generation constructed their accounts with egalitarian vocabularies.

There are, then, clear qualitative differences in the ways in which the three generations of women talked about men's participation in housework, which suggest differences in the importance attached by the women to traditional gender roles and identities. Without wishing to suggest a crude determinism, the research evidence mapping the likely historical contexts of these women's lives, (reviewed at the beginning of the chapter), can be used to interpret the differences in their accounts. Thus, for the oldest generation women (born *c*.1915), the historical context of their lives has been one where men only undertook limited household work and where a marked sexual division of labour was the norm. Data on these women's own domestic arrangements at the time of the interviews certainly showed them retaining the responsibility for the domestic work of their households, despite their husband's retirement from paid employment (see also Mason 1987). Moreover, the women were reportedly satisfied with their domestic *status quo*. The oldest generation of women can thus be said to have been socialized to invest their female identities within the domestic sphere, as dictated by the cultural expectations of their time, leading them to be resistant to the idea of significant male participation in housework (see also Arber and Ginn 1991). Such resistance was expressed through their use of traditional and neo-traditional gender role vocabularies.

The middle generation of women (born *c*.1943) had experienced a different socio-historical context, particularly in terms of changed expectations about married women working. Data on these women's own domestic arrangements at the time of the interviews showed them retaining responsibility for domestic work despite significant levels of engagement in paid work. The women, consequently, spoke of their often inequitable domestic arrangements as a 'bone of contention' between themselves and their male partners and reported various efforts to increase their partners' input (see also Brannen and Moss 1991). On the whole, they made use of egalitarian vocabularies in their talk about men and housework. Some women of the middle generation did, however, remain resistant to any significant participation of men in household work and this was expressed through the use of a vocabulary of traditional roles. The sociological theory of generations proposes that adjacent generations will be more similar in outlook than non-adjacent generations. Certainly, the finding that the middle generation employed both egalitarian and traditional vocabularies indicates that they acted as something of a 'buffer' between the youngest and the oldest generations. The fact that some women of the middle generation took the trouble to convey an identity in opposition to the view that men's doing housework is wrong adds weight to this interpretation, since this was not evident in the accounts of the youngest generation.

The youngest generation women (born *c*.1967) had lived most of their lives in a society influenced by egalitarian and feminist ideologies. Such ideologies, although rarely explicitly referenced, were implied in the emphatic and insistent tone of the youngest generation's accounts of men and housework. Although the life course stage occupied by these women cannot be discounted as an influence on their constructions of the issue of men and housework (many had yet to face such domestic situations themselves in reality), the clear theme of the youngest generation's accounts was that the participation of men in housework was non-problematical and that they held high expectations in this respect. These women, in contrast to the oldest generation of women, were not at all concerned to defend housework as an exclusively or even a primarily feminine activity, or one that was fundamental to their own female identity. It may be that, for these youngest generation women, insisting that men *do* undertake housework is an important part of their identities as women who have grown to adulthood in a society influenced by feminist and egalitarian ideologies.

Data from the British Social Attitudes survey suggests that respondents tend to be more egalitarian in theory than analysis of their actual domestic arrangements show them to be in practice (Witherspoon 1985). In the study reported here, the younger two generations of women were found to be more egalitarian in their accounts of men and housework than the oldest. However, analysis of their reported actual domestic arrangements showed, that they indeed continued to have the main responsibility for household work, despite their greater rhetoric of egalitarianism (see Pilcher 1992). Thus, whilst younger generations of women might be more likely to insist in theory that men take a greater share of household work, it would appear much more difficult to put this theory into practice (see also Brannen and Moss 1991). Younger generations of Welsh women may no longer be investing their feminine identities in the domestic sphere to the same extent as older generations; nevertheless, they seem likely to continue to invest their time and effort, alongside participation in paid employment.

References

Arber, S. and Ginn, J. (1991). *Gender and Later Life* (London, Sage).

Beddoe, D. (1988). 'Women between the Wars', in T. Herbert and G. Jones (eds.), *Wales Between the Wars* (Cardiff, University of Wales Press).

Bott, E. [1957] (1971). *Family and Social Network: Roles, Norms and External Relationships in Ordinary Urban Families* (London, Tavistock).

Brannen, J. and Moss, P. (1991). *Managing Mothers: Dual Earner Households after Maternity Leave* (London, Unwin Hyman).

Brennan, T., Cooney, E. and Pollins, H. (1954). *Social Change In South West Wales* (London,: Watts and Co).

Callender, C. (1987). 'Women seeking work', in S. Fineman (ed.), *Unemployment: Personal and Social Consequences* (London, Tavistock).

Crook, R. (1982). 'Tidy women: women in the Rhondda between the wars', *Oral History* Vol. 10, No. 2, 40–57.

Dennis, N., Henriques, H. and Slaughter, C. [1956] (1969). *Coal is Our Life: An Analysis of a Yorkshire Mining Community* (London, Tavistock).

Edgell, S. (1980). *Middle Class Couples: A Study of Segregation, Domination and Inequality in Marriage* (London, George Allen and Unwin).

Gavron, H. [1966] (1983). *The Captive Wife: Conflicts of Housebound Mothers* (London, Routledge and Kegan Paul).

Hutson, S. and Jenkins, R. (1989). *Taking the Strain: Families, Unemployment and the Transition to Adulthood* (Milton Keynes, Open University Press).

Leonard, D. (1980). *Sex and Generation. A Study of Courtship and Weddings* (London, Tavistock).

Lummis, T. (1982). 'The historical dimension of fatherhood: a case study 1890–1914', in L. McKee and M. O'Brien (eds.), *The Father Figure* (London, Tavistock).

Mannheim, K. (1952). 'The problem of generations', in K. Mannheim, *Essays on the Sociology of Knowledge* (London, Routledge and Kegan Paul).

Mansfield, P. and Collard, J. (1988). *The Beginning of the Rest of Your Life? A Portrait of Newly-wed Marriage* (London, Macmillan).

Martin, J. and Roberts, C. (1984). *Women and Employment: A Lifetime Perspective* (London, HMSO).

Mason, J. (1987). 'A Bed of Roses? Women, marriage and inequality in later life', in P. Allat, T. Keil, A. Bryman and B. Bytheway (eds.), *Women and the Life Cycle: Transitions and Turning Points* (London, Macmillan).

Mogey, J. (1956). *Family and Neighbourhood: Two Studies in Oxford* (Oxford, Oxford University Press).

Morris, L. (1990). *The Workings of the Household* (Cambridge, Polity).

Morris, L. (1985). 'Renegotiation of the domestic division of labour in the context of male redundancy', in H. Newby, J. Bujra, P. Littlewood, G. Rees and T. Rees (eds.), *Restructuring Capital: Recession and Reorganization in Industrial Society* (London, Macmillan).

Oakley, A. (1974). *The Sociology of Housework* (London, Martin Robertson).

Pahl, R. (1984). *Divisions of Labour* (Oxford, Basil Blackwell).

Pilcher, J. (1992). *Social Change and Feminism: Three Generations of Women, Feminist Issues and the Women's Movement*, unpublished Ph.D. thesis, University of Wales.

Red Flannel Films (1988). *Mam* (Pontypridd, Red Flannel Films).

Roberts, E. (1984). *A Woman's Place: An Oral History of Working Class Women, 1890–1940* (Oxford, Basil Blackwell).

Rosow, I. (1978). 'What is a Cohort and why?', *Human Development*, Vol. 21, 65–75.

Rosser, C. and Harris, C. (1965). *The Family and Social Change: A Study of Family and Kinship in a South Wales Town* (London, Routledge and Kegan Paul).

Thompson, P. (1975). *The Edwardians: The Remaking of British Society* (London, Weidenfeld and Nicolson).

Winckler, V. (1987a). 'Women and work in contemporary Wales', *Contemporary Wales*, Vol. 1, 53–71.

Winckler, V. (1987b). 'Women in post-War Wales', *Llafur,* Vol. 4, 69–77.

Witherspoon, S. (1985). 'Sex roles and gender issues', in R. Jowell and S. Witherspoon (eds.), *British Social Attitudes: The Fifth Report* (Aldershot, Gower).

Young, M. and Willmott, P. [1973] (1975). *The Symmetrical Family* (Harmondsworth, Penguin).

Zweig, F. (1952). *Women's Life and Labour* (London: Victor Gollancz).

3

The refuge movement and domestic violence

NICKIE CHARLES

The family in Wales, as in the rest of Britain, is characterized by a division of labour in which women undertake the bulk of the domestic work while, at the same time, participating in paid employment, often on a part-time basis. Men, on the other hand, are engaged in paid employment full-time and are responsible for the financial well-being of their wives and children. This is the ideal and is, of course, modified by variations in the availability and type of employment. This division of labour has found ideological expression in the notion of the Welsh Mam. The quiet, strong woman selflessly working for the good of the family, holding the purse strings, holding the family together and keeping a meticulously clean and tidy home. This representation of Welsh women bears little relation to the reality of women's lives and it is a moot point whether it has ever been the dominant pattern within Wales. Indeed, its emergence in the nineteenth century can be understood as part of the process of excluding women from areas of paid employment, such as heavy industry, which were viewed by the English ruling class and the labour aristocracy as inappropriate for women and against all norms of femininity (Barrett 1980). Despite this process of exclusion, working-class women have always sought paid employment and during the course of this century it has become increasingly available. Many women, once they were married and had children, had little chance of paid employment during the early years of the century due to the predominance of heavy industry in the industrialized parts of Wales. But this does not mean that women did not work for money, by taking in washing for instance, or lodgers, and in rural areas there has always been agricultural work available.

The myth of the Welsh Mam also hides another reality, a reality that calls into question the idea that the family is a haven of emotional support and mutual affection. It is the reality of domestic violence. Research shows that, far from the home being a place of safety for women, they are more likely to suffer violence within the family at the hands of their closest and most intimate male relatives than they are in the public domain, where the threat to women is supposed to be at its greatest (Walby 1990). For many women the family is the place where they experience violence and the terror accompanying it, the place where violence is least expected because, until recently, its occurrence was not publicly recognized and the family was regarded as a 'haven in a heartless world' for all its members. Women who experienced violence often felt they were the only ones to whom this was happening and that it was somehow their own fault. They therefore kept it hidden, leaving the myth of the happy family unchallenged. It was not until the advent of the women's liberation movement that domestic violence was brought into the light of day and its existence publicly acknowledged. This chapter explores the way in which the women's refuge movement in Wales has focused attention on domestic violence, and the nature of the support it provides for women and children experiencing domestic violence.

The emergence of Welsh Women's Aid

In the early seventies, women's groups throughout Britain began to campaign for refuges for women in order that they would be able to escape from violent domestic situations. At first these refuges were run on an entirely voluntary basis in premises which were often supplied by the local housing authority. Not that this was achieved without a lot of hard work and active campaigning. In Cardiff, for instance, after an initial meeting in June 1974 where the decision was taken to set up a refuge, a letter-writing campaign was begun in order to enlist the support of local MPs, councillors, social service departments, housing officers and the Mayor. Meetings were held with representatives of the local housing department and, eventually, the group was offered a house which could be used as a refuge. As with many other local authorities which agreed to provide houses for use as refuges, Cardiff City Council had not offered the group one of its better properties. This particular house had to be rewired, reroofed, replastered and generally repaired before the group regarded it as suitable. It was eventually ready and on 29 July 1975 the first resident arrived with her eighteen-month-old son. An article in the *Western Mail* on 8 July 1975 began: 'A sunny happy little house with stout walls, a pretty colour scheme and a small paved garden, will shortly be opening its door to women and children desperately in need of a respite from a life of beatings and bullying' (Cardiff Women's Aid 1990). This story was repeated wherever a women's refuge was opened and, in the early days of the refuge movement, state support, beyond the provision of a suitable house, was minimal. The refuges were run on a self-help basis with the women residents running them collectively. The women who set up the refuge operated as a support group for women in the refuge and a point of contact for women seeking refuge, but no one was resident in the refuge as a warden and no one was paid for the work they put in.

Prior to the emergence of the refuge movement no provision existed to enable women to leave their violent partners. There was nowhere for them to go and no one to whom they could turn. At that time, women made homeless through domestic violence did not even have the right to be rehoused; this only became law in 1977. Setting up refuges was, therefore, a very material way of affecting the situation of many ordinary women and of challenging what had hitherto gone unchallenged: the right of a man to behave towards the woman with whom he lived in any way he pleased as long as it was within his own four walls. Male violence towards women was brought into the light of day by the refuge movement and the first steps were taken to enable women to challenge it.

Refuges can also be seen as a form of alternative, feminist welfare provision offering women the sort of support that was unavailable elsewhere. This is immensely important when it is remembered that all the other agencies to which women turned, such as social services or the police, were reluctant to intervene in the private realm of the family or were limited in their ability to support women because of their statutory duties which prioritized the need to maintain the family as a unit (Pahl 1985). Women involved in refuge groups were tied by no such statutory obligations and made it a priority to support the women who came to them and to believe their version of events without question. As one refuge worker put it, 'Violence is always wrong'. No pressure was put on women to return to their violent partners and an open-door policy ensured that shelter was available to all. Equally, pressure was not exerted to persuade women to leave their partners if they themselves did not feel it was appropriate. A refuge worker who had herself been through the refuge said:

We love to see a woman go out, you know, make her own mind up what she wants to do, and whether that's to return to him and it works, then that's a success story in itself, right? And we believe that that's a good success, we're not in this to break up families or marriages.

However, impartiality, although desirable, is often difficult:

When women go home we cross all our fingers and we always feel uncomfortable about women going home. 'Cos we're of the opinion that if men are violent, they probably won't change. And it could be years before the woman comes back or she may never come back and you know it hasn't changed . . . it's difficult for us when women go back 'cos we always think it's going to happen again but we actually have to learn to give information without influencing them. Because we don't have the right to decide what other people are going to do with their lives . . . It's really hard not to influence them into leaving the man . . . But it's important that we do [not].

Despite these views, women's refuge groups were often and may still be perceived as a threat to the family because of the very fact that they provide women with a woman-centred alternative to tolerating continuing abuse.

Refuge provision

At the time of writing (1992), there are thirty-one local Women's Aid groups affiliated to Welsh Women's Aid and between them they run thirty-five refuges and thirteen information centres. A research project, completed in 1991, found that the greatest number of refuges, family spaces and information centres are located in the south of the country where the funding of local groups is higher than in other parts of Wales (Charles 1991). The only group to be relatively well funded outside south Wales is Bangor Women's Aid, which was for a long time the only Women's

Aid group in Gwynedd. The worst-funded groups are to be found in rural mid and west Wales. The exceptions to this are two poorly-funded groups in industrial south Wales, Swansea and Lliw Valley. Swansea's funding is low because the group chose to run its two refuges on the basis of unpaid volunteers rather than moving to a mix of paid and unpaid workers which other local groups had gradually done. The group changed its policy in 1991 as a response to the dwindling supply of unpaid workers. Lliw Valley is a different case. Until 1991 it had applied year after year for funding under the Urban Programme. Such applications have to be supported by the local council because, although the Welsh Office provides the major portion of the funding for the first few years, the council is expected to take over responsibility for full funding after this initial period. Lliw Valley Borough Council, year after year, refused to support the group's application. It was only in 1991 that an application for funding was successful. This was because of the work put in by one of the regional Welsh Women's Aid co-ordinators on behalf of Lliw Valley Women's Aid with the Welsh Office and the subsequent 'persuasion' that the Welsh Office was able to exert on Lliw Valley Borough Council. These two groups, Lliw Valley and Swansea, were the only refuge groups in Wales not to have a paid refuge worker in 1990.

Levels of funding do not, however, have a direct relationship to the adequacy of refuge provision in different parts of Wales, particularly if the number of family spaces available in refuges is related to the population that they serve. In 1975 the Select Committee on Violence within Marriage recommended that there be one family space per 10,000 population. This target has not been reached in any part of Wales but, perhaps surprisingly in the light of the distribution of funding and facilities, Powys is the county where provision comes nearest to that level, while provision is furthest away from the recommended level in Clwyd and South Glamorgan. The research found that in Powys there was one family space to 12,767 people whereas in Clwyd the ratio was 1:31,308 and the ratio for South Glamorgan was 1:31,030. In 1991 Powys had three Women's Aid groups while Clwyd and South Glamorgan each had one. Although Cardiff Women's Aid enjoys the highest levels of funding of any refuge group in Wales, runs two refuges and an information and drop-in centre and has a higher number of family spaces than any other refuge group, provision in South Glamorgan is low in relation to its population. Of course the concentration of population is much higher in the urban, industrial areas of Wales than it is in rural areas. So although Women's Aid groups in these areas may receive higher than average levels of funding, it means neither that refuge provision is adequate nor that it is any nearer recommended levels than in areas receiving lower levels of funding.

The fact that the refuge movement grew out of and was part of the movement for women's liberation may help to throw light on the distribution of refuge provision within Wales. The women's movement was largely a middle-class, urban phenomenon. It was made up of relatively young, well-educated, usually white women who were highly motivated to change the restrictive social structures in which they found themselves. It was local women's liberation groups that set up refuges in the seventies and, by definition, they were likely to be found in urban areas. Given these origins, it is not surprising that the first refuges in Wales were located in urban areas and that there are more refuge groups in the urban, industrial areas of Wales than in the rural areas (Charles 1991). Welsh Women's Aid has, in fact, decided to take the initiative and develop refuges in the rural parts of north Wales rather than waiting for pressure to be applied by women's groups in those areas. This is because the groups which might apply the pressure and develop a refuge simply do not exist.

The urban origins of the refuge movement may also throw some light on the disparity in funding between urban and rural refuge groups. Those groups that receive higher levels of funding tend to be those that have been established the longest and these are by and large groups in urban areas (Charles 1991). Indeed, Lliw Valley Women's Aid was set up in 1985, considerably later than the other groups in the industrial south, which had all opened refuges by the end of 1980. Most groups have had to work very hard in their local communities to convince their local councils, social services departments and the police that they are providing a skilled and essential service to the women of that area and that they deserve to be taken seriously. The longer-established groups have undoubtedly achieved this and most have good relations with the statutory agencies. It may be that these sort of relations need to be established before local authorities will agree to a long-term financial commitment to a voluntary group in their area. A minimal level of support from local councils, often taking the form of premises in which to open a refuge, may provide groups with the opportunity of demonstrating the need for refuge provision while not committing the council to any significant financial outlay. This was certainly the case in Lliw Valley where the council rented the refuge group a council house to be used as a refuge but did not support their applications for funding until 1991.

In 1991, there were nine district council areas without refuge provision, six of these were in rural north and west Wales. The scarcity of refuge provision is particularly problematic for women in rural areas as the distances they have to travel in search of assistance are often very great and may condemn them to remaining in a violent domestic situation. Some district councils, even though there is no provision in their own area, make a financial contribution to provision in other local authority areas. So, for instance, the five district councils in Gwynedd all contribute to the funding of Bangor Women's Aid. While this is very laudable and much appreciated by Bangor Women's Aid, it does not ensure adequate provision for those women in need of refuge in their *own* areas.

A handful of district councils do not support Women's Aid refuges at all and some justify this by stating that women in their locality do not become homeless as a result of domestic violence. They therefore have no statutory duty to make any provision for them. Such a position is maintained by South Pembrokeshire but the refuge group in neighbouring Preseli district is often approached by women from South Pembrokeshire. A reluctance to acknowledge the existence of domestic violence, or to recognize that women may become homeless as a result of it, often goes hand in hand with a reluctance to acknowledge a homelessness problem. The two are clearly linked because women who become homeless by leaving a violent partner are regarded as officially homeless. This means that local authorities have to rehouse them and, in the meantime, provide them with temporary accommodation. Women's Aid refuges are the best form of temporary accommodation available for women in this situation but, from the point of view of a housing authority with limited housing stock, an increased number of refuges is likely to mean an increased number of women applying to be rehoused. If local housing departments do not wish to recognize that they have a homelessness problem, or genuinely believe that they have not, and if they also believe domestic violence is best kept behind closed doors, they are not likely to welcome increased refuge provision in their areas followed by increased pressure on them to rehouse women who become homeless as a result of domestic violence. This situation is likely to become more acute as local authority housing stock diminishes and local authorities are overstretched financially.

Paid and unpaid workers

Originally, refuges were run by women on a voluntary basis. The women in the groups which set up refuges regarded their support for women and children escaping domestic violence as part of their political activity. Their commitment to refuge work stemmed from their feminist convictions and perhaps from their own experiences of male violence. One of the aims of these groups was to provide an alternative experience for women seeking refuge, not only by providing them with an environment where they were safe from the threat of violence and where men were not allowed, but also by providing them with the experience of communal living. In this way women were able to share their experiences. This is extremely important for women who have suffered domestic violence because, by talking to other women, they realize that their experience is not unique and that they are not to blame for what has happened to them. Women who have stayed in refuges often speak about the support that they receive from the other women in the refuge. A refuge worker who had become involved in refuge work after having been through the refuge herself said:

> They get a *lot* of support from one another. When women first come in they think that it's only happened to them and once they all get talking they find 'no, it isn't just me' . . . They're very supportive of one another.

Another refuge worker said:

> I had never had a family, no brothers, sisters or anything. So coming in here I had the sisters I never had before. They were supportive and they were always there.

And women often talk of this support as being more valuable than anything else in enabling them to come to terms with what has happened to them and to find the strength to start a new life away from their violent partners:

> We tend to help each other out here. If one's down we tend to look after each other . . . if it wasn't for Women's Aid I couldn't have left. Because all I'd done was get another bedsit and then go back. But it's given me the strength and independence to want to stay away.

Responsibility for the day-to-day running of the refuge lies with the women who live there. They are usually collectively responsible for cooking and cleaning and co-operate with each other and with the women on the support group to run the refuge as a collective enterprise. To this end, in most refuges, weekly house meetings are held where everyone comes together to discuss the week's events and any problems that may have arisen. Running a refuge collectively also involves sharing skills and avoiding any hierarchy of specialization or organization. All the women, those seeking refuge and those on the support group, have a say in running the refuge. In other words, refuges are organized along feminist lines.

The initial reliance on women working voluntarily as members of refuge support groups has changed over the years. While most groups still rely on unpaid workers and wish to retain a mix of paid and unpaid workers, most groups now have at least one paid worker, usually a refuge worker. Employing paid workers is dependent on groups' applying for funding; the sources of funding are continually changing and most are insecure. Obviously, those groups which were not successful in their applications, such as Lliw Valley, or which took a policy decision only to rely on unpaid workers, such as Swansea, remained wholly dependent on unpaid workers. Conversely, the groups which were successful were able to take on paid workers. Many of the paid workers, at least initially, are women who have been working as unpaid workers in a refuge group and have been able to develop the skills of refuge work in the process. Many also have themselves been through the refuge. One woman who was in this position said:

> I believe that women that have been either through the refuge or through a violent marriage themselves make the best workers, because they've been there and they *know* what the women are going through when they come in, sometimes you've only just –

you haven't got to say anything to the woman, you can just say to her 'Look, I know where you are, I've been there' and that makes them unwind a little bit.

There is considerable disagreement within Welsh Women's Aid about the desirability of increased reliance on specialist, paid workers. Most groups remain committed to the self-help principles of the organization and feel it is very important to retain a mix of paid and unpaid workers. Apart from anything else, this enables women who have been in the refuge to continue to be involved in its work after they leave. Very often they become unpaid workers, learning the many aspects of refuge work by becoming involved in it themselves. This can be regarded almost as an apprenticeship. Women working as unpaid workers in refuges become skilled workers themselves and may then apply for a job as a paid refuge worker. Indeed, this has been the route taken by several of the paid workers in local groups and such involvement can be seen as a means for working-class women to gain experience, skills and confidence in their own abilities.

This is part of the self-help philosophy underpinning Welsh Women's Aid, that women who have themselves experienced domestic violence should be able not only to escape from the violent domestic situation but also to participate in collective organization with other women. Whilst most groups now have a refuge worker who is paid, only twenty-one of them have a child worker and many child workers are employed for as little as twelve hours per week. This is a reflection of the difficulty experienced by groups in obtaining funding for child worker posts. It is often thought that child workers in refuge groups do little other than keep the children amused. In fact, children who come with their mothers into refuge groups are often disturbed and damaged by the violence they have witnessed their mothers experiencing and may themselves have been abused. They clearly need skilled support and attention in their own right and it is this which child workers should be able to provide. Even fewer groups have any other type of paid worker. As a result almost all the groups rely fairly heavily on unpaid workers to carry out much of the work of the refuge.

The groups with the highest number of paid worker hours are not necessarily those with the lowest number of unpaid workers although many groups are finding increasing difficulties in recruiting and retaining unpaid workers. This is forcing groups into a greater reliance on paid workers and was one of the factors in Swansea's decision to change its policy and apply for funding for paid workers. It also means that groups need funding in order to be able to operate at all. This is a new departure and suggests that a process of professionalization is being put in train. While funding is higher in the longer-established, urban-based groups where the number of paid workers is also higher, it appears that the ability to recruit unpaid workers may be more problematic for these groups than for those in smaller, more rural communities. Of the seven groups studied in depth for the research, the three in north, mid and west Wales found no problems in recruiting unpaid workers, while those in the south, with the exception of Cardiff, experienced extreme difficulty in recruiting and retaining unpaid workers. Support for the groups in north, mid and west Wales came not only from women in the community who were involved in refuge work on an unpaid basis, but also from their local authorities. For although the level of funding was not particularly high, the two most rural groups stressed that their local authorities were very supportive. It is interesting that these were also the groups which were most successful at fundraising. This is because higher numbers of unpaid workers are likely to mean that the support group is larger and more effective and, therefore, more likely to be engaged in such activities.

The availability in a locality of a pool of women who are prepared to work in a refuge may be affected by a number of factors. In south Wales over the past fifteen or twenty years there have been increasing job opportunities for women and more and more women have entered the paid workforce. This means that fewer women are available to do voluntary work in the way that is traditionally expected and which fits in with the domestic division of labour which assigns to them the caring role within the family and community. Women are also increasingly returning to full-time education when their children reach school age, which again means that there are not so many women available to work in refuges. Thirdly, many women working in refuges did so out of political commitment or because they had themselves been through the refuge and wanted to maintain their involvement. Because of the 'apprenticeship' nature of working as an unpaid worker, it was often possible for women to become paid workers in the fullness of time. In the interim they were able to rely on social security payments. In recent years it has become much more difficult for women on social security to work with refuge groups in this way because pressure is put on them by the Department of Social Security to look for paid employment and because Income Support levels have decreased in real terms. For these reasons it is not surprising that there are fewer women available in urban areas who are able to work unpaid with refuge groups. In rural areas, however, there are fewer occupational or educational opportunities for women and this may partly explain the continuing availability of unpaid workers in these areas.

Conclusions

Since the establishment of the first refuge in Wales in 1975, large numbers of women and children have been provided with an alternative to remaining in a violent domestic situation. In 1978, 432 women and 600 children stayed in Welsh refuges; this number had risen to 1,272 women and 1,990 children in 1991 (Welsh Women's Aid 1990 and 1991). For all these women, the existence of Welsh Women's Aid and the refuge network has meant that there is a means of escaping and challenging male violence. There is much local support for refuge groups within their communities, despite the fact that they are seen by some as threatening the 'traditional' family and invading its privacy. Indeed, if the 'traditional' family is one which is based on male authority and a man's right to exercise this authority over other members of his household in any way he sees fit, then the existence of refuges which enable women and children to escape this domination is certainly challenging the family. Refuges make it more difficult for men to continue to abuse the women with whom they live and provide women (who may be dependent upon their abusers financially and for the roof over their own and their children's heads) with a viable alternative to continued violence. The fact that Welsh refuges are almost always full and are often unable to give shelter to all the women who turn to them also throws into stark relief the extent of domestic violence. It is something which affects thousands of women and children in Wales every year. It is not pleasant to be reminded that many families, far from being happy, are riven by conflict and violence, particularly when our culture lays such a high premium on the values of family life and when, in Wales, the mythical Welsh Mam has been the object of veneration and reverence for so long. The reality is that many Welsh women experience violence and abuse from their partners and it is this reality which Welsh Women's Aid brings to our attention. It is not the family which is threatened by the refuge movement but the abuse of power by men within their homes. Providing refuges for women and children who are experiencing or are threatened with violence is one way of empowering women and beginning to redress the power balance within families which has for so long favoured men.

References

Barrett, M. (1980). *Women's Oppression Today* (London, Verso).
Cardiff Women's Aid (1990). *How we Began* (Cardiff, Cardiff Women's Aid).
Charles, N. (1991). *Funding Women's Aid Services to the Community in Wales* (Cardiff, Welsh Office).
Pahl, J. (ed.) (1985). *Private Violence and Public Policy* (London, Routledge).
Walby, S. (1990). *Theorising Patriarchy* (Oxford, Polity).
Welsh Women's Aid (1990) and (1991). *Annual Report* (Cardiff, Welsh Women's Aid).

4

Old women in rural Wales: variations in adaptation[1]

G. CLARE WENGER

Old age has been seen by some as a women's problem. Amongst those aged sixty-five or over in the United Kingdom, two-thirds are women. Over the age of eighty-five, three-quarters are women. The life expectancy of women in Wales at the age of sixty is twenty-one more years compared with sixteen for men (Welsh Office 1988). This gender difference is critical in defining the experiences of women and men in old age.

This chapter is based on data from a longitudinal study of ageing conducted in rural north Wales, which started in 1979 with the interview of 534 elderly people aged sixty-five or more, living in their own homes; 325 of them were women. In addition to extensive structured interviews every four years since 1979, the research has also included an intensive study of thirty people who were in their eightieth year or older in 1983. Twenty of these were women. Whilst using background data from the main survey relating to the identification of different types of support networks, this chapter focuses primarily on the qualitative data and case histories of women from the intensive study. It highlights the factors which are influential in the formation of different types of support network, showing how life events contribute to variations in informal support, self-image and identity in old age.

Gender and old age

The greater longevity of women has many implications. Women are more likely to be widowed than men, both because they have tended to marry men who are on average five years older than themselves and because men die on average at younger ages. For women in the age group under discussion here, a higher proportion never married, compared with men in the same age group and subsequent cohorts of women. This was the result of the high losses of young men in the First World War, and the rural nature of the environments in which many of them grew up. Gender differences in marital status are in turn reflected in household composition. Women are more likely than men to live alone. More than half the women in the north Wales sample lived alone compared with less than a quarter of the men. Not only are old women more likely than old men to live alone, but they are likely to live alone for longer periods and this likelihood increases as they get older. The same is not true for men. As a reflection of household composition, old women spend far more time alone than old men. Nearly twice as many women (38 per cent) as men (20 per cent) spent nine or more hours a day alone and for most this meant that they were alone all day and all night. Women, therefore, are more likely to be widowed, to live alone and to spend more time alone. It is not surprising then to find that women are more likely to feel lonely; we might also expect to find gender differences in the nature and composition of support networks.

Network formation

An understanding of support networks is crucial to an understanding of the experience of ageing and to the nature of identity in old age. A person's support network, and the larger social network of which it forms a part, is firstly a question of chance. Given that the core of most people's support network is the family, much depends on the marriages and fertility of earlier generations, the size of one's family of socialization and even birth order. Women are far more likely to become responsible for siblings in old age as older sisters frequently outlive their younger brothers. Sisters are also far more likely to *assume* care for a brother or sister. Elderly men, therefore, are not only more likely to be still married but are also more likely to have surviving sisters to look after them if they have no wife or available daughter. Whether or not one marries also affects one's social network. While not all marriages result in children and/or grandchildren, marriage extends the social (and potential support) network through the addition of in-laws. The importance of adult children in old age has been well documented, but gender is also important. Daughters have been shown to be more likely to provide personal care for ageing parents than sons, who provide more property maintenance or financial help. For women there is also the greater likelihood of widowhood in old age. All of these biological factors are ultimately beyond the control of the individual.

A second important imperative in network formation is migration. Here the individual has more control over her/his own geographical mobility, although the demands of employment opportunities may in reality limit choice. The individual, however, has little influence over the migration decisions of relatives, friends or neighbours. Areas with poor employment prospects or social policies geared to the mobility of labour lead ultimately to the undermining of support networks. The third factor affecting network formation is personality or temperament. Those who are loners in old age tend to be those who have been loners all their lives and those with large social networks tend to have always been sociable. Some develop personality traits which distance them from others or become so desperate for social contacts that others back away. But even the most gregarious temperament cannot alter the effects of biology and migration. It can only affect adaptation to the outcomes of these factors.

The north Wales study identified five types of support networks and life styles. These were the result of different chance combinations of the factors of biology, migration and temperament. Different types of support network were related to different sources of help, and represented different possibilities for self-help and mutual aid, and this influenced self-image and identity. Support networks were identified on the basis of the availability and proximity of family and the level of involvement with family, friends, neighbours and community. The networks are named on the basis of the old person's relationship to the support network:

1. Local family-dependent
2. Locally integrated
3. Local self-contained
4. Wider community-focused
5. Private restricted

The first three types are based on the presence of local kin, the other two types reflect the absence of local kin.

Gender and support networks

The support networks of all old people include more female members than male members and this is no different for women than men. Because many of the network members are also elderly, the gender of network membership reflects the ratio of women to men in the age group. However, women tend to have more bonds with friends, sisters and brothers and to have more multiplex ties (Mugford and Kendig 1986, Wenger and Shahtahmasebi 1990). Women are also more likely to have intimate same-sex friends (Wellman 1981, Corin 1982, Wenger 1992). While the networks of both women and men are family based, women's networks are more likely to have extra-familial ties (Corin 1982). When widowed, old men rely more on their children, while women are more likely to develop bonds with other same-generation female relatives or friends (Wenger 1992).

Reflecting differences in marital status and household composition, women tend to rely on different sources of support from men. Women develop confiding relationships primarily with their adult children or sisters, whereas most men are able to confide in spouses. Although the majority of elderly people can name a significant other on whom they rely, women are more likely than men to report that they rely on themselves or that they rely on a member of another household. Women are less vulnerable to the effects of migration. A quarter of those in the study under discussion were retirement migrants, i.e. they had moved fifteen miles or more after the age of sixty. In this respect there was no difference between women and men. However, men are less able to re-establish networks, so that moving (Corin 1982) and widowhood (Wenger 1984) are much more damaging to their networks than to women's, i.e. men's networks shrink while women's tend to remain the same size.

Although neither support network size nor network type is related to gender at a level of statistical significance, interactions *within* support networks are likely to be significantly different for women as a result of the social differences discussed previously. The following case histories illustrate characteristic patterns of self-help, mutual aid and self-image associated with the different types of network (Wenger 1993). All names and some specific details have been changed to protect the identities of the women involved.

The local family-dependent support network

The local family-dependent support network has primary focus on close local family ties with few peripheral friends and neighbours. It is often based on a household shared with, or near to, an adult child, usually a daughter. Community involvement is generally low. All support needs are met by relatives. These networks tend to be small and the elderly women are more likely to be widowed, older and in less good health than those with other types of networks, primarily because this type of network makes it possible for impaired old people to remain longer in the community. A family-dependent support network may have always been so, or it may develop, if a local family exists, in the face of the growing dependency of the elderly person.

The typical situation of old women with local family-dependent support networks is for a widowed mother to be living with or very near to a married daughter. In this context, the daughter tends to take growing responsibility for the care of the mother as the dependencies of age increase. Efforts to retain independence on the part of the mother may often be subverted by her daughter or other members of the family as they attempt to minimize risk or find that often it is quicker or easier to do things for her rather than to let her struggle to accomplish tasks alone. Family-dependent networks may also pivot on sisters or daughters-in-law, although the mother–daughter core is the most common. Such networks may reflect large local extended families, especially in more rural areas, as well as family adaptations to high levels of dependency. Old women within this type of network see themselves as fortunate to have family support and are often conscious of others who do not. They perceive themselves as having a 'good' family and, although it is rarely made explicit, it is possible to discern their satisfaction in having brought up caring children. On the other hand, most are conscious of the other demands on their children, and seek to continue to do things for themselves and resist high levels of support. The conflict between gratitude, worries about being 'a burden' and the desire to maintain some autonomy is common.

Case history 1

Typical of women with family-dependent networks was *Hannah Johnson*. Mrs Johnson, a Welsh-speaker, had lived all her life in the small village near which she had been born in 1899, one of nine children. She was a small woman, with a quiet, wry sense of humour and although she explained that she was shy, she always enjoyed my visits and talked freely as she shared her life story with me. As a young woman she had worked on a large estate where she met her husband, another estate worker. Eventually they took over the smallholding where she had been born. She had two children, a daughter and a son. When her husband's health failed, they moved to a council bungalow and their son took over the smallholding.

When first interviewed in 1979, Mrs Johnson had been widowed for fifteen years. One sister and one brother were still living within fifteen miles but she hardly ever saw either of them because all three were in poor health. However, her daughter, son and daughter-in-law came to see her several times a week and provided her with a lot of help. She was friendly with her neighbours and talked to them occasionally but described contacts other than her immediate family as 'other people who live around, no one special'. However, her next-door neighbour did come to watch her television most evenings. Mrs Johnson's sight was failing and she could no longer read or go out alone. Her daughter, daughter-in-law and son between them did her shopping, cleaning, laundry, ironing, decorating, cut her toenails, provided her with firewood and drove her wherever she needed to go.

By 1983, Mrs Johnson had had to give up her bungalow and had moved in with her daughter, son-in-law and grandson who lived in a neighbouring hamlet, about five miles away. She was now blind and had bad arthritis in both knees. She was always bright and cheerful, maintained her good sense of humour, and enjoyed telling stories about her childhood and early married life. Her son dropped in to see her frequently. She appeared to have a very good relationship with her daughter. She had no contact with her former neighbours – the one to whom she had been close had died although the nephew had been to see her once or twice. She appeared to have no close contacts outside the immediate family but took delight in her grandson's new job and his girlfriends! Other grandchildren, cousins, nieces and nephews dropped by to see her from time to time and she was always interested to hear and to relay the details of their lives. Her daughter had given up her part-time job to care for her mother and did everything for her, including helping her dress and get into bed. Her bed had been brought downstairs. She could move freely around the ground floor of the house. Despite her infirmities she was anxious to help if she possibly could and said she sometimes did the washing up.

Over the ensuing four years Mrs Johnson became more frail and more dependent on her daughter. She could only walk with a frame and was subject to dizziness and falls. Her daughter was increasingly tied to the house as she feared to leave her mother alone and had to tuck her firmly into bed with instructions to stay there until she got back in order to visit the supermarket in a town ten miles away. Mrs Johnson's son and daughter-in-law visited less frequently. After suffering a stroke, Mrs Johnson spent increasingly frequent and lengthening periods of time in the cottage hospital during the last three years of her life, eventually returning home for only occasional weekends. During these last years the marriage of her grandson and the subsequent birth of his daughter, her first great-grandchild, were highlights. Her daughter and son-in-law visited her every other evening all the time she was in hospital. She always spoke very positively about their care and attention. Her son and daughter-in-law also visited, but less frequently. She died in 1988.

Mrs Johnson portrayed herself as a true countrywoman. She identified very strongly with the small local area in which she had lived most of her life. She was conscious of having worked hard and being a good and tolerant neighbour. She continued to take pride in her friendly interactions long ago with tramps and gypsies who were common in the area in her early years. Her interest in natural history and her pride in her competence in raising and caring for large numbers of small animals – both commercially and as pets – were still part of her self-image. She had obviously been a resourceful woman. Her life had been family and locality focused and she strove to continue to make a contribution to the household as long as she was able. In her last years she gave the impression of a woman satisfied with her self-perception as a loved mother and grandmother, who could still make people laugh and who had been a good wife and mother and a hard worker.

The close mother–daughter bond is common amongst women

in local family-dependent networks, as is the gradual concentration of all caring responsibilities onto one person. Shared care is more common at lower levels of dependency. The low salience of friends and neighbours is also typical of this network type at high levels of dependency. The network type is found in all types of communities but is particularly common in the most rural areas with scattered settlement patterns.

The locally integrated support network

The locally integrated support network includes close relationships with local family, friends and neighbours. Many neighbours are also friends. It is usually based on long-term residence and active community involvement in church and voluntary organizations in the present or recent past. These networks tend to be larger on average than others. Women with locally integrated support networks have typically lived in the same house or at least the same neighbourhood for many years. Neighbours tend to be also long-standing friends and, together with relatives from the same or adjacent community or neighbourhood, combine to form a supportive milieu in which network members have long-term knowledge of each others' lives. Expectations of mutual aid are part of a *modus vivendi* deeply enmeshed with family, friends and neighbours and based on an ethos of generalized reciprocity.

Old women within these networks perceive themselves as a part of the community. They show an interest in and concern with the experiences of a wide range of local families. In early retirement they are likely to conform to our 'salt of the earth' stereotype, anxious to help out as and when needed by other community members – offering sympathy and advice and visiting the sick and bereaved. They identify with the community and tend to see themselves as good neighbours and friends. Being a responsible and participative community member is an important part of their self-image. While also including local family in their networks, it is the local *community* which is the focus of their lives.

Case history 2
Blodwen Griffiths had a locally integrated support network, despite having a large extended local family. She was born in 1900 near the same market town in which she had lived for most of her

life, and spoke Welsh. When first interviewed in 1979, she had been widowed for fourteen years and her only sister had died ten years previously. She had seven children ranging in age from thirty-seven to fifty-two. She lived with her youngest daughter, son-in-law and granddaughter. Two other daughters and one son and their families lived within five miles. She had ten grandchildren and growing numbers of great-grandchildren. Various members of her family dropped in to the house during the day. Every year she went to stay with her other children in different parts of the country.

Mrs Griffiths had been born on a farm just outside the town and had worked in domestic service before she married. Her husband worked in forestry all his life. They originally lived in a small cottage with only two bedrooms and no bathroom, where she had brought up her seven children who were all at home together for a short time. Although she could not imagine later how she had managed, she remembered it as a very happy time. Subsequently, they moved to a three-bedroomed council house.

Mrs Griffiths had a very positive, accepting personality and gave the impression of being prepared to see the best in other people. She had been living alone when her husband died, after a long illness, but her youngest daughter had come to stay with her for a few months, her other children provided additional support and a friend helped by taking care of all her washing. In the final weeks the district nurse came daily.

Mrs Griffiths's daughter worked part-time in the mornings and Mrs Griffiths was busy in the house making luncheon for her daughter and son-in-law, cleaning and ironing. She had a lot of energy and enjoyed housekeeping tasks. Her daughter used to worry that she was overdoing it. She also helped out her daughter-in-law who lived nearby and worked full-time. This occasionally involved caring for her son who was an invalid and sometimes needed nursing care. She took pride in the academic successes of the granddaughter, who lived at home when not away at college, and the fact that her married granddaughters and her grand-daughters-in-law came to visit her often after they had dropped their children off at school.

Mrs Griffiths was well known on the council estate where she lived and in the town beyond as someone who was involved and helpful in the many voluntary organizations. She had many friends, some of whom were neighbours. Particularly close relations existed with the next-door neighbour and the two families looked out for and after each other in times of sickness. When she was younger Mrs Griffiths had cleaned the chapel and private houses. She continued to be a faithful member of the chapel and a good friend to the schoolteacher for whom she had cleaned. The schoolteacher was now suffering from the early stages of dementia and Mrs Griffiths visited her regularly and monitored and valeted her personal appearance. If anyone she knew was ill or recently bereaved, Mrs Griffiths could be relied on to visit and offer support and help.

Mrs Griffiths's life-style continued with little change until, in 1986, she had a stroke. She was quite ill for some weeks but seemed to make a good recovery. She resumed her household activities and visits to friends and neighbours although she did slow down. While she was ill she was visited by family, friends and neighbours. After this illness her daughter helped her to bathe and handled most of her financial affairs. However, she still maintained her social contacts and had recently been spending a lot of time sitting with her son who was by then very ill, or with her closest neighbour who was recovering from a mastectomy. By this time she had ten great-grandchildren and it was becoming difficult to keep count! In 1990 her son died, and shortly afterwards his wife – two people to whom she was particularly close. However, her active and involved life-style continued although she was becoming rather frail. She died in 1992.

Mrs Griffiths's life-style was a clear continuation of her earlier life. She saw herself as energetic and independent and enjoyed her role as trusted friend and confidant both within the family and beyond. She took her role as comforter and supporter very seriously. Her relationship with her youngest daughter was friendly and they enjoyed going on trips together. Her daughter's efforts to restrict her activities – such as standing on chairs to clean windows or exercising the lively puppy – were brushed aside with wry expressions and humorous comments, much to her daughter's frustration. She very obviously saw herself as an active, competent woman, needed by her family, neighbours and friends.

The interest and involvement with the local community is typical of those with locally integrated support networks. Membership of chapel, church, Women's Institute or Merched y

Wawr (sometimes both) and pensioners' groups is common. Other women with the same network type were less active than Mrs Griffiths, but even after becoming housebound, established ties meant that friends, neighbours and co-members of voluntary groups often continued to visit and keep in touch. Women with this network type tend to give help and support willingly and unstintingly and receive, accept and appreciate help from others in their turn. In failing health and increasing dependency, much help is received from neighbours or local family, even when formal statutory services are involved. The shared care between family, friends, neighbours and services makes it possible for independent living to be maintained and self-help reinforced even at quite severe disability levels. This was the most common network type in the study, although more common in the larger villages and small towns than in areas of dispersed settlement.

Local self-contained support networks

The local self-contained support network typically has arm's-length relationships, or infrequent contact, with at least one relative living in the same or adjacent community or neighbourhood, often a sibling, niece or nephew. Childlessness is common. Reliance is focused on neighbours, but elderly people with this type of network tend to adopt a household-focused life-style. Community involvement, if any, tends to be low key. Networks tend to be smaller than average.

The local self-contained support network was a minority type and appears to be associated with population sparsity and restricted opportunities for social contact in earlier phases of life. The privatized nature of this life-style means that old women, in the absence of a spouse, tend to rely primarily on self-help and crisis interventions from neighbours. However, many have never married and few with this network type have children. These women tend to opt out of reciprocal exchange, seemingly preferring to be self-sufficient, although they may accept help with long-interval needs, such as shopping. In stable communities, they may benefit from the ethos of generalized neighbourhood reciprocity and neighbours may adopt a pattern of arm's-length surveillance.

Old women within this network type tend to project themselves as emotionally self-sufficient and are likely to say that they keep themselves to themselves. Daily activities tend to be household centred, solitary or limited to role exchanges. While they are likely to perceive the community or neighbourhood as non-threatening, their relationships outside the household tend to be fairly superficial and they are unlikely to confide easily in others. If married, they are likely to say that they don't need others. Some may be quite cordial and conversational with neighbours but refrain from close relationships. Disappointments about not having married or not having had children were sometimes expressed. Relationships with existing relatives are often distant or infrequent. Resistance to asking for or accepting help is common.

Case history 3
Typical of those with local self-contained support networks was Mary Jenkins. Born on a farm in 1900, Miss Jenkins was one of six children and was also a Welsh-speaker. She went into service at eighteen when her father died and worked at several jobs in English towns. She returned to her native village during the Second World War and lived with and looked after her mother while working locally as a cook. At fifty-two she gave up work to look after her mother full-time. She was fifty-nine when her mother died, since when she had lived alone. She moved into an old person's bungalow in 1966.

By 1979, all Miss Jenkins's brothers and one sister had died. Her one surviving sister lived twelve miles away but she saw her infrequently. She could name no friends and was unwilling to ask anyone for help when faced with hypothetical situations. Miss Jenkins was always very courteous and deferential. She was shy and quiet and seemed lonely. Although she had infrequent contact with them, she spoke at length about her nephews and nieces. She seemed to expect visits more often than these materialized. She related how one nephew and his wife had visited just before Christmas 1983 but had not had time to sit down or have a cup of tea. She was hoping a great-niece would come to live in the village. This was a frequent topic of conversation but did not happen. She also had two cousins living in the village but seemed to see little of either of them.

Although Miss Jenkins had no friends in the village when first interviewed, she did have a friend who lived about twenty-five miles away. Each summer she managed to go once or twice by bus to meet this friend, returning the same day. During the study period, a woman she had known in her youth moved in opposite her and subsequently they went to church together. Regular church attendance was an important part of Miss Jenkins's life, but in the winter she sometimes found it too cold to go. She belonged to a pensioners' group in the village but did not attend regularly. When she did attend, she usually went with her dementing cousin at the request of a younger relative, who picked her up and took them both and delivered her home afterwards. Her descriptions of her participation in group meetings and outings gave the impression that she adopted an onlooker role.

From 1984, Miss Jenkins's health began to deteriorate. She had a several falls. One occurred when she was walking to the village shop and a heavy lorry thundered past her. The proprietor of one of the village shops picked her up, took her to the doctor and then took her home. She was very shaken by the experience. She had spoken about having a telephone installed but decided her hearing was too bad. Subsequently, after suffering another fall, she spent some time in hospital. She decided to stay in her bungalow for the summer months but to find a residential home before the winter. She had previously said that when her health failed there was no other choice open to her but 'a home'. Despite the fact that visits from her nephews and nieces had been few and desultory, a nephew was contacted by the doctor. A decision was made to move her to a local-authority residential home thirty miles away, but convenient for the nephew to visit her. He took her there in July 1987. She had wanted to go to a private home near the village where her 'friends' could come to see her, although at other times she said that all her friends were dead.

When I last saw Miss Jenkins she did not recognize me but was very grateful for my visit. She told me that she had decided that she should look for a place in a home while she was still well enough to make her own decision and had thought that she would then have had more choice. She had been in this home for a year. She still wanted to move to the other home. The officer in charge told me that she had come in at first to 'see how she liked it', and from the beginning she wanted to leave. Her wishes appeared not to be taken seriously because she was often confused. The other home would also be too far for her nephew to go to visit. Her nephew came to see her once a fortnight but he was the only one who ever came.

Miss Jenkins was always extremely polite and deferential when I visited. Her home was spotless and early in the study period her garden was always very neat and tidy. She would serve coffee on a neatly laid tray with a clean napkin, but never took any herself. She spoke with pride of the professional families for whom she had worked and their appreciation of her high standards. She said that she was shy, and she was certainly a very private person, responding politely and willingly to my queries but talking little about her feelings. It was clear that she prided herself on doing the right thing. She had cared for both her parents in their final years but seemed to feel that she had been taken for granted by them and by the rest of the family; although this was expressed coolly, without hostility – it was presented as an unmarried daughter's expected role. She obviously saw herself as someone competent, and one who accepted her responsibilities. She had no expectations of help from others and, although she compared her old age with that of her own parents, she clearly felt that she was responsible for herself.

Findings presented elsewhere (Wenger and Shahtahmasebi 1990) have shown that normative expectations of care in old age exist only for spouses and adult children. However, in the absence of other kin, nieces and nephews will accept legal responsibility. Women with local self-contained support networks typically recognized existing norms of family responsibility and did not expect care from relatives other than adult children. Childlessness is common in this network type and the acceptance of the inevitability of residential care is a realistic stance. At low levels of dependency, neighbours can be expected to provide some help but early admissions to homes are common in crises. Some old women, like Miss Jenkins, seek to avoid crisis admissions by making their own arrangements, before the decision is taken out of their hands.

Wider community-focused support networks

The three networks described so far are associated with local provenance or long-time residence. The wider community-focused support network and the private restricted support network are typically associated with the absence of local kin. The wider community-focused network is a common middle-class adaptation and is associated with migration, particularly retirement migration. It is associated with active relationships with distant relatives, usually children, and high salience of friends and neighbours. Absence of local kin is typical. The distinction between friends and neighbours is maintained. Local friendship support is important. Neighbour relations are different from those in the locally integrated support network. Here, neighbour help is asymmetrical with no expectation of help being returned, i.e. it has more of the character of charitable help. The old people are generally involved in community and/or voluntary organizations. Networks tend to be larger than average.

Old people with this type of network place very high value on independence. Maintaining health and mobility are important. In the face of deterioration of health and the need for help, old women with these networks are likely to make concerted efforts to make their own arrangements, including the use of privately contracted paid help. They are likely to become their own care managers. Mutual aid in this type of network may involve long-distance family support, such as telephone contact and emergency visits in times of crisis.

Self-image for old women within this network type is based on independence and autonomy. In contrast with those within local self-contained networks, who may accept residential care as inevitable, these old women tend to expect to find ways of remaining in the community by managing their own case. They typically have wide friendship networks. Activities with friends, often through voluntary groups, are regular and frequent. The maintenance of reciprocal friendships is also part of their self-image as is being a good parent. Contact with distant children is frequent, two-way and undemanding. Pride in children is presented in terms of accomplishments and continued contact rather than day-to-day support and help. The independence of their children is often seen as evidence of their good parenthood, i.e. non-controlling.

Case history 4
Typical of women with wider community-focused support networks is *Caroline Jackson*. Mrs Jackson was born in Liverpool in

1897, the fourth of six children. Her mother died when she was a child. Her father, a civil servant, was in a position to hire staff to help him bring up the family and she had a comfortable middle-class childhood. After school she went to university and on graduation, became a teacher. Her father lived with her and on her marriage to another schoolteacher, a Welsh-speaker, they moved to north Wales. She had to give up teaching when she married because that was the rule at the time, but over the years she played an important role in community and regional voluntary organizations. Her father lived with them until his death.

She and her husband lived in the same small seaside resort town continuously after they were married. They had two sons who joined the professions. When interviewed in 1979, Mrs Jackson had been widowed for over three years, having nursed her husband for five years before his death. Two years before he died, they had moved into a large detached bungalow on a new estate. Both of her sons were living on the south coast of England. Both were married and she had six grandchildren and three great-grandchildren. Only one sister survived and she also lived in the south of England. Mrs Jackson saw each of her sons about four times a year and her grandchildren less frequently. One granddaughter came with her three small children regularly each summer for a seaside holiday, but Mrs Jackson wished she saw more of her family. She never saw her sister, although they kept in regular touch by telephone. The telephone was very important. Both her sons telephoned weekly and she had a wide circle of friends with whom she also kept in touch.

Mrs Jackson's mainstay in terms of local support was her privately contracted daily help, who lived nearby and came five mornings a week to tidy up and do any necessary cleaning. She checked that Mrs Jackson was all right and did any required errands. She also popped in on Saturdays and Sundays. The husband of her daily help served as odd-job man. She paid him for each job and had in fact been using his services before she engaged his wife. Work in the garden was done by a local contract gardener.

At the start of the study, Mrs Jackson was still driving her car. She was a keen bridge player and played regularly. She explained that she had two distinct groups of friends. One group was based on women she had known most of her life in the town. These were primarily local professional people who had been young wives and mothers together and whose children had grown up together. The other group were mainly retirement migrants whom she had met on the new estate where she lived. She had other friends too, one or two of whom had few other contacts and relied on her friendship. She belonged to local voluntary groups and attended fairly regularly. Mrs Jackson attended church regularly, to which she was given a lift by her parish priest. She also received regular visits from two nuns from a nearby convent.

Mrs Jackson was an outgoing, interested and interesting person. She read a great deal and listened to the radio, so she was never short of a topic of conversation. She received visits and telephone calls from her many friends as well as from her family. She gave the impression of being in control of her life and took a pride in her independence. Although looking well and claiming to be in good health, she suffered from angina and arthritis. Her arthritis was such that she found taking a bath difficult and always arranged to take one when her helper was in the house just in case she could not get out.

During the study period, her health deteriorated. She was admitted to hospital for major abdominal surgery. Her sons and their wives came and stayed in her house over the time of the operation. When she was discharged from hospital, one daughter-in-law and the wife of one of her grandsons, who was a nurse, came and stayed with her for a fortnight, after which the district nurse came regularly for some weeks. Her household help came daily as before. She received many cards, letters and visits when she was in hospital and said that she had been overwhelmed by how kind and thoughtful people had been.

She resumed her previous life, but decided to give up driving her car and attended her bridge sessions less regularly. She continued to telephone her sister every week, although her sister was now in a residential home suffering from dementia. She extended the hours of her daily help who now came every day, helped her to dress and was prepared to come immediately if telephoned in an emergency. Subsequently, she accepted the help of the community nursing service with bathing and had meals on wheels three times a week. She resisted the invitations of both sons to go to live with them and maintained as independent a life-style as possible, buying help as needed and keeping up contacts with her large circle of friends. At ninety-four, she was still very much in charge of her own life.

Mrs Jackson was a very self-confident, outgoing woman, whose self-image was clearly that of an intelligent, independent and competent person. Both her sons had at different times tried to persuade her to go and live with them. She resisted because she wanted to maintain her autonomy and to be allowed to do what she wanted, including taking the risks she felt were justified. She had enjoyed her short teaching career and still took a professional interest in national debates on education and the discipline of children. She still felt she had something to offer and maintained a friendship with a younger woman in her seventies who she felt needed support and guidance, but whose company was personally unrewarding. She was constantly impressed by the fact that she had so many friends who still regularly contacted or visited her. This reinforced her self-image as a worthwhile person, one not a burden on others.

The combination of reliance on distant family and on local friends demonstrated in Mrs Jackson's support network, is typical of the wider community-focused type. In many cases, however, this type of network is associated with migration later in the life cycle, particularly after sixty. In these cases, membership of local voluntary groups is a common strategy for meeting people and making friends in the new community. Friendship networks including other retirement migrants are common, and widows with this type of network tend to support one another. However, it has been found that in the face of growing impairment, chronic illness and especially the onset of dementia, friends in this type of network are likely to withdraw (Jerrome 1990) because part of their self-image is dependent on being identified with others who are able and competent. Wider community-focused networks may become private restricted with the onset of dependency.

Private restricted support networks

The private restricted support network is typically associated with absence of local kin, other than in some cases a spouse. Contact with neighbours is minimal. These old people have few nearby friends and a low level of community contacts or involvements. In many cases a low level of social contact represents a life-long adaptation. Networks are smaller than average.

Those with private restricted support networks can be one of an independent married couple, often retirement migrants, who adopt a self-sufficient lifestyle with few contacts with others. Such couples may have moved often during the life cycle and adopted a couple-focused adaptation to life. Often they abhor the perceived parochial perspectives of more rooted contemporaries and tend to relate to the community in terms of its scenery and amenities rather than its social components. Alternatively, they might be without sources of informal support as a result of bereavement and ill-health or have adopted an isolated life-style early in the life cycle. In the absence of a spouse and in failing health, they must rely on self-help or formal services. The life-styles associated with this network type seem to represent an opt-out from mutual assistance patterns. While neighbours may assume a watching brief, old women with this type of network are unlikely to ask for informal help. With the development of the frailties of old age, they may perceive the community/neighbourhood as hostile, unhelpful or inappropriately curious. Those with a history of mental illness tend to come to old age with private restricted networks as do many of those whose earlier life-styles have been constrained by the responsibility of long-term care for ageing parents or spouses, particularly if mental illness has been involved. Indications of paranoia are not uncommon. A self-image of being alone against the world is also not uncommon.

Case history 5
One of those with a private restricted support network was *Cecily Bryant*. Born in 1887, Miss Bryant was the oldest woman in the intensive study. She had been born on the Wirral, where she had lived most of her life until soon after she retired. She had been employed as a private children's nurse and after retirement had looked after her father. When her father died, she had moved to a village in north Wales where she had a friend living. Subsequently, she had moved into an old people's bungalow, which was heated only by a coal fire and had an inconvenient and cold kitchen.

Miss Bryant had been one of nine children, but only she and a younger sister were still living. She had some contact with her sister by letter but never saw her. Three surviving sisters-in-law were never seen, but one nephew visited her occasionally. In 1979, she named two neighbours whom she could ask to do favours for her, one of whom would let her use the telephone if need be. One turned out to be her home help. She said she did have one or two friends in the area but could only name one, who it turned out had been in the local geriatric hospital for over two years. Her support network at that time consisted of: a nephew, seen maybe three or four times a year; two neighbours, one of whom was her home help; and a friend who had been in hospital for over two years.

She had belonged to the church all her life but only attended occasionally. She did not belong to any voluntary associations. However, she appeared to be remarkably active for ninety-two years of age. She claimed that she did a lot of sewing, knitting and gardening. She said that she would like to see more people dropping in but that she was not spiritually lonely. However, the 1979 interviewer reported that Miss Bryant seemed very lonely and talked for ten minutes in answer to each question.

By 1983, Miss Bryant was ninety-six and her sight was failing, but she kept her house tidy and was proud to show how tidy all her drawers were. She still knitted and crocheted, mainly things with straight edges such as shawls and dishcloths. She listened to the radio and took a keen interest in current events. Her nephew was able to come and see her even less frequently, because his wife had suffered a stroke and he was looking after her. Neither of the neighbours she had mentioned earlier were still involved. Her friend had died,

> . . . so I have no intimate friends and no one to talk to. The only friend I had died twelve months ago . . . She was the only friend I ever had. We were at school together.

She had a new home help who came twice daily and was also visited five days a week by a community nurse, who came to attend to her eyes and once a week to give her a stand up bath. Although very reliant on and grateful for her home help and district nurse, she remarked that 'they don't make friends with you', suggesting that friendship was something she wanted. Despite this she claimed that she was rarely lonely and had always been very self-sufficient. However, she seemed to be very lonely. She had not been out of the house for over a year and particularly missed the fresh air of the garden and the flowers. She gave the impression of a very lonely woman who was trying to put a brave face on a very isolated situation.

Over the following years, Miss Bryant lost her sight and withdrew from even those contacts she had, making it difficult even for formal helpers to gain access to her house without negotiation. Neighbours, who had earlier made attempts to establish contact, gave up trying. However, her nephew came to see her approximately once a month. During this time she fell and broke her arm, raised help by shouting, was taken to hospital by ambulance, refused to stay overnight and returned alone to her bungalow. She continued to live alone with daily support from the statutory services. She received home help twice a day, seven days a week. She spent more and more of her time in bed. Eventually, she was persuaded to have a holiday organized by social services in a residential home. She appeared to enjoy this, but insisted on returning to her own home and solitude. However, her social worker was surprised when the following year she applied to go again. She remained in her bungalow until she finally agreed to go to live in the home where she had been on holiday, a few months before her death at the age of 102.

Miss Bryant was an intelligent woman who was frustrated by the infirmities and indignities of old age. She frequently stressed her competences – often belligerently. She clearly felt beleaguered by the shortcomings of her body, the housing department and the outside world in general. She had always stood on her own feet and obviously felt that that was the only way to live. Although she indicated that she was lonely and wished for friendship from her statutory helpers, it is likely that her resistance to admitting her need for help in her desire to maintain her independent identity may have kept them at arm's length.

Those with private restricted support networks tend to be a more heterogeneous group than those with other types of networks. However, a high proportion of these women have never married and/or have been carers for parents. Those who have been married tend to be the widows of independent married couples. Loneliness is common but not universal. The determination to put a brave face on social isolation appears to be typical. Most women with this network type, like Cecily Bryant, struggle to maintain autonomy and independence, even if it means social isolation.

Table 4.1 Support networks, identity and self-image

Network type	Predisposing life situations	Typical factors in identity and self-image
Local family-dependent	Family-focused life pattern. Local adult children and/or other relatives. If single, large local extended family. Long-term residence. Expectations of family help.	Fortunate to have good family support. Satisfaction with good family relationships which reflect on self-image. Good parent role important. Can rely on family help if needed but autonomy often undermined by family care.
Locally integrated	Community-focused, reciprocal life pattern. Long-term residence. Active involvement local family, friends and neighbours. Expectations of mutual help/reciprocity.	Integrated into community. Helpful and considerate. Participative and responsible. Expectations of mutual assistance deserved/earned.
Local self-contained	Household-focused life pattern. Singleness and childlessness common. Low levels of community/neighbourhood involvement. Perception of community as benign. Low expectations of family help.	Independent and autonomous. Emotionally self-sufficient. Friendly but not demanding of others. Does not need help.
Wider community focused	Friendship-focused life pattern. Geographical mobility. Distant family. Involvement in voluntary organizations. Family help short-term/friendship may be withdrawn in the face of disability.	Independent and autonomous. Good parent – allows children independence. Good supportive friend. Active and involved. Can arrange own help.
Private Restricted	Socially isolated life pattern common. No local family. (Heterogeneity)	Independent and autonomous. Self-sufficient, does not need others. Perceives community as unhelpful. Does not accept help easily.

Data from the study of networks and social work (Wenger 1994) indicate that adjustment to residential care is often difficult for those who have always been loners. Not all women with this network type are as physically impaired as Miss Bryant, but one of the characteristics is that dependency may be well-advanced before anyone recognizes the need for help.

Discussion and conclusion

What I have tried to do in this chapter is to show the differences and similarities in the lives of old women living in Wales. The five women described in the case histories typify the life-styles associated with five different types of support networks identified in the study. The type of support network one has in old age is determined largely by factors of marriage, fertility, migration and temperament, over which one has little control. Table 4.1 summarizes predisposing life situations and typical factors in identity and self-image as they apply to each network type. It can be seen that in many ways self-image is formed by adaptation to the hand that life deals. Those within stable residence patterns and local family develop identities based on mutual reciprocity and expectations of help from others in old age. Those who have no close family or who have moved around during the life course have adapted through the development of identities in which independence and self-sufficiency are the key elements.

The important finding with respect to gender is that as a result of differential longevity, women who survive into old age are likely to be living alone and as a result are likely to adopt far more self-sufficient and independent life-styles than old men. The drive to retain autonomy and independence in old age is a dominant theme in all the life histories presented in this chapter. Whatever type of support network these old women have, they all strive to hold onto control of their situation and to retain as much independence as possible. The common message in their presentation of self is repeatedly: 'I am competent, I am capable, I want to stand on my own two feet.' The degree to which this objective can be reached depends on the nature of the support network which the exigencies of life have given them.

Note

[1] The research on which this chapter is based was funded by the Department of Health (Welsh Office) and the Economic and Social Research Council, whose help is gratefully acknowledged.

References

Cole, C. (1984). 'Marital quality in later life', in W. H. Quinn and G. A. Hughston (eds.), *Independent Aging: Family and Social Systems Perspectives* (Tunbridge Wells, Aspen Systems).

Corin, E. (1982). 'Elderly people's social strategies for survival: a dynamic use of social networks analysis', *Canada's Mental Health*, Vol. 30, No. 3, 7–12.

Jerrome, D. (1990). 'Frailty and Friends', in *Journal of Cross Cultural Gerontology*, Vol. 5, No. 1, 51–64.

Lopata, H. (1979). *Women as Widows* (New York, Elsevier Natn. Holland).

Mugford, S. and Kendig, H. (1986). 'Social relations: networks and ties', in H. Kendig (ed.), *Aging and Families: a social networks perspective* (Sydney, Australia, Allen and Unwin).

Quinn, W. H., Hughston, G. A. and Hubler, D. J. (1984). 'Preservation of independence through non-formal support systems: implications and promise', in W. H. Quinn and G. A. Hughston (eds.), *Independent Aging: Family and Social Systems Perspectives* (Tunbridge Wells, Aspen Systems).

Shahtahmasebi, S., Davies, R. and Wenger, G. C. (1992). 'A longitudinal analysis of factors related to survival in old age', *The Gerontologist*, Vol. 23, No. 3, 404–13.

Stephens, R. C., Blau, Z., Oser, G. and Millar, M. (1978). 'Aging, social support systems and social policy', *Journal of Gerontological Social Work*, Vol. 1, No. 4, 33–45.

Stinnett, N., Carter, L. M. and Montgomery, J. E. (1980). 'Older persons' perceptions of their marriages', in M. Fuller and C. A. Martin (eds.), *The Older Woman: Lavender Rose or Grey Panther* (Springfield, IL, USA, Sage).

Wellman, B. (1981). 'Applying network analysis to the study of support' in B. H. Gottlieb (ed.), *Social Networks and Social Support* (Beverly Hills, Sage Publications).

Welsh Office (1988). *Health and Personal Social Services Statistics for Wales* (Cardiff, HMSO).

Wenger, G. C. (1984). *The Supportive Network: coping with old age* (London, Allen and Unwin).

Wenger, G. C. (1992). *Help in Old Age – Facing up to Change: A longitudinal network study* (Liverpool, Institute of Human Ageing, Liverpool University Press).

Wenger, G. C. (1993). 'The formation of social networks: self-help, mutual aid and old people in contemporary Britain', *Journal of Aging Studies* Vol. 7, No. 1, 25–40.

Wenger, G. C. (1994). *Support Networks of Older People: A Guide for Practitioners* (Bangor, Centre for Social Policy Research and Development).

Wenger, G. C. and Shahtahmasebi, S. (1989). *Network Variation: demographic correlates of network type* (Bangor, Centre for Social Policy Research and Development, University of Wales, Bangor).

Wenger, C. G. and Shahtahmasebi, S. (1990). 'Variations in support networks: some social policy implications', in J. Mogey (ed.), *Aiding and Aging: the coming crisis* (Westport CT, USA, Greenwood Press).

Wenger, G. C. and Shahtahmasebi, S. (1991). 'Survivors: support network variation and sources of help in rural communities', *Journal of Cross-cultural Gerontology,* Vol. 6, No. 1, 41–82.

II. *Public Lives: Education, Training and Work*

5

Women and paid work in Wales

TERESA REES

Historically, relatively few women have been in paid work in Wales. In the last two decades, patterns of industrial restructuring are creating more 'women's jobs', often in part-time work in the service sector, while 'men's jobs' in heavy industries such as mining have been decimated. The male bread-winner, female home-maker stereotypes are being challenged as a result. The proportion of women in paid work in Wales is now nearly on a par with the rest of Britain. Traditional roles are challenged by new realities. The vast majority of smartly dressed commuters I see every day on the Valleys train to Cardiff are women office workers, but accessorized by shopping bags rather than briefcases.

What impact is this increase in the number of working women having on identities in Wales? How are schools adjusting to this situation in preparing young people for adult life? Are women beginning to break through the old-boy network into top jobs? And how do different women experience the return to learning, the pressure of credentialism, and the 'double load' of work and home responsibilities? This section of the book explores some of these questions. This introductory chapter begins with a review of changing identities for the working woman, and reviews the prospects for women getting top jobs in Wales.

Working women: fractured identities

Dramatic changes in modern European society have led to a fragmentation of structures and institutions with which people relate, and from which, to an extent at least, they derive their sense of identity. As a consequence, Hall et al. (1992, 9) maintain, 'some of the social identities which stabilised the modern world and gave individuals firm locations in the cultural landscape of modernity are being dislocated'. Stable institutions and structures provide a backcloth against which 'traditional' roles and patterns of behaviour emerge. Individuals are judged against those roles, as fitting in or not, as 'belonging' or not: even those who consider themselves outside or independent of such structures have identities cast by others in terms of them. In a post-modern context then, identities become 'de-centred'. Individuals increasingly experience a plethora of context-specific, conflicting identities. Different identities and roles are assumed according to time and place.

For women in Wales, the de-centring of identity is fuelled by major shifts in the economic, political and social life of Wales, and in particular, in changes in sets of expectations about the role of women in the labour force. The image and identity of woman as wife and mother is challenged by the dramatic increase in the number of economically active women in Wales in the post-war period. Women returners are advised in manuals and courses to 'avoid looking mumsie' in job interviews: 'Mid-career, middle-aged women returners often signal under-confidence and look like someone's mum the minute they walk through the door' (Spillane 1991, 140). Mother and worker are incompatible images.

Masculine management styles are regarded as the norm: budding managers are trained, with the assistance of films such as *High Noon*, to model themselves on the 'harsh but fair' squadron leader; job descriptions of managers identify potentially successful applicants as being 'lean, mean and aggressive' (Coyle and Skinner 1988). Women seeking promotion to the top lack mentors, networks and most of all role models with which to identify. Some 93 per cent of male managers are married, compared with 58 per cent of women managers, and only half of married women managers have children, compared with 90 per cent of male managers (Rolfes 1991, 12). Women bosses have to avoid being cast into stereotypes such as 'superbitch', 'dragon' or 'whore' (Breakwell 1985).

The elusiveness of the 'New Man' in Wales means women juggle work and home responsibilities, and home and work identities. The increase in women's paid work and addition of new, work identities has not been matched by a concomitant increases in men's contributions to domestic work or assumption of a pro-active domestic identity. While men may 'help' more, (see Pilcher, this volume) particularly if their partners have returned to work full time, responsibility for domestic work remains that of women (see Gershuny et al. 1986). This inevitably sets up conflicts and tensions between women's two roles: in work and in the home. Expectations about what women will do and who they are conflate women's own views of themselves.

These tensions felt at the individual level are, it is argued by many feminists, the manifestations of tensions in the articulation between our economic system, capitalism, and our sex-gender system, patriarchy (Walby 1990). In other words, women's labour is sought after both by employers and by men: women's lives are marked out by the inevitable balancing act that is required to satisfy these two masters. The tensions between the two systems come to the fore in wartime, for example, when the State and employers will address the issue of women's childcare responsibilities by providing nurseries and canteens, only to remove them when war is over and a ready supply of male labour is available. The tensions are reappearing in the late 1990s, in a period of anticipated labour shortage exacerbated by an increase in the demand for skills. There is a growing effort to ensure that women as a human resource are used more effectively. Positive action measures are back on the agenda.

Young women making option choices at school face a fundamental contradiction between the roles of mother and worker into which they are being socialized. To have a successful career, all the evidence demonstrates, it is advisable to gain qualifications (preferably not in female-dominated subject areas), to work continuously rather than take career breaks, to be prepared to move for promotion, and to work long hours. For men, having a spouse and children is an advantage, it indicates a steady worker with financial responsibilities to ensure reliability and hunger for promotion; for women, it implies a mind not on the job: it is better to be single and child-free (Collinson et al. 1990).

For women to follow this pattern conflicts with the role of wife and mother, into which young girls are also being prepared. It is hardly surprising to find then, that in Wales most young girls continue to make gender-based option choices. Many continue to find difficulty in taking their future work roles seriously, in planning strategically, or in making sufficient investment in their education and training, given that they anticipate interrupted work lives, and know that returning to work, perhaps on a part-time basis, means that they will inevitably be restricted to low-paid, low-skilled work. The exception to this is some well-qualified, largely middle-class girls moving into some of the professions (Pilcher et al. 1988; Rees 1992a).

In 1991, 69 per cent of female school-leavers opted to remain in full-time education, compared with 56 per cent of males (Careers Service in Wales 1992). But these figures disguise remarkable patterns of gendered choices. For example, of the 200 school-leavers who entered engineering science or technological employment or training in 1991, only 4 per cent were female (Careers Service in Wales 1992). This is despite the fact that the 1980s were characterized by a series of measures such as Women into Science and Engineering (WISE), and various Women's Training Roadshows designed to encourage more girls and women into these areas. Diversifying schoolgirls' option and career choices is essential to break down the rigidities of gender segregation which constrains so many able women in segmented labour markets with few opportunities for promotion. It is necessary, too, in order to supply the labour market with high-level skills in the growing technical and managerial fields. Some initiatives have been introduced in Wales at school and teacher-training level in an attempt to increase awareness of the limitations of gender-stereotyped choices (these are considered by Daniel, this volume).

Despite the persistence in patterns of schoolgirls' option and career choices, there have been considerable changes in the roles and expectations of women in Wales, in particular the growing importance of women's contribution to public life. The anti-discrimination legislation of the 1970s, the growing climate of 'social justice' and the development of concern about efficient use being made of human resources all testify to an acknowledgement that gender as a discriminator in the allocation of opportunities is not wise or as politically acceptable as it was, even though it remains widely practised. Women are being encouraged to be more active in public life. However, this has not been accompanied by facilitating measures such as childcare provision, or by changing attitudes on the part of many men, as partners or employers. Men can block or be unhelpful to women's progress both at home (see Garland, this volume) and at work (Ashton, this volume).

Women in Wales then, face a de-centred identity. Roles both in work and home are affected by gender relations. A woman may have an active and responsible role at work, but be obliged to be subservient at home. She may feel equipped and qualified for promotion, but face rejection on the grounds of gender (the 'face not fitting'). She may be admitted to the ranks of senior management, but have to change her image, her style of management, her clothes, to resemble better a man. She may be allowed into the professions, only to be segregated into low-status specialisms, or to see the status of the professions themselves downgraded, or indeed, she may have to gain more qualifications in order to stay still (see Salisbury, this volume).

The focus on gaining equality of opportunity in the workplace has been at the expense of allowing expressions of difference, and valuing difference. For women wanting to get to the top, considerable conflicts of identities and confusion of roles and images are faced, especially for women from ethnic minorities. This chapter argues for a politics of difference, which allows a diversity of identities for people in top jobs, rather than expecting women to become superwomen or surrogate men. It sets the scene for chapters which follow in this section which illustrate the experiences of women in the context of a changing economic climate, one where there is growing awareness of the contribution women can make, where credentialism is valued more, and where women's contribution to family businesses, while hidden, may shortly begin to be recognized.

The chapter outlines changes in the patterns of women's participation in the labour force in Wales. It then considers the nature of the 'glass ceiling', which women can feel, but not see, preventing their rise to the top. It examines positive action initiatives designed to encourage employers to make more and better use of women as a resource, such as Business in the Community's Opportunity 2000 in Wales, and the indigenous Welsh project Chwarae Teg, an initiative promoted by a consortium of organizations in Wales to promote 'fair play' for women in the workplace. The chapter concludes with a discussion of the de-centring of women's identity, and the need for a politics of difference so that women can reach the top without 'becoming men'.

Women in the labour force

The substantial increase in the numbers of women in the work-force in Wales in the post-war period is largely due to patterns of industrial restructuring. Decline in the coal and steel industries, and the growth of the service sector has led to a decrease in skilled full-time jobs, largely occupied by men, and a growth in semi-skilled and unskilled work in the service sector, much of it available on a part-time basis: these jobs have largely been taken by women. Despite the growth, female economic activity rates remain among the lowest in Britain at 62.2 per cent in 1991 (OPCS 1993). Male rates, too, are low and have been declining (81 per cent in 1991). As elsewhere in Europe, there are distinct patterns of gender segregation in work, both by industry and occupation. Women tend to be concentrated in service-sector fields, particularly education, welfare and health, clerical work, selling, catering and other personal services. The financial services sector employs a small (12.4 per cent) but growing number of women in Wales. They are also found in the manufacturing sector, particularly in Mid Glamorgan, but overwhelmingly in semi-skilled manual work. Compared with England, there are relatively few women professionals working in science, engineering and technology.

Women in work in Wales, then, are in a worse position than those in English regions. They are more likely to be in a low-paid sector and less likely to be in highly paid professional and technical posts. Female occupations tend to be deemed low skilled and are poorly remunerated accordingly. In 1992, the average weekly earnings for full-time workers was £218.70 for women, as opposed to £299.20 for men (Employment Department 1992a). Nearly half (45.7 per cent in 1991) the working women in Wales work part-time, compared with 7.8% of men (Employment Department 1992b). And there are fewer women at the top in Wales. But how are current shifts in the Welsh economy likely to affect these patterns in the future?

Shifts and changes in the Welsh economy

Despite conflicting views over whether Wales is leading the UK out of the recession (Wales TUC 1993), it is the case that gender segregation is more extreme in Wales than elsewhere, and that this is a matter receiving growing attention. This has been prompted by two major factors. The 'demographic challenge' facing Europe is the fact that 80 per cent of the workforce of the year 2000 are already of working age. Secondly, competing effectively with low wage economies of the rapidly developing Pacific rim countries, and the global evening out of access to technology, mean that European countries need to focus on quality goods and services to survive. This implies a highly skilled workforce. Skill shortages in high-level technology, management and engineering already exist in the European Union (IRDAC 1991, Rees 1992b). The development of training is, therefore, key, and training women, given that they are more likely to be in jobs deemed low skilled (Clarke 1991), in particular warrants urgent attention. These two factors are now considered in more depth.

The *demographic challenge*, recession notwithstanding, is expected to make women in far more demand from employers, because of the projected labour shortfall brought about as a consequence of the drop in growth of the supply of school-leavers joining the labour force, and the anticipated overall growth in the demand for labour. In Wales, there is an approximate drop of 4 per cent of school-leavers per annum from 1986–7 to the mid-1990s (Careers Service in Wales 1992). The mismatch is commonly misunderstood by employers who expect an overall decline in labour supply rather than a slow down in its growth at a time of increasing demand (NEDO/TA 1989). Employers' response has tended to focus on stepping up recruitment among school-leavers, through promotion videos, developing links with schools, compact schemes and so on. In tight labour markets where recruitment difficulties are acute, other sources of labour have been explored, and it is clear that women have been identified as the main supply: both women currently at home with children and those already in work, but in danger of leaving to look after children over the next few years.

There are growing *skill shortages* in specific kinds of work. Technological changes mean that there will be a net increase in scientific, technical, managerial and professional jobs and a reduction in low-skilled work. There are specific shortages already in people with skills in new technologies.

These two trends put a significant emphasis on training and credentialism, and in particular, training and retraining adult women.

The net demand for top-level jobs is a particular issue for Wales where the 'glass ceiling' appears to be double glazed. Women are far less likely to be in senior positions in Wales than in other regions of Britain, as the following section illustrates.

The glass ceiling in Wales[1]

The effects of the glass ceiling preventing the rise of women to top jobs in Britain was documented in a series of reports in the late 1980s. They consistently revealed how women had difficulty reaching beyond certain grades. This applied to both the public and private sectors: access to senior management positions was shown to be particularly problematic. The Hansard Society Commission on Women at the Top (1990), for example, documented and decried the relative dearth of women in top jobs across a wide range of industries and sectors. The Women in Management Association (1989) showed how, despite the growth in management jobs in the post-war period and the increase in women's educational level, the number of women in managerial jobs had only reached 20 per cent.

Despite legislation banning the exclusion of women from many professions passed in 1919 (the Sex Disqualification (Removal) Act), it is only in the last twenty years that women have been entering the professions in significant numbers. Moreover, they remain in a minority, they are not represented on professional ruling bodies, and the professions have done little to accommodate their needs (United Kingdom Inter-Professional Group Working Party on Women's Issues 1990). A study of the minuscule number of women on the boards of top British companies found that they tended overwhelmingly to have family connections with other members of the board, an Oxbridge degree and/or a title (Holten and Rabbets 1989; see also Howe and McRae 1991). The situation in Wales is even worse, as Sarah Fielder and I discovered during the course of a study on women in top jobs commissioned by HTV Wales (Rees and Fielder 1991; 1992). Indeed, Wales compared badly with the rest of Britain in every arena. A summary of the picture appears in Table 5.1. Moreover, a recent survey in south Wales by the Welsh Development Agency found that over half the employers questioned had no women managers at all (Rees and Willox 1991).

Table 5.1 Women as a percentage of top grades in selected
sectors in Wales, 1991

Sector	%
Civil Service (grade 1-4)	3.0
Local Government	
(principal officer in county councils)	3.5
Solicitors (partners and single practitioners)	9.6
Management (company directors)	2.3
Higher Education (university professors)	1.3
Education (secondary school heads)	6.9
Health Service (consultants)	13.3

Source: Rees and Fielder (1991)

One argument that is often made in response to this situation is
that as more women are now working their way through education
and training systems, it is merely a matter of waiting until they
appear in top jobs. However, this does not tackle the structural
and cultural barriers facing women: it puts the onus on women to
fit in with an organization designed for men's typical trajectories.
It is important to note, too, that for different reasons, men have
been making great progress in female-dominated professions,
reducing opportunities for women to travel in the 'glass elevator'.[2]
In teaching, for example, the number of women secondary school
heads in England and Wales fell, from 23 per cent to 16 per cent in
1989 (DES 1991). In Wales, renowned for producing teachers, the
figure dropped to as low as 6.9 per cent (Welsh Office 1990). This
is largely the result of the abolition of so many single-sex schools
when the comprehensive system was introduced. However, the
number of women primary heads has been dropping too. In
nursing, too, men have been making great strides: they take far less
time to reach managerial grades than do women, even those
women who do not take a career break or work part-time.

There are both institutional and attitudinal blocks (identified by
Hammond and Holten 1991) which consistently prevent women
from rising to the top, however many manage to congregate in the
middle tiers. Institutional blocks include rules, regulations,
customs and traditions, such as the premium put on seniority or
unbroken service in promotion. They include lack of childcare
facilities and career-break arrangements, an expectation of long
hours and insistence upon candidates being prepared to move for

promotion. Cultural barriers include how people think, feel and act: the 'old boy network' (Coe 1993), the male language of management, the masculinization of technology, recruiters' preference for taking on people like themselves, and the 'chill factor' operated by groups to exclude people whose characteristics are not like their own (Hammond and Holten 1991). Special action measures are needed to address this situation, not simply to retain women in the workforce and entice women at home with children back to work, but to ensure that they can break through the glass ceiling. The projected labour and, more importantly, skill shortage, has led to the development of some 'positive action' measures.

Positive action

Positive action has been defined as

> any measure contributing to the elimination of inequalities in practice and which allows an organisation to identify and eliminate any discrimination in its employment policies and practices, and to put right the effects of past discrimination.
> (Commission of the European Communities 1988, 10)

In other words, it is about creating (in well-worn phrases) 'a level playing field', or 'untying the hand behind women's backs'. It seeks to recognize that existing institutional arrangements and cultures are not gender neutral, they benefit men. For example, women are more likely to take career breaks, to have domestic commitments, to have less time available for work, fewer opportunities for employer-sponsored training and so on. Hence to treat people 'equally', without recognizing their different circumstances, is in fact to treat them unequally, and to reinforce the differences between them. Positive action addresses existing inequalities in men's and women's starting positions, and allows women to compete on equal terms. It is not about giving women an unfair advantage (and should not be confused with positive *discrimination*, which is illegal in Britain), but simply recognizes the advantage already enjoyed by men. It is used in particular to encourage women (and men) into occupations and professions which are particularly the preserve of the other gender.

Positive action measures can be characterized into three groups: *family-friendly measures,* which seek to overcome the fact that women undertake the major responsibility for domestic work, including childcare; *training measures* which seek to address the fact that women are less likely to have educational qualifications, or access to training; and *organizational and cultural measures* which seek to tackle the androcentricity of the organization, that is, to recognize that it is currently organized in a way that facilitates men to rise to the top, but puts barriers up for women to negotiate (Rees 1992a). The company seeks to identify those barriers and reorganize itself, its culture and climate. Where employers engage in all three forms of positive action measures, by making themselves 'family friendly', by addressing the training needs of existing and returning staff, and by reorganizing structures and changing the culture to facilitate women's rise to the top, then women stand a good chance of breaking the glass ceiling and reaching the top. This will create role models and mentors for younger women, and introduce alternative perspectives into senior management.

Positive action programmes started in the late 1970s in Britain in the banking sector and some local authorities. By 1990, some 26 per cent of major organizations were found to have introduced measures to retain women employees in response to labour shortage. They tended to be larger companies and public-sector bodies. The Equal Opportunities Commission (EOC) set up an Equality Exchange whereby employers interested in equal opportunities could exchange experience and best practice. Business in the Community launched an initiative in 1991 whereby sixty-one organizations pledged themselves to improving the quality and quantity of women's participation in the workforce (see Pollert and Rees 1992).

Within the Single European Market, there are significant reasons why positive action needs to be welcomed in Britain as a whole and in Wales in particular. Patterns of gender segregation are more marked here than in the rest of the EC. The pay differential between men and women is between 8 and 10 per cent greater than anywhere else except Portugal. Britain comes second only to Portugal for the lowest provision of pre-school childcare in the European Union (EU); and in Wales, there were only seven places per 100 children under five in 1991, compared with ten places in England (Hanney et al. 1993). Moreover, 38 per cent of single mothers are in employment in Wales (Eurostat 1991). There are fewer women in higher education and training than in most EU member states, and the UK is the only country to restrict access to training to unemployed women on the grounds of their marital status. Men work longer hours in the UK than the rest of the EU, and more women work part-time here than anywhere except Denmark (Marsh 1991). Maternity leave protection and other rights are more restricted than elsewhere in the EU. Given that the situation of women in the Welsh workforce is worse than the British average, positive action measures in Wales are especially urgent.

Positive action in Wales

In January 1992, a consortium of employers in Wales, led by the Welsh Development Agency with Business in the Community and the Equal Opportunities Commission, launched Chwarae Teg, an initiative designed to focus attention on and encourage fair play for women in the workforce in Wales. At its launch, the Secretary of State for Wales, Mr David Hunt, challenged the consortium's steering committee and Business in the Community to find twenty key employers in the Principality willing to sign up to Opportunity 2000 by the end of the year. In his own words:

> This challenge is really for the business world to stand up and be counted. Declare your commitment to the promotion of equal opportunities and spell out the steps that you intend to make this commitment a reality and I believe in due course all of Wales will reap the reward.
>
> (Hunt 1991, 4)

The challenge was heeded and in May 1992 Opportunity 2000 was duly launched by the Secretary of State in Wales. In the same year, Sir Wyn Roberts, Minister of State in the Welsh Office, was given special responsibility as Minister for Women in Wales. For once women's employment issues appeared to be on the agenda with an enthusiasm not witnessed since the Second World War. But do these initiatives represent a good opportunity to break down the extremely rigid patterns of occupational segregation which characterize the Welsh labour force? Unfortunately, there are reasons why such endeavours are unlikely to make much impact. The first set of reasons relate to the limitations of positive action generally, and the second to Wales specifically.

Positive action: radical change or window dressing?

Hammond and Holten (1991), the authors of the report which informed the setting up of Opportunity 2000, identified four main ingredients to success in achieving a balanced workforce. The first is a demonstration of commitment from the top. Secondly, to achieve change in behaviour, ideally equal opportunities should be identified as a goal as part of the business strategy: goals need to be set and monitoring mechanisms put in place to measure change. Training in the objectives needs to be given throughout the organization. Thirdly, it is important to 'build ownership' of positive action, so that it is everyone's responsibility, and a performance criterion. Finally, investment is needed, of resources, time and people.

Few employers fulfil the four determinants of success in positive action as identified by Hammond and Holten. Indeed, as Cockburn (1992) has shown, the agenda of top management may be short term, to facilitate a few able, qualified and experienced women to move into top management by behaving like men, rather than revolutionizing the entire organization culturally and behaviourally to allow women as a category to move upward on equal terms. Her study of organizations that have introduced some positive action measures reveals that equal opportunities officers may have a longer agenda for change, but that this can be resisted by male backlash. This supports Hammond and Holten's claim that top-level commitment needs to be shared by decision-makers further down the organization. Ensuring widespread 'ownership' of positive action is extremely difficult. Nevertheless, there are successful examples: when Canadian police chiefs' pay bonuses were linked to the proportion of women they had promoted to senior ranks, then there was indeed radical improvement.

While it is too early to judge to whether the employers signed up to Opportunity 2000, both nationally and in Wales, are on course to achieve their aims by the turn of the century, early signs are not promising. The recession has hijacked attention away from the most effective use of human resources, to the subject of redundancies. Banks in particular, who led the way on positive action, have been laying off thousands of workers. Few participating employers set themselves targets, most were less specific about what they hoped to achieve. Many signatories outlined their plans for

UNIVERSITY COLLEGE
LIBRARY
SWANSEA

cultural change in terms of Total Quality rather than a commitment to removing inequalities. This has the advantage of linking the issue in with good business sense, but allows the specifics of positive action to elide.

Impediments to positive action in Wales

In Wales, there are particular structural factors impeding the success of positive action measures. In the first instance, very few employers have signed up to Opportunity 2000, or to the Equal Opportunities Commission's Equality Exchange in Wales. This is not surprising. It is major national and international companies and large public or ex-public sector organizations which have shown most enthusiasm for positive action in Britain as a whole. They tend to have head offices informed by recruitment and retention difficulties in the south-east of England. While the Welsh regional and local branches of such companies may be expected to follow national guidelines, it is evident that managers have some discretion in how they interpret company policy at regional and local level, in a labour market context where recruitment difficulties are not nearly as acute.

Secondly, the economy of Wales is numerically dominated by small and medium-sized enterprises, which tend not to have the flexibility or the cultural inclination to embrace 'equal opportunities' in such a thoroughgoing sense. Many use highly gendered informal networks to fill their vacancies (see Rees et al. 1990), thus perpetuating existing patterns of occupational segregation.

Thirdly, where positive action measures have been introduced in Wales, they tend to be of the family-friendly variety, which while welcome, do not *of themselves* necessarily change women's occupational life chances except indirectly. For example, if seniority is a criterion for promotion, then childcare provision can clearly help women overcome their disadvantage. It is usual for superintendents in the police force to have twenty-five years of service or more: in 1989, in the South Wales police force, only four women satisfied this criterion because of career breaks. However, a positive action measure which examined barriers to women's promotion would question the premium put on seniority in the first place; it would involve the construction of alternative, less crude methods of assessing whether an individual was the best person for a job for promotion. This is not to say that family-friendly measures are unwelcome. But in isolation their impact on segregation will be marginal. When the demographic pendulum swings in the opposite direction, as it will towards the end of the century, or if the 'green shoots' of economic recovery prove to be illusory, or if economic growth is found, as some forecasters predict, to be no longer linked to job growth, then childcare measures, flexible working arrangements, and so on can easily be dismantled.

Chwarae Teg is a unique partnership of private and public sector organizations including the Welsh Development Agency, Training and Enterprise Councils, local authorities, the Employment Service in Wales, the EOC, and the National Health Service (NHS) in Wales (the NHS, after all, is the largest employer of women in western Europe). It has been extremely active and reasonably successful in raising awareness among employers in Wales of the economic need to expand the role of women in the workforce (Venus 1993). It has also produced guidelines for employers on action. It has focused on family-friendly policies, especially childcare initiatives and flexible working; training, and facilitating women returners back to work. It remains to be seen to what extent raised awareness and will translate into positive action, and positive action into the breakdown of gender segregation in the workforce.

Conclusion

In Wales, in response to the increasing demand for skills and efficient use of human resources, and encouraged by initiatives such as Chwarae Teg, Opportunity 2000 and the Equality Exchange, employers are being made aware of the need to consider how work is organized, to recognize the importance of training for women, and to examine cultural attitudes which construct glass ceilings. While the waste of women's talents is immense, there are few signs that employers are tackling organizational and cultural barriers in a thoroughgoing, thought-through fashion. The discourse remains at the level of equal opportunities, whereas, as Cockburn (1992) argues, what is needed is not more training courses designed to hone women's 'killer instincts', but a tolerance of difference. There is a need to shift from an ideology of 'equality', individual women joining a male culture, to an ideology of 'parity', women as a sex having full representation in the organisation.

(Cockburn 1992, 233)

There is a danger that while positive action may facilitate women wanting to remain in or return to the workforce in greater numbers, they will leave the male-centred culture of the workplace intact. Only women who can accommodate the demands of this culture will survive and reach the top. Women generally are still likely to find their gender determining what sector they enter, what training and promotion opportunities are offered to them and, how seriously they are taken as potential top management material.

Messages of a so-called post-feminist age, and the supposed era of 'equal opportunities' conflict with the realities of women's everyday lives. Women struggle to fit in, they try to accommodate organizations and cultures (rightly dubbed 'greedy institutions') not designed for them and their domestic responsibilities. Many women at the top seek to become invisible, to obscure their gender through their clothes, actions and behaviour (Breakwell 1985). Others feel all too visible: their actions interpreted and judged by their gender. The majority make decisions, and have decisions made for them largely on the basis of their gender, which mean they will never gain access to the competition for top jobs at all, irrespective of their desires or capabilities. The effects of the de-centring of these conflicting identities of women are heard in the following chapters.

Notes

[1] There are in reality many glass ceilings operating at different tiers. This paper focuses on the most well known one, between middle and senior management.

[2] The term 'glass elevator' refers to women's enhanced opportunities to rise to the top in female-dominated occupations and professions where, however, it is interesting to note, there are fewer top jobs.

References

Breakwell, G. (1985). *The Quiet Rebel: Women at Work in a Man's World* (London, Century Publishing).

Careers Service in Wales (1992). *Pupil Destination Statistics in Wales 1991* (Careers Service in Wales).

Clarke, K. (1991). 'Women and Training: A Review' *EOC Research Discussion Paper No. 1* (Manchester, Equal Opportunities Commission).

Cockburn, C. (1992). *In the Way of Women: Men's Resistance to Sex Equality in Organisations* (London, Macmillan).

Coe, T. (1992). *The Key to the Men's Club: Opening the Doors to Women in Management* (London, Institute of Management).

Collinson, D., Knights, D. and Collinson, M. (1990). *Managing to Discriminate* (London, Routledge).

Commission of the European Communities (1988). *Positive Action: Equal Opportunities for Women and Men. Third Medium Term Community Action Programme 1991–1995* (Brussels, Commission of the European Communities).

Coyle, A. and Skinner, J. (eds.) (1988). *Women and Work: Positive Action for Change* (London, Macmillan).

Department of Education and Science (1991). *1988 Secondary School Staffing Survey, Statistical Bulletin 18/91* (London, DES).

Employment Department (1992a). *New Earnings Survey* (London, HMSO).

Employment Department (1992b). *Employment Gazette* (London, HMSO).

Eurostat (1991). *Labour Force Survey* (Luxembourg, Office for Official Publications of the European Communities).

Gershuny, J., Miles, I., Jones, S., Mullings, C., Thomas, G. and Wyatt, S. (1986). 'Time budgets: preliminary analyses of a national survey', *Quarterly Journal of Social Affairs*, Vol. 2, No. 1, 13–39.

Hall, S., Held, D. and McLennan, G. (1992). 'Introduction' in S. Hall, D. Held and T. McGrew (eds.), *Modernity and its Futures* (Cambridge, Polity).

Hammond, V. and Holten, V. (1991). 'A Balanced Workforce? Achieving Cultural Change for Women: a comparative study', research project sponsored by the Women's Economic Development Team, Business in the Community for Opportunity 2000 (Berkhamstead, Ashridge Management Centre).

Hanney, M., Holterman, S. and Stone, M. K. (1993). *An Audit of Childcare* (Pontypridd, Chwarae Teg).

Hansard Society for Women at the Top (1990). *Report of Hansard Society for Women at the Top* (London, Hansard Society for Women at the Top).

Holten, V. and Rabbets, J. (1989). 'Pow(d)er in the Board Room: Report of a Survey of Women on the Boards of Top UK Industrial Companies' (Berkhamsted, Ashridge Management Centre).

Howe, E. and McRae, S. (1991). *Women on the Board* (London, Policy Studies Institute).

Hunt, D., Secretary of State for Wales (1991). Keynote address delivered at the launch of Chwarae Teg at the Holiday Inn, Cardiff.

IRDAC (1991). *Skill Shortages in Europe – IRDAC Opinion* (Brussels,

Industrial Research and Development Advisory Committee of the Commission of the European Communities).

Marsh, C. (1991). *Hours of Work of Women and Men in Britain* (Equal Opportunities Research Series, London, HMSO).

National Economic Development Training Office/Training Agency (1989). *Defusing the Demographic Time Bomb* (London, NEDO).

Office of Population Censuses and Surveys (1993). *1991 Census: Welsh County Reports* Part I (London, HMSO).

Pilcher, J., Delamont, S., Powell, G. and Rees, T. (1988). 'Women's Training Roadshows and the "Manipulation" of Schoolgirls' Career Choices', *British Journal of Education and Work*, Vol. 2, No. 2, 61–6.

Pollert, A. and Rees, T. (1992). 'Equal Opportunity and Positive Action in Britain: Three Case Studies', *Warwick Papers in Industrial Relations No. 42* (Coventry, School of Industrial and Business Studies, University of Warwick).

Rees, C. and Willox, I. (1991). *Expanding the Role of Women in the South Wales Labour Force* (Cardiff, Welsh Development Agency).

Rees, G., Winckler, V. and Williamson, H. (1990). *Employers' Recruitment Strategies, Vocational Education and Training: An Analysis of a Loose Labour Market* (Cardiff, School of Social and Administrative Studies, University of Wales College of Cardiff).

Rees, T. (1992a). *Women and the Labour Market* (London, Routledge).

Rees, T. (1992b). *Skill Shortages, Women and the new Information Technologies* (Brussels, Commission of the European Communities).

Rees, T. and Fielder, S. (1991). *Women at the Top in Wales: A Report for HTV Wales 'Wales This Week'* (Cardiff, Social Research Unit, University of Wales College of Cardiff).

Rees, T. and Fielder, S. (1992). 'Smashing the Dark Glass Ceiling: Women at the Top in Wales', *Contemporary Wales: An Annual Review of Economic and Social Research*, University of Wales Press, Vol. 5, 99–114.

Rolfe, R. (1991). *Europe's Glass Ceiling: Why Companies Profit from a Diverse Workforce* (Brussels, The Conference Board Europe).

Spillane, M. (1991). *The Complete Style Guide from the Color Me Beautiful Organisation* (London, Piatkus).

United Kingdom Inter-Professional Group Working Party of Women's Issues (1990). *Women in the Professions* (London, The Law Society).

Venus, J. (1993). 'Chwarae Teg (Fair Play) Evaluation and Feasibility Study Report' (Pontypridd, Chwarae Teg).

Walby, S. (1990). *Theorising Patriarchy* (Oxford, Blackwell).

Wales TUC (1993). *Tackling the Low Pay, No Jobs Economy* (Cardiff, Wales Trade Union Congress).

Welsh Office (1990). *Statistics of Education in Wales: Schools* (Cardiff, Welsh Office).

Women in Management (1989). *The Female Resource – An Overview* (London, Women in Management Association).

6

Educating Rhian: experiences of mature women students

PAM GARLAND

Introduction

Despite changes in the patterning of women's lives and the family life cycle, when we think of wives and mothers in north Wales today, we still tend to hold to an image of a woman either working in the home, or possibly in tourism or agriculture in addition to her household tasks. In recent years, however, a steadily increasing number of wives and mothers in north Wales have made the decision to enter university as mature students. This sets the individual on a new pathway through life, and thus marks a turning point in the life course. Nevertheless, it remains a pathway that relatively few adults take; despite the increasing popularity of mature age study, life on campus is still dominated by the young, and the university environment is still largely geared to their needs and life style. In consequence, the role of the mature student is somewhat ambiguous to say the least; clearly stereotypes of young, fancy-free, politically active students do not accord with being thirty or forty, with home and family commitments and limited time for extra-curricula activities. Embarking on a student career in adulthood can thus be regarded as an unusual course of action, a transition that brings with it a specific set of problems. It certainly has implications for the individual's sense of identity, in so far as the individual's perceptions of who she is are inextricably bound up with the status positions she occupies, the concomitant roles she enacts, and the meaning she attaches to these roles. One's identity is not a constant given, it is forged and negotiated through relationships with others, it undergoes revision and modification as new roles are acquired, existing roles adjusted, and other roles lost (McCall and Simmons 1966, Strauss 1962).

This phenomenon of mature age study raises a number of questions. Why do mature women choose to return to education? What adjustments have to be made to their existing roles as wives, mothers, daughters and friends in order to accommodate the student role? How does their return to education affect their interpersonal relationships? What are the implications of their experiences for their self-image, the way they see themselves, their identity? This chapter is concerned with thirty such women from north Wales, who, at a particular point in their lives, made a decision to enter higher education as mature students; in so doing they took a path that was to transform their lives and their self-image.

Returning to study: thirty north Wales women

The main focus of this chapter is the changing identity of thirty north Wales mothers during their time as students at the University College of North Wales (UCNW) Bangor. Any explanation of change must necessarily begin at a point before transition takes place, as change can only be assessed in retrospect, by a comparison between the before and the after. This section provides a brief profile of their background and circumstances on entering university.

The majority of these women could not be considered earlier 'failures' of the educational system: 47 per cent (fourteen) left school with 'O' Levels, 13 per cent (four) with 'A' Levels, although the remaining 40 per cent (twelve) had no academic qualifications. On leaving school, the destination for most of them (80 per cent or twenty-four) was the labour market and 'typical' female jobs within it. Some 60 per cent (eighteen) entered routine white-collar jobs, while nursing proved the most popular choice among those who chose to follow a vocation.

The ages of the women ranged from twenty-nine to fifty-five; nevertheless, the majority (eighteen or 60 per cent) were between thirty-six and forty-five years of age. Family size was generally small with only 6.5 per cent (two) of these mothers having more than three children. Their families were at various stages of the family life cycle, however; certainly the majority (sixteen or 53 per cent) had school-age children, but 17 per cent (five) had a child under the age of five and 30 per cent (nine) had adult offspring. Few of the women were indigenous to the area, in fact the majority had moved to north Wales with their husbands. Husbands, or, in some cases, ex-husbands, were typically located in white-collar occupations (twenty or 66.6 per cent), one third (33.3 per cent) of these women being either separated or divorced when they entered university.

Their employment histories were largely discontinuous: twenty-six (86 per cent) of the women had been full-time housewives for at least part of their lives, and in all cases cessation of employment occurred on the transition to motherhood. These career breaks were typically long, 40 per cent (twelve) had been out of the labour force for nine years or more. Some had remained full-time housewives until the day they entered university. Mothers who had re-entered the labour force typically returned to part-time jobs that could be fitted in with family commitments (43 per cent or thirteen). Nevertheless, education had played a part in the lives of most of the women, 82 per cent (twenty-five) having undertaken a course of study as an adult.

This section has sought only to provide a quantitative overview of the women's background, and it must be borne in mind that such an approach, by emphasizing general tendencies, fails to capture the rich diversity of the women's experiences. Therefore, in order to comprehend the reasons why they chose to become mature students, and the importance and meaning they attached to their multiple roles during this period of their lives, it is essential to turn to the accounts provided by the women themselves. The remainder of the chapter is thus devoted to the women's explanations of their experiences.

Why am I putting myself through this? Why now?

Mature students are largely free of the parental and peer group pressures that can affect the decisions of the young. So what factors influence a woman's decision to enter university? The majority of the women at UCNW suggested that higher education would assist them in the attainment of multiple goals. They spoke variously of their need for self-fulfilment, confidence, intellectual development and independence, of their desire for a career, or a new career. For some, the frustration of 'just being a housewife and mother' played a part in their return to education, others stressed the importance of their economic contribution to family finances. The response of the student quoted below is typical of many:

> Self-fulfilment, to broaden my life experiences, to enable me to have a career. To try to improve my financial income through future employment, to better myself.

Their reasons alone do not provide a complete explanation of their decision to enter university. Previous research suggests that the factors which propel adults back into education are complex and vary as a function of age, gender and life stage (Charnley, Osborne and Withnall 1980). In this study, nineteen (63 per cent) of the women claimed that the idea of getting a degree had long been on their minds, but other considerations had deterred them. It appears that the complexity of the female life course prevents a return to full-time education at an earlier point in time even though the desire to do so may be strong. Ultimately the decision to enter university is reached through a negotiation of 'push and pull' factors acting on women at various stages in their lives, through a weighing of costs and benefits involved. Certainly the expansion of educational opportunities in the area, combined with a more flexible approach toward mature age study on the part of the university, contributed to the timing of their entry, but it was a change in their life situation that enabled the women to take advantage of these opportunities. Of the women who had wished to enter university in the past, the majority cited home responsibilities as the main barrier to earlier entry. Not unsurprisingly then, the main factors contributing to the timing of their entry to UCNW were inextricably bound up with the family, or more specifically with their children. Even those women who had not wanted to undertake degree level study in the past, tended to cite changes in the family as the main impetus to their return to education.

The majority of the women in the survey (53 per cent), and particularly the single parents among them, identified 'the children becoming more independent' as the most significant influence on their decision. Nevertheless, it is interesting to note that the women varied in their interpretations of a child's greater independence, for example:

> All my children were attending primary school.

The age of the children, they were 17 and 18.

> The children had left home, I felt free to pursue a university degree. Previously I would not have been able to give the necessary single-minded concentration for such an undertaking.

It was the older women among them who suggested that their children were dependent until they reached their late teens, or in some cases until they left home. Hence these different interpretations of a child's independence are perhaps linked to the increasing participation of mothers in the formal economy (Martin and Roberts 1984), and a concomitant change in the meaning that motherhood has for women in successive cohorts (Bush and Simmons 1981), and thus a move away from traditional female roles over time.

The fact that the children were growing up was not the sole influence on the timing of college entry however, rather it was the implications that their growing independence had for the mothers. For some it brought the realization that the 'empty nest' phase of their life was fast approaching:

> The kids were doing 'O' Levels and they encouraged me to try. Also I was thinking at the time they were growing up and what would I do when they left home.

For others it meant a change of career or a return to work, and a discovery that employment opportunities in the area were limited:

> The children were older, they were both at school, and I couldn't get what I'd call a decent job. I could get part-time jobs in hotels, shops etc., which I found fairly boring.

A few of the women also identified their move to Wales as a decisive factor in their return to education:

> Youngest child started school, recently moved to Wales, needed to master the language so that I could gain employment in the area.

A number of factors, either alone or in combination, drew these women back into education: unstable marital relationhips, disillusionment with the mother/housewife role, growing children, the economic situation of the household, limited occupational opportunities and the expansion of educational opportunities for adults in north Wales. All of these were variously cited by the women in the study; such factors either triggered new aspirations and led to the pursuit of a new goal, or else made possible the realization of a deferred goal. What is clear is that no matter what their situation at their time of entry, they saw themselves, or at least had expectations of themselves, in terms of roles other than those confined to the domestic sphere.

University life: making the transition

Generally we enter roles that are consistent with our gender, age, and social class. Even if we have no experience of enacting the role in question, we are usually familiar with it through our acquaintance with others who have taken it on, or perhaps through the media's portrayal of it. In consequence, we have some idea of what the role entails. When a new role is inconsistent with what is normally expected of persons of our social status, we are unlikely to find many role models from whom we can draw ideas of what is required of us. Making such a transition, then, is often fraught with ambiguity and uncertainty, and can necessitate a considerable degree of adjustment. Entering the role of a university student in middle adulthood is one such transition; where and how do such individuals fit into life on campus?

On the basis of the women's explanations of their initial response to university life, it would appear that they had mixed feelings about the path they had chosen; the words 'terrified' and 'excited' were used simultaneously to sum up their emotions. However, few of the women expressed doubts about their academic ability at this stage; for many their success at various courses prior to entry had served to build up their confidence and prepare them for further study. Their main concerns tended to centre around fitting into the academic setting and relating to fellow students:

> I felt terrified absolutely terrified. I spent freshers' week locked in the loo . . . I felt really intimidated by the building and the set up, you know a seminar! What the hell was a seminar? All I'd seen was American TV programmes about college. And the people, everywhere there were people and I didn't know a single soul here, I felt really intimidated.

The first day here, well the first term was horrendous. I was absolutely terrified, you know. I walked into the main foyer and thought 'Oh my God what have I done'.

Initially it was a sense of isolation, of being alone in a strange environment, combined with an assumption that everyone else was confident and could cope, that proved most distressing. These insecurities were eventually overcome by finding, and talking to, other mature students; discovering that they too were prone to the same anxieties:

If that's what stress feels like I was extremely stressed, I felt ill, I had butterflies in my tummy, I couldn't eat, I lost half a stone in the first week. Anyway I stuck it out, I got worse toward the end of the first week, but then someone came up to me, another mature female student, and said 'Do you know I feel absolutely dreadful', and I realized that there were other people who felt just as bad as I did.

The schools of the college vary in the structure and organization of their courses, and in the composition of their student populations; consequently some of the women's experiences were unique to their particular school of study. Of the thirty women in this study, five (16.6 per cent) were located in the science faculty, the majority (sixteen or 53.3 per cent) took a social science course and the remaining nine (30 per cent) took an arts subject. As a result the women who opted to take a physical science course were in a clear minority among their fellow students and had few age peers with whom to confer. No matter which school they were in, and despite their different life situations, there was almost universal agreement among the women that their first year had been the most difficult to negotiate; it was a time of adjustment and adaptation, uncertainty and, for many, hard work. Some felt there was a lack of direction as far as academic work was concerned. Coping with what for many were new forms of learning – seminars, tutorials, practicals, all proved threatening initially. The stress arising from a perceived failure to cope adequately with new learning situations was in part reduced by collaborating with others who felt themselves to be in the same boat.

For a few, the option of 'dropping out' during their first year and returning to the relative security of non-academic life seemed appealing at times, especially among women who had been full-time housewives and mothers for many years. Their continued participation at the university was in fact the outcome of strong determination:

> I hated the first year, I suppose I was adapting to something new, the work I thought was very hard. During the first year I was on the verge of packing it in a lot of the time, but as I progressed it became more enjoyable.

> The first year was the worst, I felt like giving up a few times, well, most days I would think, looking back.

The majority however did not mention giving up; indeed, for some of those who had been in full-time employment prior to entry, university was found to be preferable to work:

> I was happy after the hassles of work. It was such a relief, maybe that was part of it, being answerable to no one but myself, being in control of what I did and how I did it, and when I did it, and to what extent and depth I did it. There was a lot of good things that suited me.

Generally they were in agreement that it did all become easier with the passage of time, they gained a greater understanding of what was required of them, became more able to access resources, and acquired the necessary writing skills for producing academic work. They started to gain more confidence in their academic ability and this was combined with a greater sense of ease within the academic setting. There was certainly little evidence to suggest that the women felt alienated or marginalized by dint of their mature status, once they started their degree course. They were not without their problems even so; some were carried over from the first year, others were specific to a particular year of study. It is to the women's later experiences of both university and home life that we turn our attention in the next section.

Managing multiple roles: university and home life

The women's adaptations to, and experiences of, the student role were in large part shaped by influences external to the university setting itself, that is by their family roles, by the networks of support upon which they could draw, and by the circumstances that had led them into higher education in the first place. The women in effect employed strategies of time management in order to cope with, and reduce, stress levels. Unfortunately this often meant missing courses in which they were interested, for example:

I chose courses for time really rather than interest value.

There were a couple of courses I didn't do because I had to be back by half three for children.

Courses were selected not only on the basis of lecture times but by their slot in the weekly timetable. Many of the women lived a considerable distance away from the university, and, in rural areas with busy secondary roads, their journey back and forth could take two hours or more. For those with no transport of their own, the situation was more complex. They either had to arrange lifts with friends and so fit in with their timetable, or rely on public transport, which in rural areas was infrequent, if indeed there was a service at all. In consequence, they opted for courses that fell on the same day, thereby minimizing the number of days in a week they had to attend university. Even so, they found that seminar or practical times were arranged after the start of term, necessitating that they come in for just one hour on an otherwise free day. This they found increasingly irksome as they became more time conscious.

Producing academic work in the allotted time caused consternation for the majority of the women throughout their university career; they all wanted to do well and set high standards for themselves, which they strived hard to achieve. The considerations outlined above also acted to deter involvement in extra-curricular activities; socializing was, therefore, fitted in between classes, and restricted to the coffee shop and student union. Over time strong support networks were established between students, these provided for the mutual exchange of information, sympathy and reassurance, as well as acknowledgement of each other's successes.

If university life was time managed, so too was time in the home, as far as was possible. The women coped in various ways with the demands made upon them, but in all cases the needs of the family came first; in this respect the mother role took priority. For most of the women it was a case of arranging their college work around the needs of their children, particularly when they were still at primary school. Mothers did college work when the children were at school or had gone to bed; for those with older children, the problem of evening study centred around trying to find a quiet peaceful place, free of interruptions, in which to work. For the most part things worked well, it was the unexpected events, such as a child's illness, that caused problems, especially when such an event conflicted with essay deadlines or examinations. Women who were either indigenous to the area, or had been resident within it for a number of years had support networks in their community to which they could turn for help, such as a mother, mother-in-law, siblings or friends. Those who were relatively new to the area however had no such support. When children were ill they simply had to take time off, and this sometimes caused long-term anxieties. One such student, who was absent for the first three weeks of term due to a child's illness, feared that she would never catch up, and felt herself to be under immense pressure for the remainder of that term.

The competing demands made on the women necessitated that they restructure their lives in some way. All of them reported that, in terms of the allocation of their time, university had gradually taken over a bigger part of their lives. Support networks, although a valuable resource, could take up precious time in so far as these relationships were reciprocal. Indeed a few of the women noted that their relationships with friends outside university deteriorated over the course of their studies. This was partly due to their having less contact with them because of university commitments, and partly to their own changing interests, and the realization that they now had less in common with old friends. Even those few women who had been used to working full-time discovered that college work, unlike paid employment, impinged on their family time: it was brought home with them and was always there to be done. So too was the housework, although their attitude toward it changed; moreover, it was one activity they could cut back on. One student explained:

> If the housework's not done, at one time I'd have been 'Oh my God, I've got to get this done' and that doesn't bother me the same anymore, if it's not done, it's not done.

Another student commented:

> It [education] alters your perspective on life, like having clean windows isn't very important anymore, and there are greater things in the world to think about.

Certainly those women with a husband or partner, or with older children, could have eased their workload somewhat by delegating household chores to other family members; nevertheless, there was little evidence of this occurring. This is not to say that all partners did nothing to help around the home; some did nothing while others helped with childcare, and/or cooking from time to time. However, the women were quick to point out that these were things that their partners had done before they came to college, so in the majority of cases partners contributed very little extra help. It appears that they were sometimes perceived as being supportive as long as they were not being obstructive, for example:

> He's not gone and done things for me just because I'm on the course, but he's not stood in my way at all, so tacit consent. Occasionally dropping things off at college for me, or getting something photocopied, so that kind of support but nothing else.

Indeed, many of the women, when asked about their husbands' attitudes toward their return to education, produced similar replies:

> Oh I think he thought it was a good idea as long as it didn't affect him in any way. He didn't alter his routine in any way.

> I don't think he thought about it, as long as it didn't affect him he didn't mind.

Husbands also varied in the amount of emotional support they provided; certainly some of the women did experience strain in their marital relationships, and a withdrawal of their partners's support over time. As the comment of the student cited below demonstrates, some of the women had not only to contend with pressures of work but also with emotional stress:

> My relationship with my husband finally improved, but due to deterioration and coming out the other side. Myself and another student think the university should carry a warning: WARNING: UNIVERSITY CAN SERIOUSLY DAMAGE YOUR MARRIAGE.

Another student explained:

> Over the three years his tacit support wavered, his backing up, his support for me doing it began to change. By the third year he was glad it was over and he was rubbing it in, you know things about me not earning.

It should perhaps be pointed out that husbands did not suddenly become awkward without reason; certainly, when the pressure was on, women had less time to spend with their partners. In the majority of cases, though, it was more likely to be changes in the home and more particularly a change in the wife that caused the friction. This is given further consideration in the following discussion of personal change.

Personal change

Clearly the women had various goals in view when they first entered university. Toward the end of their second year, and certainly at the end of their third year, they had accomplished a great deal, and they had changed in the process. Buhler (cited Strom, Strom and Bernard 1989, 28), has emphasized the importance of setting goals, and their periodic revision for progressive individual change. New choices and responsibilities contribute to alterations in the individual's identity, self-esteem and interpersonal relations. The evidence presented below tends to confirm Buhler's assertion. All the women claimed that they had changed as a result of being at university; they had more self-confidence and improved self-esteem, and had gained new perspectives and horizons. One of the women, in talking about personal change, also added one note of regret:

> Well my expectations have changed, my way of thinking, my way of looking at things has changed. I have a lot more expectations now than I ever did before. I just wish, perhaps, that I had done it earlier.

Underlying much of what they said was a sense of empowerment; in essence they perceived themselves differently. On entering the student role they took on a new identity, which, over the course of time, led them to question the meaning they attached to their other roles, and to a reappraisal of them. They had developed a new, stronger sense of their own identity, as separate from the family; they felt more competent and had valid, informed opinions which deserved to be heard. They had coped successfully with competing pressures and felt a sense of achievement, but they were less tolerant of, and less affected by, other people's negative attitudes toward them. They were more sure of their own worth as individuals, they were equipped to stand and fight their ground when necessary, be this in the competition for employment or within the family. These voices echo the sentiments of many of the women in this study:

> I stood up for myself more, I realized my point of view was as important as anyone else's. I didn't take kindly to being put down, in that sense I did gain confidence. Relationships were better from my point of view, but it didn't go down well with my husband, he was used to me agreeing with him.

> It has made me more confident and aware of myself and of him (husband), so that in itself can cause conflict. Things like, 'Don't you talk to me like that', that sort of thing.

Some women were keen to emphasize that, although they had changed, university had merely brought out in them what was already there. One observed that women were good at organizing and juggling, attending to more than one thing at a time, indeed they need to be if they are to accomplish all their daily tasks; for her, university had helped to improve on these skills. It brought out qualities that were always there, as another student explained:

> I don't know if it has changed me as a person, no, all this was there before, it has just brought ME out.

Another student observed that:

> I think I have regained, rather than changed, the sort of person I was before. It also alters your perspective on life, so it has changed me in that way, but really it has just taken me back to where I was before, twenty years ago, and I like that. I'm a much happier person, it's rejuvenated me.

Despite the fact that these women encountered problems that placed them under considerable stress on numerous occasions, not one of them regretted their decision to undertake a degree course.

For the most part they had enjoyed their time at Bangor, and in their opinion the benefits gained outweighed the costs incurred. In fact, a number of those in their final year expressed regret at having to leave the university.

Conclusion

This chapter has been concerned with thirty mothers resident in the north Wales area. Their decision to enter university as mature students was directly related to their current life situation, and the changing expectations and aspirations that arose from it. Some had been disillusioned with their existing roles, finding that the reality of their situation failed to live up to the ideology of domestic bliss, others had become frustrated at the limited occupational opportunities in the area. Nevertheless, the timing of their entry to university was inextricably bound up with family life stage, reflecting both the constraints that family life places on women, and the changing ideology of the mother role over time. Higher education was not an easy path to follow by any means; they muddled, struggled and juggled their way through both university life and home life, in order to meet the competing demands made upon them. In large part these competing demands could have been reduced by a more flexible approach to mature age study on the part of the university; modularization and part-time degree courses, for example, could enable such women to study the courses in which they were interested, and allow them more time for other equally demanding commitments. Certainly none of the women complained about the structure of courses, they merely accommodated themselves to what was available. Moreover, the majority of them were more than satisfied with the constructive support provided by the staff. By and large, however, the college itself continued to function as an institution geared to the needs of young single students.

Family matters always rated highly on the women's list of concerns. Ensuring that the children did not suffer in any way was always a priority, so too was an accession to a partner's needs. In respect of the latter, what does become apparent is the relative lack of support for these women within the home, on the practical side at least; most of the domestic chores remained their responsibility, and the degree was undertaken in addition to their other duties. For some women there was also a concomitant withdrawal of their partners' emotional support. On the home front, then, many of the women's lives would have been made easier by greater tolerance and sharing on the part of their husbands or partners.

According to these women, it was worth the stress and strain; university did not simply provide them with academic knowledge, it gave them much more. On entry they sought the goals of self-confidence and self-esteem and they attained them; in the process their perceptions of their potential and their roles in life underwent a transformation. In addition, nearly all of them expressed a desire to embark on a career on the completion of their degree. Whether or not their ambitions were, or will be, realized remains a matter of conjecture as no follow-up study has been carried out. It is only to be hoped that their accomplishments and their potential will be fully recognized by the wider community, and particularly by the employers within it.

References

Bush, D. M. and Simmons, R. G. (1981). 'Socialisation Processes Over the Life-course', in M. Rosenberg and R. H. Turner (eds.), *Social Psychology Sociological Perspectives* (New York, Basic Books).

Charnley, A., Osborn, M. and Withnall, A. (1980). *Review of Existing Research in Adult and Continuing Education, Vol. 1, Mature Students* (Leicester, National Institute of Adult Education).

Martin, J. and Roberts, C. (1984). *Women and Employment a Lifetime Perspective: The Report of the 1980 DE/OPCS Women and Employment Survey* (London, HMSO).

McCall, G. J. and Simmons, J. L. (1966). *Identities and Interactions* (New York, Free Press).

Strom, R. D., Strom, R. K. and Bernard, H. W. (1989). *Human Development and Learning* (New York, Human Sciences Press).

Strauss, A. (1962). 'Transformations of Identity' in A. M. Rose (ed.), *Human Behaviour and Social Processes an Interactionist Approach* (London, Routledge and Kegan Paul).

7

The farmer needs a wife: farm women in Wales

SHAN ASHTON

Despite the recent and increasing prominence given to studying women's issues in Wales it can be rightly claimed that we are 'shockingly ignorant' of many aspects of their lives, especially with regard to women in rural areas (Winckler 1987). This chapter will focus on a particular group of rural women in Wales – women who are involved in farming, not as independent farmers or as waged farm workers, but as farmers' wives on family farms.

What we know of farm women in Wales is limited to fleeting glimpses of their lives as described or interpreted in literature (Vaughn 1951), in community studies (Rees 1950) or in biographies (Williams 1958). The images drawn from these works suggest a domestic idyll where the woman's natural role was that of wife and mother, the nurturer and upholder of moral values, with the home as the ideal setting for her life. Such images fit well with the idea of a 'rural idyll' which

> incorporates highly specific ideas on the relative roles of men and women. These are witnessed in all aspects of women's lives . . . and epitomised in the importance attached to women's domestic role.
> (Little 1987, 339)

It has been suggested that the domestic and rural idylls share many common features and that the home,

> like the village community . . . was seen as a living entity . . . harmoniously related parts of a mutually beneficial division of labour. The male head of this hierarchy, like the country squire, took care of and protected his dependents.
> (Davidoff et al. 1976, 152)

Thus the cult of domesticity arose, exacerbated by far from accurate representations of women in labour-force statistics and further prejudiced by narrow and biased concepts of 'work' (Beneria 1988; Rees 1988, 1992).

Together these led to an apparent separation, both social and spatial, of production and reproduction, home and work, domestic and waged labour, and men's and women's lives (Foord and Gregson 1986). What resulted was a gross underestimation of women's participation in economic activities and a tendency to regard women's work, especially their domestic work, as secondary and subordinate to men's activities. Women's labour was lost from sight, concealed by familial, rural and economic ideologies.

As with all myths, that of the home-based woman not involved in economic activities has *some* basis in fact (Rees 1988). With the mechanization of farming in industrial societies, women's role in primary agricultural production usually diminished (Bradley 1989) but to claim that it was removed completely (Bouquet 1985) is erroneous (Gasson 1986b). Yet such views continue to hold credence, not only with agricultural and rural policy makers, but also amongst rural dwellers themselves.

> Images of the home, of the domestic idyll and of women at the centre of the family still remain an important part of rural social organisation as a powerful element of the rural ideology.
>
> (Little 1987, 339)

One result of this prevailing image is that at a time of agricultural crisis, when governments are promoting diversification as a means of cutting the cost of farm income support, farm wives are being called upon to 'work' on behalf of the family enterprise, to generate additional income by running small enterprises within the farm household. Yet these calls are being made without detailed knowledge of what farm wives are actually doing already and without much consideration of their perceptions and attitudes to their lives as farm wives in contemporary Wales.

This chapter explores the views and activities of farm wives in north-west Wales.[1] The study area is one of predominantly hill/livestock farming, with an established specialization in sheep farming on varied scales of production. Agriculture is the dominant land use, the ownership of which is varied, with individual farmers and landed estates being the most important. There are numerous small towns situated along the northern and western edges of the study area but these offer few alternative industrial employment opportunities to farming. There is an established tourist industry in the area. Opportunities for farm tourism such as bed and breakfast, camping and caravan holidays and farm visits are increasing. The growth in the area's popularity as a retirement location and for second homes and holiday lets has had an impact on both towns and rural hinterland. Being in a National Park area exerts particular pressures on land use, especially with increased use as a recreational area combined with an environmental emphasis leading in new directions. Considering the dearth of published statistics on farm wives' labour activities and the problems associated with gaining a full picture of their working day, a questionnaire was sent to ninety farm wives, across two distinct farming areas (hill and low), of whom fifty-two (58 per cent) replied.[2]

The purpose of the investigation was twofold: firstly, to gain information about farm wives' activities and the gendered division of labour on the farms; and, secondly, to gain information from the women themselves about their work across the various labour spheres in which they might operate (domestic household labour, agricultural labour, non-agricultural but on-farm labour, off-farm waged labour and community work). This chapter focuses on the replies and subsequent interviews of the twenty-four responding hill farm wives.

The working day

The most striking feature of the farm wife's day was the sheer volume and variety of work:

> Up at six, breakfast for the family (six in all), do dishes and put laundry in machine to hang out later. Tidy and hoover downstairs and make sure father (in-law) is right for the morning. Answer phone three times before 9.00 a.m. – all to do with the farm. 'Ministry' arrived at 9.30 a.m. to scan 'Chernobyl' sheep – help husband drive and catch these. Finished at 2.30 p.m. – but make lunch for everyone in between and got washing on the line. Went food shopping (15 miles away) and called in at the vet's and farmers' co-op to pick things up for the farm. Did banking and

called in at the accountants to sort out some business problems. Home, got dinner for everybody and washing off the line. Husband and son off to (rented) lowland to check stock there, so I fed the dogs (5), washed dishes and helped other children with homework. Did some ironing and went to village for carnival committee meeting (fundraising for community centre). Home around 10.30 p.m. supper for family then did some work on accounts before bed at 12.00 midnight.

(Mary Evans)

This is an extract from one farm wife's diary at a 'non-busy' time, where it can be seen that her contribution to the running of the family household and farm business is many sided. Although it is convenient to consider her activities separately, in reality they overlap to such an extent that it is difficult to disentangle them for the purpose of measurement and analysis. It is this point that makes the position of these women particularly interesting to feminist analysis because here the conventional distinction between domestic and productive work is blurred (Haney and Knowles 1988). Whilst other studies (Gasson 1991) have shown that the wife's contributions may vary by size and type of farm business and according to her age and background, in this study, economic necessity was the most significant factor in defining the wife's activities. These were not greatly altered by the number of children or stage in the family life cycle; that is, her non-domestic workload was just as great regardless of the size and stage of the family. As one respondent put it:

I did take a year off when the first (child) arrived . . . with the others (children) it was ten days off for each and back to business.

(Judith Jones)

Domestic household labour

Domestic household labour was the farm wife's primary area of responsibility and labour activity. It was seen by all as 'women's work' and it was the consistency of the wives' predominant responsibility for work in this area, regardless of their other labour activities, age or background that was the most striking characteristic of domestic household labour. This division of labour was not unexpected:

> It is in large part a consequence of its familiarity that the material features of domestic household labour, and hence a major element of farm wives' work, have remained largely unexamined in the farm labour literature.
>
> (Whatmore 1988, 140)

Yet this labour is essential, as the wife supplies all the services necessary for the daily functioning of the family farm in that she provides for the basic needs of its constituent members. In addition, she produces, rears and socializes successors into their roles, and this is crucial to the survival of most farm businesses (Gasson 1980).

The tasks that make up this area of the wife's labour consist of child-rearing and care, food provision, housework, laundry and shopping (Oakley 1974; Collins 1985). In this investigation, fourteen of the wives defined their weekly work as being mainly domestic with three quarters of the sample spending forty hours or more a week on domestic duties. With the exception of childcare, where only half of the households had children of pre-school and school age, all the main domestic tasks were carried out by all the farm wives. Where there were children in the household, it was the women who were the primary carers. Three of the households without school-age children still had adult offspring, all sons, living in the home. In these instances, the mother continued to provide all domestic services. In addition, in three of the households questioned, domestic labour extended to the care of elderly relatives living in. In all cases these were relatives of the husband/farmer. A further quarter of the respondents pointed out that they regularly spent time caring for or helping out elderly relatives living elsewhere.

The labour contribution of other household members to the domestic workload of the wives was negligible, with the partial exception of childcare. Here it can be seen that a quarter of the wives received regular help, one half enjoyed occasional help, whilst the remaining quarter received no help whatsoever with childcare. Where help was available across the task areas it was largely explained by the presence of teenage daughters living at home. On occasions, especially at times of greatest need, help with domestic household labour was received from relatives or friends (always female) on an unpaid basis. None of the wives in this survey employed paid help in relation to these domestic tasks.

Table 7.1 Number of wives receiving help with domestic tasks

Frequency of help	Childcare	Food preparation	Housework	Laundry	Shopping
		Task			
Regular	3	3	1	0	2
Occasional	6	3	6	3	9
Never	3	16	17	21	13
Total	12*	24	24	24	24

* Total number of households with children of pre-school and school age

Agricultural labour

As well as contributing significant labour to the administrative sphere of the farm business, farm wives, contrary to popular belief, play a far from negligible role in agricultural production. Administrative activities ranged from skilled work such as book-keeping and secretarial duties to tasks such as running errands and dealing with enquiries. All the wives were involved in the 'dog's body' jobs of running errands and dealing with enquiries. Skilled office work, such as keeping farm accounts, involved sixteen of the wives.

Although one might expect wives to be closely involved in the management and decision-making processes of running a *family* business, nearly a third were totally excluded. This is despite the fact that fourteen were actually registered as business partners. In day-to-day management decisions, seven of the wives were involved on a regular basis whereas a slightly larger number (ten) were included in longer-term major policy decisions, such as land acquisition/disposal or changes in enterprise.

Despite their substantial input in this sphere, much of the work was invisible or seen as a 'natural' extension of the wives' domestic duties. As one wife complained:

> He (her husband) doesn't see me spending hours over it (the paper-work) so he thinks it doesn't exist. And then when it's needed, because of all the hard work put in before, it's sorted out quite easily, he thinks it's not difficult to do.
>
> (Liz Griffiths)

Another respondent put it differently:

> I do the paper (work) and the money but all the stuff from the bank and the accountants, the ministry and so on, it's all addressed to him. If I go to the bank they think I'm the little wife carrying messages for him in between the shopping and the hairdressers, not a business partner. It's not my husband, you know, it's them (outside agencies) that don't include me.
>
> (Mary Evans)

Whilst their contribution to manual labour was not uniform, what becomes evident, once the narrow and restrictive methods of officially measuring work are dispensed with (Beneria, 1988), are high levels of participation in manual activities. The vast majority of the wives (twenty-two) were involved in some way in manual work, almost a third on a regular basis. 'Busy times' (such as lambing and silage making) again involved nearly all farm wives (twenty-three) with three-quarters as regular workers. These high levels of participation are not unique (see Gasson 1991) or unusual on family farms though they remain for the most part unrecognized or undervalued by all barring, on occasions, the farmer himself. As one husband put it:

> I don't know where I'd be without her really, she can turn her hand to anything on the farm. She'll do what's needed, when it's needed and still gets dinner on the table at night . . .
>
> (David Davies)

The tasks involved in manual work were more wide-ranging than has hitherto been popularly imagined, that is the wives did far more than 'keep a few hens or feed a . . . few lambs'. They regularly helped with, and were often responsible for, livestock feeding; they also shepherded alongside their husbands, especially at times of greatest need such as at lambing time and in winter.

Just over one half of the wives had primary responsibility for particular agricultural tasks, although these were predominantly secondary farm enterprises that ran alongside the farm's main agricultural production activity. These 'sidelines' included, for example, a small beef enterprise, specialist sheep-breeding aside to the main flock, calf-rearing and sheepdog-breeding and training. Here the women enjoyed a high degree of self-determination although the subsequent control over the income generated was often limited.

At 'busy times' the wives, the ultimate in flexible workforce terms, came into their own and turned their hand 'to anything on the farm'. Lambing involved taking their full share of the twenty-four hour shift system that is necessary at this time, and involved using many skills that earn others (the farmer or the vet for instance) professional status and identity. Shearing days involved helping in the sheds, often doing the same work as the men, as well as feeding the day's workforce of twelve or more. If she was not actually involved in the shearing, the wife 'stood in' for her husband and did the usual farming activities that he was unable to do during this time.

Silage harvesting or haymaking for many hill farms means working 'lowland' (rented or owned) away from the home farm, and so involved much travelling before and after work:

> It's a sixty-mile round trip each time. We often leave here at 6.30 in the morning and don't get home till midnight. You have to take all your food with you, it's hell if you forget something . . . like the teabags! It's a long day, you know . . . I try not to think of all the work piling up at home.
>
> (Mary Evans)

Although the manual work that the wives undertook was of a more wide-ranging nature than has perhaps been generally believed, there existed nonetheless an axiomatic gender division of labour in terms of the actual activities, their site of operation and the relations under which they were carried out. The agricultural tasks wives perform tended to be limited to secondary enterprises and activities; their work sites were generally restricted, except at busy times, to the farmyard and its immediate surroundings – the 'ffridd'[3] perimeter being the commonest limit; their labour was of a responsive rather than of an initiatory and directive nature. Subsequently the majority of the wives had little control over the products of their labour, the disposal of those products or the income generated from them. Only a small minority received direct payment, the majority worked for up to forty hours a week in return for a notional share of the profits or, worse still, for their 'keep'.

As mentioned earlier, the wives' contribution to agricultural labour was far from uniform and perhaps it was this diversity that had contributed to the lack of recognition of the extent of their agricultural labour input – after all, what they all had in common was their domestic identity. Yet the traditional explanation for the 'lack' of women's participation in agricultural activities – their domestic responsibilities – does not hold in the face of the evidence found here. In this study, only three women with childcare responsibilities claimed to perform no agricultural labour at all. Yet, on closer analysis, even they performed some 'small' manual tasks, such as feeding the dogs, 'pet' lambs and chickens on a regular basis. A number of wives also contributed directly to the farm business and household budgets through running diversified businesses or by taking off-farm jobs.

Off-farm work

Those that participated least in regular farm manual work tended to be wives with better paid and more career-structured off-farm jobs such as teaching. Nonetheless, even these wives were active in the farm business administration sphere. As shown elsewhere with regard to rural women (Little 1987), the majority of women who performed off-farm waged labour were restricted to jobs of low socio-economic status, i.e. part-time or seasonal work in the tourist sector mostly domestic in nature, often poorly paid and offering little long-term security. According to Little (1987), 'such opportunities both constrain and are constrained by women's domestic role'. Whilst this is certainly the case generally speaking, for the farmer's wife her agricultural role is a further factor. The wives themselves offered up mainly economic reasons for taking up such work, although all valued the social benefits gained. The nature of the work also enabled them to fulfil their domestic and farm responsibilities. On working the evening shift in the local hotel after a full day's work on the farm and in the home, one wife commented:

> The money is very handy, especially when you've got children . . . and really a change is as good as a rest. It's a good crowd to work with, lots of chat after a day on your own. That's it, really, and I can still see to the family and do my bits on the farm.
>
> (Alice Jones)

She had already been working fourteen hours and had another three hours on her shift before going home. On querying the worth of the money she earned in relation to the hours she worked, her answer was: 'It means that we don't use "farm money" for "extras" . . . '

What few opportunities that are available, are difficult to capitalize on when one considers the sparse service provision in rural areas. Services such as formal childcare and transport in rural areas are facing cut-backs. For women generally these cuts have greater implications than for men, but this is especially so for rural women. Scattered population and, therefore, scattered sources of potential help mean that women have to travel significant distances in order to accomplish the basic everyday activities necessary for family, work and social requirements. Combined with poor rural transport systems, the logistics are often almost impossible to solve:

> It's never ending, here, there and everywhere all the time. Shops one way, school another, work the other, and then the farm work is scattered all ways!
>
> (Ann Roberts)

On-farm diversified activities

A third (eight) of the farm wives have, over the last ten years, developed non-agricultural, income-generating enterprises on the farm. These 'diversified' activities have been hailed by various agencies as the 'way forward' for farm businesses and as a means of protecting their incomes. For the women these activities might be expected to reduce to some extent the fragmentation of their working day, and enable them to gain higher social and economic status and identity.

Five wives ran a holiday cottage on or near the home farm, a further two operated bed-and-breakfast businesses within the home, and one ran a caravan site on farm land. The hours spent working these enterprises varied between ten and forty a week, according to seasonal pressures and requirements (tourist and agricultural). Some help was forthcoming, usually from the husbands in the form of maintenance activities. Only four of these projects operated independently of the farm business and of these only two claimed to reinvest the income in enterprise improvement or expansion. The income earned was, for the most part, used in the household budget, though occasionally it was used directly for farm business purposes. Not one of the respondents used the income for personal benefit. All but two of these women also worked regularly on the farm and in the household, whilst a further three accomplished these tasks and held off-farm jobs. This multiplicity of roles leads to enormously long working hours with just over half the total sample working upwards of eighty hours a week regularly; four wives worked more than one hundred hours but only three worked less than sixty hours per week when *all* labour activities are taken into account. They all suggested that diversification schemes such as theirs were unavoidable these days, and most felt they had gained from the experience. One respondent felt that

> I'm not just an 'assistant' to my husband now but do my own bit for the business . . . it gets used . . . for the family, but that's what it's for, isn't it?
>
> (Ann Roberts)

As for non-diversified respondents (sixteen), a minority felt that they were in 'this' for farming and if they wanted to run bed and breakfast they'd 'buy a house in Llandudno'. Others felt that the area and their particular farm was not suited to such schemes:

> This is a sheep farm. You can't do nothing only keep sheep on the mountain.
>
> (Dorothy Griffiths)

The majority had considered developing projects but felt obstructed or constrained from doing so. Tenants were restricted by terms of contract and, anyway, felt unable to invest their own capital and time in developing property that was not theirs in the long term. Others were limited by time constraints imposed by farm work or outside jobs:

> There's no time really. I have the family and all the housework, a part-time job and I help on the farm . . . it's about eighty hours a week already. There's six of us . . . where would I keep visitors . . . the house is full.
>
> (Mary Evans)

Nearly all respondents cited bureaucracy and lack of finance as standing in their way. The fact that the majority live in a National Park has ramifications, especially planning restrictions:

To do it up like they want – slate, stone and style, costs money we haven't got . . .

(Ann Roberts)

This point is all the more relevant since the axing in January 1991 of a 25 per cent capital costs grant available for converting farm buildings into tourist accommodation.

That was little enough help to farmers . . . this cut in grant will mean many farmers will not be able to diversify into tourism . . . It seems that just as farmers start to gear up for new initiatives the Government pulls the rug on them.

(Pugh 1991, 22)

It must be noted that all the wives also provided essential support to their hard-pressed husbands, who belong to a group increasingly prone to suicide under the present difficult agricultural and economic conditions:

It's very hard for the farmer's wife because she is . . . always having to absorb a lot of the stress.

(Gasson cited in the *Guardian* 12.2.92, 17)

Indeed, fourteen of the respondents in this survey said their most important task was as a twenty-four-hour support system – 'succour to the fainthearted' as one woman succinctly put it.

Community life

As well as performing their various roles as farm wives and wage labourers, the women played a very important part in community life, contributing extensively to local social, cultural and political life. This also earned status for the family when farmers are increasingly losing their own status as a result of the present crisis. With the reduction of service provision in rural areas becoming more acute, women's roles as unpaid carers and providers become increasingly important, within their families and within the community. Substantial fund-raising on behalf of a variety of local causes, especially in relation to provision in the pre-school, education and health areas, is a major activity. Their involvement in cultural and social activities was extensive and ranged from preparing the local *papurau bro* (Welsh-medium community newspapers), performing with local choirs and drama groups, to organizing a variety of local social events and entertainment.

Much of their voluntary work consisted of activities that can be viewed as an extension of their domestic role and it was seen as 'natural' for them to be involved in such work. Although this work is essential within the community, it does little for the women but reinforce their domestic role and position within the family (Little 1987). Indeed, their 'public' role appears to mirror that of their 'private' role – unpaid, underestimated and viewed as of secondary importance. This image is further reinforced when one considers how few (three) of the women belonged to the more formal local power structures such as the local councils and school governing boards; similarly, few women belonged to either of the farming unions. These institutions are dominated by men; where women do partake, they rarely operate in an official capacity except as secretaries or clerks.[4]

Although this gender division of voluntary labour suggests, yet again, a secondary role for women, this was not how the women themselves saw it:

> Well, yes, a lot of it is 'domestic', I suppose, but we have the skills and we're using them, and they're doing some good if it means we have a scanner in the hospital and computers in the schools.
>
> (Julia Jones)

Another criticized the author for questioning the nature of such institutions as the WI and for suggesting that they reinforced women's domestic role:

> It's not just jam and Jerusalem or whatever they say . . . we also have talks by women who've climbed in the Himalayas and travelled all over, business women and their work . . . now that gave me some ideas.
>
> (Ann Williams)

Through membership of such groups as Merched y Wawr (a Welsh-medium organization similar to the WI) and Mudiad Ysgolion Meithrin (Welsh-medium nursery groups), for example, rural women participate in far more than pleasant social activities. They become involved in locally pertinent political activity, albeit (generally) in an implicit or indirect way, on issues such as rural housing, language matters, nursery provision and transport.

An underestimated and undervalued contribution

The aim of the chapter thus far has been to make visible the extensive and varied labour activities of the contemporary farm wife in north-west Wales; to do away with the prevailing image of her as 'someone who bakes cakes and feeds hens'. Yet it is this image that predominates despite evidence to the contrary. Although *all* respondents recognized the worth of their own labour, three-fifths felt their efforts were appreciated by no one. The remainder complained that, whilst the farming community valued their input, the general public and various official agencies did not. The latter rarely addressed the women in their own right. This situation is not difficult to comprehend when it is realized that much of their labour is not officially recorded or even recognized as 'work' in many instances.

As suggested earlier, the fragmented and diverse nature of the wives' work also contributed to the lack of recognition of the extent of their labour input. What they all had in common was their almost exclusive responsibility for the domestic arena. According to Long 'work generates specific identities for those involved in specific forms of it' (1984, 16) and so the continuous underestimation and undervaluation of farm wives' other roles follows on from the low value society attaches to women's domestic work. This is further exacerbated by their marital status and the fact that they are working in a family business where

> Women working with their husbands in small businesses, where they don't receive a wage, are in a position which reproduces dependency very similar to that of domestic labour.
>
> (Westwood and Bhachu 1988, 6)

The situation is made worse when businesses operate from the home where little differentiation is made between domestic labour and the work done by the wives at home on behalf of the family business. Thus, the popular identity generated for these farm wives is one of a domestic nature, regardless of what they *actually* do.

Conclusion

Long (1984) suggests that control of specific identities generated by particular forms of work 'often implies control over the values ascribed to them.' This control, from the point of view of a feminist analysis, is rooted not only in the basic processes of capitalist exploitation but also in patriarchal practices within and beyond the family. Thus, the farm wives' varied labour activities are appropriated through family and kinship relations which are sustained by a familial ideology which stresses the role of women in the home as wives and mothers (Gasson 1980). A significant minority (eight) of the respondents apparently subscribed to such an ideology. They emphasizd their willingness to put up with the 'muck, long hours and poor returns' in return for benefits derived by them from 'working together as a family', 'helping my husband' and contributing towards 'the children's future'. A willingness was also expressed by a small majority (thirteen) to put up with the same in order to 'keep the way of life here as it is', for the 'closeness' and 'friendliness' of rural life and, amongst the Welsh respondents, to secure a specifically 'Welsh way of life' as they see it.

As part of the restructuring of the British economy, significant changes are being wrought in the agricultural sphere with emphasis on creating a more self-supporting enterprise culture, encouraged by substantial cuts in farm income support. Within the 'family farming' system of Wales 'the family' by definition, can always be called upon as a resource. But it is also a gendered system where a readily available and cheap resource is always to hand – the farm wife's labour, a point made by this study's analysis. Yet these wives cannot simply be seen as a one-dimensional class of dually exploited women, when the nature of their everyday working lives and experiences is so diverse. Their response to the present crisis was similarly varied and stemmed from a complex interaction between the differing factors that structured their lives and themselves as active agents within that process.

Although they were frustrated with the lack of recognition that their labour efforts earn, the majority (sixteen) expressed a pride in their ability to contribute to the family farm and to generate income for the family business and household. Therefore, whilst it is possible, in an analytical sense, to view labour power as exploitative, not all the women necessarily saw themselves as exploited. With the exception of those wives (three) in career-orientated, well paid and relatively secure jobs, it must be recognized that paid work off the farm is not always a 'liberating experience' – especially given the poor range of opportunities available to most women in this study area. In many instances it does little more than add a third burden to the double-day they already experience for generally low, though necessary, economic returns. On the other hand, the danger of the alternative, staying 'at home', is a return to the invisibility of yesterday.

Nevertheless, as a result of the continuing agricultural crisis and the changing of ideologies that have, in the past, closely defined women's lives, many farmers' wives may now have the opportunity to renegotiate their gendered position within the family and farm labour system. For the respondents (eight) who have diversified into non-agricultural business activities, the impact of their earnings could lead to a shift in the balance of power between men and women as well as a shift in attitude towards these women from the 'public' sphere:

> Some of these businesses are doing better than farming.
> (Rowlands cited in *Golwg* 13.3.91, 17)

Involvement in the farm business could empower those respondents (ten) who identified more closely with the agricultural aspects of farm life, especially those with a defined legal and active position as partners in the family firm. It is increasingly possible for these women to have access to the products of their labour, even if they do not yet have absolute control.

It must be recognized that work is not just 'a technical process' but involves exposure to new contexts and ideas. Within this context, farm wives are learning to organize with regard to their activities. Such organization ranges from more informal self-help groups, particularly in relation to non-agricultural diversified activities, through to becoming active at the highest policy-making levels of the farming unions in Wales. Similarly, work is not just about economic gains but is also about gaining a positive sense of self and identity. These aspects were certainly expressed by a number of the respondents whatever their working focus – farming, domestic or waged labour.

In relation to the various points outlined above moves are being initiated at various levels to alleviate the discrimination and injustices that these women endure. The unions are already moving in this direction with the National Farmers' Union claiming the intention is: 'for us to move away from talking about farmers' wives and have more women farmers' (Dillon-Roberts cited in the *Guardian* 12.2.92, 17).

At the European level, the European Parliament has requested action to be taken 'on spouses in agriculture and family businesses'. These actions include spouses contributions to be 'legally recognised as work' and for these women to have 'rights, relating to income, professional status and social security, commensurate with this fact' (OJEC 1989).

In the meantime and in conclusion, despite the varied constraints imposed upon them, these farm 'wives' continue to work out pragmatic responses and viable strategies as women and workers in the context of the material reality of their everyday lives.

Notes

[1] The data reported in this chapter form part of a wider study of gender roles and relations on the family farm in north-west Wales.

[2] The National Farmers' Union and the Farmers' Union of Wales provided a core list of twelve farm wives in the two districts. These wives then provided further names and addresses to create the full sample framework.

[3] 'Ffridd' perimeter − commonly refers to the walled/fenced boundary between the lower levels of the farm unit and the open mountain.

[4] Exceptions in this instance are three women who chair major policy committees within the Farmers Union of Wales.

References

Beneria, L. (1988). 'Conceptualising the Labour Force: The Underestimation of Women's Economic Activities', in R. E. Pahl (ed.), *On Work: Historical, Comparative and Theoretical Approaches* (Oxford, Blackwell).

Bouquet, M. (1985). *Family, Servants and Visitors* (Norwich, Geobooks).

Bradley, H. (1989). *Men's Work, Women's Work* (Cambridge, Polity Press).

Collins, R. (1985). 'Horses for Courses: Ideology and the Division of Domestic Labour' in P. Close and R. Collins (eds.), *Family and Economy in Modern Society* (London, Macmillan).

Davidoff, L. et al. (1976). 'Landscape with Figures', in J. Michel and A. Oakley (eds.) *The Rights and Wrongs of Women* (Harmondsworth, Middlesex, Penguin).

Dillon-Roberts, A. (1992). In C. Fitzsimons, 'The Lie of the Land', *Guardian* 12.2.92, 17.

Foord, J. and Gregson, N. (1986). 'Patriarchy: Towards a Reconceptualisation', *Antipode* 18, 186–211.

Gasson, R. (1992), in C. Fitzsimons, 'The Lie of the Land', *Guardian* 12.2.92, 17.

Gasson, R. (1991). *Farmers' Wives – Their Contribution to the Farm Business*, paper given at Agricultural Economists Society Conference (unpublished).

Gasson, R. (1986b). Review of Bouquet's 'Family, Servants and Visitors', in *Journal of Agricultural Economics* Vol. 37, 423–4.

Gasson, R. (1980). 'Roles of Farm Women in England', *Sociologica Ruralis* Vol. 20, 165–79.

Little, J. (1987). 'Gender Relations In Rural Areas: The Importance of Women's Domestic Role', *Journal of Rural Studies* Vol. 3, No. 4, 335–42.

Long, N. (ed.) (1984). *Family and Work in Rural Societies: Perspectives on Non-wage Labour* (London-New York, Tavistock Publications).

Oakley, A. (1974). *The Sociology of Housework* (London, Martin Robertson).

OJEC (1989). Document A2–416/88 'Resolution on Spouses in Agriculture and Family Businesses', *The Official Journal of the European Communities* No.C96/160–163, Thursday 16 March 1989.

Pugh, S. (1991). 'Tourism and Latest Developments', *Y Tir and Welsh Farmer Journal of the Farmers Union of Wales*, February/March, 22.

Rees, A. D. (1950). *Life in a Welsh Countryside* (Cardiff, University of Wales Press).

Rees, T. (1993). *Women and the Labour Market* (London, Routledge).

Rees, T. (1998). 'Changing Patterns of Women's Work in Wales: Some Myths Explored', *Contemporary Wales* Vol. 2, 119–30.

Rowlands, J. (1992). In R. Gwyn and S. Sutton 'Mamog, Mwd a Menywod', *Golwg* Cyfrol 3, Rhif 26, 13.3.91, 16–17.

Vaughn, R. (1951). *Moulded in Earth* (London, John Murray).

Westwood, S. and Bhachu, P. (eds.) (1988). *Enterprising Women: Ethnicity, Economy and Gender Relations* (London, Tavistock).

Whatmore, S.J. (1988). *The Other Half of the Family Farm* unpublished Ph.D. thesis, University of London.

Williams, J. (1958). 'Dros Fy Ysgwydd', in *Fferm a Ffair a Phentre* (Aberystwyth, Cymdeithas Llyfrau Ceredigion).

Winckler, V. (1987). 'Women and Work in Contemporary Wales', *Contemporary Wales* Vol. 1, 53–71.

8

Chasing credentials: women further-education teachers and in-service training

JANE SALISBURY

The drive for credentialism and professionalism is leading people from many walks of life to seek more qualifications mid-career. This chapter reports on the quest for a 'more professional identity' of six women teachers from further education in south Wales. Unhappy with their unqualified status and discontented with their inadequate 'chalkface socialization' as further-education teachers, the women pragmatically pursue a teaching credential. In their 'talk', the women reveal changing perspectives both on the realities of their work with post-sixteen-year-olds, and also in their views about themselves. The chapter is based on research on six women on a part-time in-service Certificate of Education (FE) course situated at a university department of education, in Wales.[1] It sets out to show how the women, who have diverse occupational biographies, both traditionally female ones and traditionally male ones (a hairdresser, a quantity surveyor, a radiographer, a secretary, a typist and a social worker), experience professional training and make the transition in identity to qualified teacher status.

Women have traditionally always been teachers, particularly in Wales, but more typically they have worked with school-aged children, in particular in the primary sector. Over the last decade or so, however, women have increasingly been entering the further education and tertiary sector, not as newly qualified teachers, but more usually as untrained but 'occupationally experienced' staff to teach on appropriate vocational courses. Further education in England and Wales has changed and is metamorphosing rapidly. A movement towards professionalism has generated a credential-conscious further-education workforce.

In the two sections below it will be seen how increasingly important it is for women in further education to possess qualifications and credentials. Not only are these 'portable' – a competent occupationally qualified person will usually have few difficulties taking his or her qualifications elsewhere (Crompton and Sanderson 1990) – but such 'bits of paper' may provide shelter in the changing and uncertain labour market of further education.

Women in further education

Women became a larger part of the teaching force in further education in England and Wales in the late 1980s, increasing their numbers from 17,214 in 1986 to 19,006 in 1988 (DES 1987, 1988). A closer inspection of the distribution of women staff, however, reveals an alarming paucity in senior posts. In 1986, only 292 women were heads of departments in further-education establishments compared to 2,327 men, and although by 1987 women had gained an extra thirty head of department posts, they continued to be under-represented at Reader and Senior Lecturer grades. In both further and higher education (HE), women are over-represented in the lower grades and enormously under-represented in the higher ones. Such under-representation, argues Spencer (1987, 3), indicates that dynamics of exclusion and marginalization are operating, which 'clearly make Further and Higher Education a discriminating environment for women'. Table 8.1 (p.142) lends support to Spencer's argument and suggests that women's careers are constrained by their gender and that, despite their graduate status and training, women lecturers are often 'tracked' into low-status positions.

The information in Table 8.1 is an outline of the situation and may conceal major trends of the employment of women within further education. *Statistics of Education for Wales 1991*, (DES 1991), for example, reveals a continued rise in the number of part-time teachers in further and higher education not in regular service, which has increased by 69 per cent since 1986. Though official sources do not differentiate these part-time staff by gender, other sources indicate that women's employment in further education is increasingly marked by temporary contracts (NATFHE 1991). The stories of the women in this chapter illustrate the point that women's work histories in further education are more varied,

Table 8.1 Full-time lecturers in further and higher education establishment by sex, age range, graduate status, training and average salary, 1988–1989

	Women	Men
Total number employed	25,000	69,000
Age Range	34–54 yrs	30–59 yrs
	(17,000	(54,000
	employees)	employees)
% Graduate status	47.6	47.4
% Trained	65.5	59.9
Average salary	£15,488	£17,412

Source: Calculated from Government Statistical Service (1991). *Educational Statistics for UK* (London, HMSO, 9,10; tables 9 & 10).

briefer and more often characterized by part-time work than those of men.

Women in further education need to look out for themselves. The development of a dual labour market with a shrinking core of permanent well paid (predominantly male) staff and a swelling periphery of part-time and temporary staff (mainly female) is increasingly likely. Under the incorporation of FE colleges in April 1993, efficiency measures and cost cutting will, argues Johnston (1992, 9), lead to the formation of a large industrial reserve army of labour.

The importance of in-service training for women teachers

In-service education and training is increasingly important for all teachers. Not only does it provide opportunities for professional development at a time when promotion prospects are limited, but it also equips teachers to deal with rapidly changing responsibilities within their schools and colleges. In further education, Gleeson (1991) asserts that changes have been, and will continue to be 'anarchic'. For women, in-service training may be particularly important, especially for those who have taken a mid-career break or who have entered teaching following other earlier occupations. Further, for women teachers in further education who are seeking promotion or a permanent contract, such training may be especially important. Competition is severe and despite the slowly increasing numbers of women in this field, the majority of senior lectureships and head of department posts are held by men. Such patterns of under-representation cannot be attributed solely to women's domestic and parental responsibilities. However, as Acker (1992, 2) points out, career plans on the stereotypically male professional model are highly unrealistic for women teachers, as real life produces 'an unpredictable mix of health and illness, domestic stability and upheaval, childbirth and miscarriages'. Such planned and unplanned events, with resulting discontinuities and shouldering of heavy domestic responsibilities, undoubtedly had their effects on the women whose lives are touched upon here. Brief biographical details for each one of them are presented in Table 8.2. Planned or not, the opportunity to 'professionalize', i.e. to obtain qualified-teacher status via in-service training, was valued by each of the women. In the sections which follow, data are presented which show how such a credential was perceived as having the potential to transform occupational life chances and make more secure promotion possibilities. Before moving to empirical material, however, it is necessary to sketch in a few details about the further education in-service teacher education course on which the women were participants.

The in-service course: Reflecting on the 'nuts and bolts' of teaching

The FE in-service course has been running for over twenty years and annually enrols around forty trainees. Participants are usually involved in 'post-sixteen' education, and may come from further education, the new universities, agricultural colleges, the armed forces, nursing and the paramedical professions. The time needed to obtain the qualification is just over a year; attendance is required in the University for eight weeks (June and July) in each of two consecutive years, with supervised teaching practice in the trainee's own institution during the intervening period.

The aim of the course is to improve teaching skills, or what the course director terms 'the nuts and bolts' of teaching, and the trainees are given a variety of lectures, tutorials, seminars and micro-teaching experiences to develop their teaching skills. Trainees' practical and written work is continuously assessed. Particular emphasis is placed upon the daily writing of a Journal, in which students are required to 'interrogate' their own experiences, and 'reflect' upon the curriculum of the course and how it applies

Table 8.2 Biographical details of six women further-education teachers

Name	Age	No. of years married	Children's ages	No. of years teaching in FE part-time	full-time	Teaching subjects	Occupations/work history before teaching	Qualifications/ training
Alice Bristow	47	27	26 19 16	9 years	5 years	Hairdressing	Apprentice hairdresser Mother Part-time hairdresser Salon owner Part-time teacher Full-time teacher	City and Guilds Advanced Cert. in Hairdressing
Sharon Hughes	34	–	–		6 years	Social Care	Undergraduate 4 yrs Social worker for Barnardos Social worker, Social Services Full-time teacher	3 'A' Levels BA degree in Social Admin. and Social Work
Clare Jones	35	13	10 7	18 months	2 years	Surveying and Construction Studies	Student for HNC Worked as surveyor Mother Part-time student for degree Part-time teacher Full-time teacher	2 'A' Levels HNC in surveying. Degree in surveying (via extension course)

Table 8.2 (cont.)

Name	Age	No. of years married	Children's ages	No. of years teaching in FE part-time	full-time	Teaching subjects	Occupation/work history before teaching	Qualifications training
Rhiannon Moore	38	20	20 8	12 years	2 years	Business Studies, Word-processing	Mother Evening-class student Part-time evening-class teacher Full-time teacher	'A' Levels. Secretarial qualifications. Computing. City & Guilds FE Teaching Certificate Stage 1 & 2
Margaret Reynolds	45	21	12 15	5 years		Secretarial Subjects Medical secretaries course	Trainee Radiographer Radiographer Mother Part-time teacher	3 'A' Levels. Diploma in Radiography. Wordprocessing qualifications. RSA Teacher Certificate.
Cecilia Taylor	42	18	11	4 years	1 year	Wordprocessing	Typist/Secretary Mother Part-time secretary Part-time teacher	Secretarial qualification e.g. 18 Shorthand Certificates. RSA Teaching Certificate.

to their own teaching. On successful completion of the course, the variously experienced participants, some of whom are graduates and others non-graduates, are awarded either the 'Postgraduate Certificate in Education' or 'Certificate of Education' respectively, conferred by the University of Wales.

Why enrol for the certificate of education?

The logic of credentialist exclusion does not appear to operate for teachers in further education, at least not at an overt level. Indeed, where teaching qualifications are concerned, though deemed highly desirable (Haycocks Report 1977), such credentials are not a prerequisite for securing a teaching post in a college of further education. Thus the motivations for undertaking an unnecessary qualification deserve some attention.

About the study, about the women

The women whose voices and views are presented in this chapter were opportunistically sampled from a larger group of forty-two men and women, all enrollees on the Certificate of Education (FE) course, an in-service course, designed to improve teaching skills for experienced but untrained teachers. All six women were currently teaching in colleges of further education in south Wales.[2] Their ages ranged between forty-seven and thirty-four years; five of them were married with children, only one of them had entered teaching on a full-time basis. Between them they had worked thirty-one years as part-time teachers and sixteen years as full-time teachers. Each of the women had trained for and worked in other occupations (see Table 8.2 for brief cameos), deciding only later to take up teaching. And finally, a second common feature of their individual biographies was the fact that each of them had entered the college classroom as unqualified, untrained teachers.

> I remember my first day as a teacher clearly, it's a funny story but I was actually a part-time secretary for the Vice-Principal of the College at the time. Well, a woman in Business Studies was taken ill – she died a few days later actually – and the Principal asked me to step in to help the Department out . . . so I was a typist one

morning and a teacher the same afternoon . . . I was really thrown in at the 'deep end'!

(Cecilia Taylor)

Though not as dramatic as Cecilia's initial foray into teaching, the other women share tales of how they had 'muddled through', or taught 'along the lines of good teachers' they had encountered in their own schooling. Sharon, who had joined a college of further education direct from a social services department, where collaboration and team work were the norm, reported how her new colleagues had refused to share handouts and teaching aids:

The only advice and help that I, or anyone else got was where to find the paper and pens!

(Sharon Hughes)

Describing and recounting such initial encounters and experience as untrained teachers occurred with marked frequency over the period of training. All trainees, including the six women, shared personal stories both informally and in structured tutorial discussions. This 'talking shop' (Marsh 1987) was a distinct feature of the in-service Certificate of Education course. These unelicited accounts, along with data from semi-structured interviews, provides much of the material on which this chapter is based. In the sections which follow, the women's motivations towards the course and their experiences of certain aspects of the training programme will be examined.

Enter six women

We now turn to the voices of six women teachers and open this empirical section by uncovering their mixed motives and optimistic beliefs for undertaking an unnecessary qualification! When asked about their reasons for pursuing the Education Certificate, the women revealed both instrumental and altruistic motives:

I'm here (on the course) for two reasons – to improve my teaching and get some ideas to take back to work and, I suppose more privately, I'm keeping my fingers crossed it (the qualification), the piece of paper, will help me get Head of Department in three years time!

(Rhiannon Moore)

Having optimistically mapped out her 'career' (Lyons 1981), Rhiannon was candid in disclosing her motivations for undertaking professional training. Instrumental orientations were displayed by other female trainees. Margaret admitted:

> I'm after a Course Leader's role in my College. I'm virtually doing the job anyway! Our Principal has a policy of getting all his staff qualified as teachers so I'm trying to 'fit the bill' as it were.
>
> (Margaret Reynolds)

And Alice confessed,

> I know that I'll get an increment for getting Qualified Teacher Status. So that's a good enough reason don't you think? The chances of moving into other colleges are increased if I get the Certificate.
>
> (Alice Bristow)

Whether the Certificate of Education would help the women achieve promotion and job mobility is debatable. Other research (Simmons and Stanford 1987) shows that although female teachers attend in-service courses and pursue more substantial qualifications, such as the B.Ed., more than men, there is little relationship between such courses and subsequent career trajectories.

For two of the women (Sharon and Alice), release for their in-service training was part of a planned programme of staff development initiated by their college and staff development officer, whilst for others (Clare and Rhiannon), time off to undertake the education course was largely negotiated and initiated at their own prompting:

> The men in my section have all done this course, and two of them did the City and Guilds Stages as well. I heard one of them talking about it [the course] and it sounded good, . . . so I asked the Staff Development Officer if I could do it. But I've been waiting a year to come here as another chap asked before me and I was told that there was a queue. Still, I'm here now!
>
> (Clare Jones)

Similarly, Rhiannon applied to her principal for three consecutive years for permission to undertake the in-service course:

> I applied again this year and waited for over a month for the Head of Department to tell me I had been granted leave of absence. I

nearly missed it again – but recently I heard on the Q.T. [quiet] that she didn't support my application. Perhaps she feels threatened at the idea of me getting a proper teaching qualification, I don't know really.

(Rhiannon Moore)

In these statements can be detected the belief that the Teaching Certificate mattered, being seen as a credential with currency both in the internal labour market of a college of further education and as a 'portable' qualification (Crompton and Sanderson 1990).

Critical thoughts about the course

The women found fault with structure, content and delivery of the course and did not always see it as relevant. At various stages some of them were highly critical. Hodgson and Whalley (1985) insist that the key to success for in-service courses for experienced teachers is that the knowledge and techniques delivered update participants and can be applied by them on returning to their institutions. Many criticisms centred on 'relevance' and 'applicability'. Clare, while recognizing the value of the 'nuts and bolts' section of the course, refuted a lecturer's point that Bloom's taxonomy of educational objectives[3] was a necessary starting point for planning lessons:

When I do cavity walls with a class, the technician wheels a model in on a trolley; I give students handouts and I talk about cavity walls . . . dimensions, air space, brickties – I just tell them the facts . . . things that I want them to know – that the syllabus specifies. In my notes I have a simple list of points I want to cover – I don't pour over that taxonomy formulating objectives – it's not necessary.

(Clare Jones)

Similarly, while Clare could teach without 'Bloom', Alice felt that:

Some of the theory stuff is a bit airy-fairy, a waste of time for me – it's of no use to me in my teaching and I don't understand it anyway!

(Alice Bristow)

Both Alice and Rhiannon tended to use the word 'theory' to label and diminish anything which did not directly conform to their personal views of what was useful and relevant. In contrast, two of the female students expressed concern at the lack of theoretical content in the training course. Sharon admitted that she felt disappointed and let down by the curriculum:

> I thought it (the course) would be a more intellectually challenging . . . that we'd examine larger issues impinging on classrooms and learning like [pause] class, race and gender.
>
> (Sharon Hughes)

Cecilia was also irritated to find out, on returning for the third stage of the course, that the Equal Opportunities and Sociology modules had been dropped. Complaining to the course director, she argued:

> If theory isn't present on a course like this, then teachers like us will miss out; I think that there are very few of us who would work through different books to get some differing perspectives. Sociology has lots to offer us, surely?
>
> (Cecilia Taylor)

Such complaints about the atheoretical nature of the course were untypical of the student group as a whole; most participants, both men and women, had revealed an antipathy towards two early lectures on Memory and Learning Theory. Evidence from various studies suggest that teachers are resistant to the disciplines of Education as subjects (Elliott 1991). As far back as 1968, Jackson observed that 'not only do teachers avoid elaborate words they also seem to shun elaborate ideas' (1968, 144). Since then, various authors have identified themes of anti-intellectualism and cynicism in teachers' culture (Hargreaves 1972, 404–7; Lieberman and Miller 1984; Sikes 1992). It has been shown that teachers firmly believe that their instructional needs are practical, not theoretical; knowledge skills which are deemed useful to classroom practice are valued over abstractions or theoretical knowledge which teachers find obstruse and irrelevant. Several writers have argued and shown that teachers draw on personal knowledge rather than abstract theory (Pollard 1987; Nias 1989; Cortazzi 1991).

Course participants were encouraged to be 'reflective practitioners' (Schon 1983) via the writing of a daily Journal. Though required to 'interrogate their own experience' and draw upon personal knowledge, the trainees were suspicious, confirming the assertion of Squirrel et al. (1990) that both experienced and student teachers tend to be wary of teacher education programmes which lay emphasis on reflection. Worried about confidentiality, Cecilia saw the writing of the journal as an intimate and private document which she was reluctant for others to see or grade:

> Cecilia: My Journal is very personal . . . I've opened up in it and admitted weaknesses and problems from my early days in teaching – when I was just given a class and told to get on with it!
>
> *JS: You mean details from when you were in at the deep end?*
>
> Cecilia: Yes, exactly . . . It's not that I haven't enjoyed writing it, I have really, it's been a sort of, . . . a catharsis working through of things . . . But it's private and as for anyone assessing it, well I suppose I'm not really happy about it.
>
> (Cecilia Taylor)

With different concerns, Clare (drawing upon the irreverent acronym of a male student in her tutorial group) admitted that she found the journal writing tedious:

> Clare: I do it [write the journal] because we have to, it's instead of an unseen examination isn't it? . . . But its all a bit of a con. Like Clive said 'FO FO, fuck off and find out.' The lecturers give us a taste of a topic and then we're supposed to go off read up and write about how it applies to our work as teachers!
>
> *JS: You sound unhappy with it Clare?*
>
> Clare: That's putting it politely! The journal is a way of keeping us busy – but we don't have the time for all this reflection – not to do it well anyway!
>
> (Clare Jones)

Clare was not alone in her cynicism, along with the majority of further-education teachers on the course, she saw reflection as too time consuming. The problematic nature of the word 'reflection' has been addressed by Rudduck (1991, 324), who points out that it

> seems to hint at a different, more leisurely life style – and it is easy to see how teachers valuing the reality of a more active self-image,

might reject 'reflection' and see it, along with 'theory' as belonging to the world of dreaming spires that they think HE staff inhabit.

The lecturers and tutors who staff the in-service course did not escape criticism. The women students were irritated by inefficiencies and bad practice:

> I didn't travel over sixty miles to be read to! We've been taught how to do it properly – how to take pains over presentation – Why on earth don't they practice what they preach!
>
> (Margaret Reynolds)

> It was stressed to us that telling wasn't teaching and we were made to explore other ways instead of chalk'n'talk – but the staff here, most of them just carry on in the same groove.
>
> (Rhiannon Moore)

> Didn't somebody say, 'Those who can't teach teach teachers'?
>
> (Clare Jones)

> He's all slap on the back and arm round the shoulders and 'How are we doing my lovely?', but in terms of proper tutorials, he has a very narrow agenda . . . The journal stuff comes back with a pencil tick in the base of each page – no comments and he's incredibly slow to turn it around. Does it mean that my 'reflections' are okay?
>
> (Margaret Reynolds)

Following a heated discussion towards the end of the course Sharon, sympathizing with tutors, lecturers and in particular the course director, pointed out to members of her tutorial group that:

> The course is unlikely to suit everyone – you just have to look at the range of experience between the ten of us here! Leave alone the other thirty-odd students on the course! Individual needs are so varied that designing a course to suit everyone is, well, [gasps] . . . I think JA [the course director] has got an unenviable task.
>
> (Sharon Hughes)

Teaching practice: performances in the workplace

> I don't practice. I do it for real. I'm paid for it and I've been doing it six years!
>
> (Sharon Hughes)

The women were united in their views that their assessed teaching practice was extremely stressful. Each one had gone to great lengths to implement and display methods and strategies that had been taught on Stage 1 of the course:

> I spent literally hours rewriting my usual lesson notes with aims, behavioural objectives, methods resources to suit my tutor. But during the lesson I didn't refer to them once! [laughs] By the time I came to perform them I knew them off by heart!
>
> (Sharon Hughes)

> My overheads [overhead projector-transparencies] were brilliant – I'd done some glossy, professional looking ones but he [the tutor] could see my pen shaking as I pointed to each heading. I was in such a nervous state!
>
> (Rhiannon Moore)

> Even though I do the job day in day out I found the whole idea of being assessed and watched really stressful. I did loads of work for the tutor's visit.
>
> (Alice Bristow)

Tutors assessed the teaching skills over three or four pre-planned visits. Several of the women explained to me how they had arranged to be seen with 'good' groups:

> I made sure that every time he came I had decent classes – if they want us to do things properly then I had to have a group of students who would behave properly.
>
> (Margaret Reynolds)

> When JA (the tutor) was on the phone negotiating dates and times for his visits I deliberately left out my second year classes – they're far too cheeky. I used my first year groups for all of his visits and I told them what it (the tutor's visit) was all about. I knew they'd be angels – and they were!
>
> (Clare Jones)

All the course participants, men and women, without exception saw teaching practice as something to be endured, requiring 'a show', 'a display', a 'performance' for staff to witness. To write cognitive objectives routinely, prepare glossy visual aids and teach so self-consciously, it was felt, was an impossibility. There was a sense that the in-depth preparation and exhausting performance required for the sample lessons was both untypical of, and unrealistic for teachers in further education:

> I was glad to get the teaching prac. [sic] over with and get back to normal . . . if I had to teach like that for every lesson, or every course I'd give up – But then nobody expects it, there's not enough hours in the day for perfection!
>
> (Alice Bristow)

With varying occupational experience, different educational backgrounds and resulting needs, the women found the course far from perfect. The next section however, presents the women's perceived gains more positively, and identifies aspects of their training that they found useful.

Being 'more clued up' – benefits and gains of training

Though citing different aspects of the in-service training course, each of the women found various parts of it useful, at both personal and professional levels. Much of the information gathered in interviews and observations does not necessarily fit neatly under personal or professional headings; however, a selection of typical evaluatory comments is presented below:

> The really useful bits of the course for me were the sessions we did on lesson and course planning. Now that I'm in a post that involves designing courses and writing up BTEC submissions, I needed guidance. Before, well I just muddled through, you know – Aims, Methods, Resources . . . but now I'm clearer about how to break down material and topics into learning objectives. You should see the schemes I now write, they are completely different . . . I cringe when I look back over the stuff I used to write!
>
> (Clare Jones)

Commenting on the effects of the training course after returning to her college workplace, Margaret insisted that it had produced benefits for her students:

> Apart from being more informed about teaching methods and ways of delivering knowledge to a class, I think that I'm more confident, and they [the students] sense it.
>
> *JS. How do you mean exactly?*

Well . . . before, I'd usually teach straight forwardly you know –
Handouts, explaining out at the front of the room. Most lessons
were the same format. But now, I'm getting them to do more for
themselves. I think, I honestly think that they are happier not to be
so spoonfed, so dependent . . . I think far more carefully about
coursework assignments and already the projects they are producing are a better standard. As well as a better learning experience
hopefully they should have better exam results!

(Margaret Reynolds)

Cecilia also felt that the course had made her more aware of the
way she used classroom time,

I'm much more self-conscious and aware of the limited time I have
to cover a syllabus. I think this resulted from the teaching project
assignment. I have to admit that I had never ever planned and
mapped out my teaching and the students' work so carefully before
. . . I'm now thinking more about the what and the how of
teaching

(Cecilia Taylor)

Halpin, Croll and Redman (1990, 196) acknowledged that there
are difficulties with teachers' own reports of changes in their practice in that they may exaggerate the nature and extent of the
change. The women's claims about improved practice however,
were not the result of direct questions but offered as part of an
unstructured interview. Similar unelicited accounts were also given
in tutorial discussions in the final stages of the course.

Apart from the individually identified gains and benefits of the
in-service course, four of the women also reported gains in self-
confidence. The words of Alice summarize her shifts in
occupational status, while at the same time hint at an emerging
identity as a professional:

I've been a hairdresser, mother, a salon owner, a teacher. I know
I'm good at these things but this course has made me feel that I
know my subject. It's daft really, but being here at a University and
studying for a teaching qualification makes me feel more professional . . . It's difficult to put into words but, I know I'm more
confident. I speak more at meetings which I never did. My husband
was reading a bit of my journal the other night and he said, 'Just
look at you Alice, you're much more clued up.' He put it in a nut-

shell really – I am more clued up about teaching and educational matters!

(Alice Bristow)

For three of the women, the in-service course was the first 'outside' contact they had experienced for some time, and they welcomed an interlude from the isolation of their classrooms. An important aspect of the course for all of them was the contact it offered for meeting, sharing experiences and collaborating in projects with other untrained teachers.

> Because we are all unqualified there's a feeling of 'We're all in this together' . . . We might have different backgrounds and subjects but . . . It's great to learn other people's horror stories – you don't feel quite so useless about your own bad lessons.
>
> (Cecilia Taylor)

Most individuals, but particularly those with school-aged children, spoke of 'getting through' or 'surviving' the course, but occasionally it was referred to as being a 'foundation for continued professional learning' (Cecilia) and 'a platform for possible promotion' (Rhiannon). The women saw the gaining of a qualification not only as a successful end to a period of training but as a potential lever for securing a permanent contract, a full-time position or a promotion in a college of further education.

'A useful bit of paper' – the Certificate of Education as currency?

> I'd only completed the first phase of the course when I was made discipline director, so it had spin-offs for me . . . I was even wondering whether to complete the second phase [laughs] . . . – no seriously. I'd got what I wanted without the bit of paper.
>
> (Clare Jones)

Both Rhiannon Moore and Sharon Hughes, like Clare, experienced a change of role and enhanced status during their participation in the in-service teacher education course. The positions of course leader and course director were allocated to them before their successful completion of the course. Clearly it would be foolhardy to attribute the credit for such job changes solely to the in-service course; however, those women who had been promoted and given extra responsibilities felt sure that the qualification (and being seen to be pursuing it) can have done them little harm!

> It was noted by my head of department and the powers-that-be that I was here (on the in-service Certificate of Education Course), then, in the following September I spoke up more than usual in a few meetings. I think I probably knew more than them about NVQs (National Vocational Qualifications) and APL (Accreditation for Prior Learning) and well, I think they saw me in a different light!
>
> (Rhiannon Moore)

Commitment and credentials for a better career

Teachers on vocational courses in colleges of further education are expected to have experience of the work for which they are preparing their students. Each of the women in this study fulfilled that criterion. However, like the women further-education teachers studied by Black (1989), they also recognized the importance of a formal teaching qualification. Three of them (Rhiannon, Margaret and Cecilia), had used their free time to pursue City and Guilds or Royal Society of Arts Teaching Certificates in evening courses. All six of them were prepared to lose eight weeks summer vacation to participate in the in-service course. They travelled daily distances ranging from 120 miles (Margaret), to four miles (Sharon).

Unlike the negative or non-committed teachers described by Cole (1985) who had 'drifted' into teaching, the women all displayed a positive commitment to their work as teachers:

> I love my job teaching. I love seeing the youngsters coming along; they change so much during their course and they leave us able to perm, colour, cut, do everything – it's fantastic work!
>
> (Alice Bristow)

> I remember the boredom of working in an office. I'm never bored now, the work is so interesting and there's more responsibility attached to teaching. I think it's the human element – getting involved with young people; helping them get qualified. No, I could never go back to office work!
>
> (Cecilia Taylor)

When reflecting upon earlier occupations, individuals identified numerous satisfying aspects of their teaching roles. Not only had part-time teaching enabled them to fulfil family duties (Acker 1989, Beechey 1986) but such work also paid the women what Siltanen (1986) terms 'a component wage', allowing them to contribute to household income. A final and significant 'satisfier', though variously expressed, was the 'improved self-image' (Cecilia) and 'more professional identity' (Rhiannon) that becoming a qualified teacher had given the women. It is perhaps this latter gain, or shift in identity that is most vividly captured in the words of Alice (a former hairdresser), which appropriately bring this chapter to a close.

> I can now say I've been to university! [laughter] I had to work very hard but it worked. I've got a teaching certificate now, so no HMI [Her Majesty's Inspector] can embarrass me again by asking if I'm qualified. I'm a proper teacher with a proper certificate!
>
> (Alice Bristow)

Notes

[1] The data presented in this chapter derive from a larger doctoral research project which is a qualitative study of training experiences of further education teachers. Ethnographic fieldwork was undertaken over the fourteen months' duration of the In-Service Certificate of Education Course for untrained further-education teachers. Participant observation and interviews formed the main research methods.

[2] Pseudonyms are used throughout the chapter to provide confidentiality and protect the women's identities.

[3] Bloom's (1977) Taxonomy of Educational Objectives is a classification system which divides educational objectives into a hierarchical order and which helps teachers to plan lessons and student learning more thoroughly.

[4] A special thank-you must be recorded to the six women. They gave willingly of their time – participated in an in-depth semi-structured interview and allowed me to observe their discussions and 'teaching performances'!

References

Acker, S. (1989) (ed.). *Teachers, Gender and Careers* (London, Falmer Press).

Acker, S. (1992). 'Travel and Travail, a critical introduction', in J. Gaskell, *Gender Matters from School to Work* (Milton Keynes, Open University Press).

Beechey, V. (1986). 'Women's Employment in Contemporary Britain', in V. Beechey (ed.), *Women in Britain Today* (Oxford, Oxford University Press).

Black, E. (1989). 'Women's Work in a Man's World: Secretarial Training in a College of Further Education', in S. Acker (ed.), *Teachers, Gender and Careers* (London, Falmer Press).

Cantor, L. M. and Roberts, I. F. (1986). *Further Education Today: A critical review* (London, Routledge and Kegan Paul (3rd edition)).

Cole, M. (1985). ' "The Tender Trap?" Commitment and Consciousness in Entrants to Teaching', in S. J. Ball and I. F. Goodson (eds.), *Teachers' Lives and Careers* (London, Falmer Press).

Cortazzi, M. (1991). *Primary Teaching How it is: A Narrative Account* (London, David Fulton).

Crompton, R. and Sanderson, K. (1986). 'Credentials and Careers; some implications of the increase in professional qualifications amongst women', *Sociology* Vol. 20, No. 1, 25–42.

Crompton, R. and Sanderson, K. (1990). *Gendered Jobs and Social Change* (London, Unwin Hyman).

Department of Education and Science (1987). *Statistics of Education Teachers in Service, England and Wales* (London, Department of Education and Science).

Department of Education and Science (1988). *Statistics of Education Teachers in Service, England and Wales* (London, Department of Education and Science).

Elliott, J. (1991). 'A Model of Professionalism and its implications for Teacher Education', *British Educational Research Journal* Vol. 17, No. 4, 309–18.

Gleeson, D. (1991) (ed.). *Training and its Alternatives* (Milton Keynes, Open University Press).

Government Statistical Service (1991). *Education Statistics for the United Kingdom* (London, HMSO).

Halpin, D., Croll, P and Redman, K. (1990). 'The Effects of In service Education', *British Educational Research Journal* Vol. 16, No. 2, 163–78.

Hargreaves, D. (1972). *Interpersonal Relations and Education* (London, Routledge and Kegan Paul).

Haycocks, N. (1977). *The Training of Full-time Teachers in Further Education* (London, Association of Colleges for Further and Higher Education).

Henderson, E. S. (1975). 'Attitude change in in-service training', *British Journal of In-service Education* Vol. 2, No. 2, 113–16.

Hodgson, F. and Whalley, G. (1985). 'Evaluating In-Service: The question of criteria', in *British Journal of In-Service Education* Vol. 12, No. 1, 44–52.

Jackson, P. W. (1968). *Life in Classrooms* (New York, Holt Rhinehart and Winston).

Johnston, R. (1992). 'Alfred Marks to Enter Education', in *The Lecturer*, National Association of Teachers in Further and Higher Education (NATFHE), No. 6 August 1992, 9.

Lieberman, A. and Miller, L. (1984). *Teachers, Their World and Their Work* (Alexandria, V.A., ASCD).

Lyons, G. (1981). *Teacher Careers and Career Perceptions* (Windsor, NFER-Nelson).

Marsh, I. (1986). ' "Feel the width": Teachers' Expectations of an In-service Course', *British Journal of In-service Education* Vol. 13, No. 2, 76–86.

Marsh, I. (1987). 'Teachers' Perception of an In-service course: You can't please all of the people all of the time', *British Journal of In-service Education* Vol 14, No. 1, 56–63.

NATFHE (1991). 'Towards a Charter for Part-time Teachers', *National Association of Teachers in Further and Higher Education*, No. 3, Summer 1991, 3.

Nias, J. (1989). *Primary Teachers Talking: A Study of Teaching as Work* (London, Routledge).

Pollard, A. (1987). 'Primary Teachers and their Colleagues', in S. Delamont (ed.), *The Primary School Teacher* (Lewes, Falmer Press).

Rudduck, J. (1991). 'The Language of Consciousness and the Landscape of Action: Tensions in Teacher Education', *British Educational Research Journal* Vol. 17, No. 4, 319–31.

Schon, D. (1983). *The Reflective Practitioner* (London, Temple Smith).

Schon, D. (1987). *Educating the Reflective Practitioner* (San Francisco CA, Jossey-Bass).

Sikes, P. (1992). 'Imposed Change and the Experienced Teacher', in M. Fullan and A. Hargreaves (eds.), *Teacher Development and Educational Change* (London, Falmer Press).

Siltanen, J. (1986). 'Domestic Responsibilities and the Structuring of Employment', in R. Crompton and M. Mann (eds.), *Gender and Stratification* (Cambridge, Polity).

Simmons, K. and Stanford, J. (1987). 'Women and Inset: The road to promotion', *British Journal of In-service Education* Vol. 13, No. 2, 99–101.

Spencer, A. (1987). 'Foreword and Introduction', in Coombe Lodge Report, *Women in Further and Higher Education Management*, The Further Education Staff College, Vol. 20, No. 3, 131–8.

Squirrel, G., Gilroy, P., Jones, D. and Rudduck, J. (1990). 'Acquiring Knowledge in Initial Teacher Education: reading, writing and the PGCE course', *Library and Information Research Report No. 79* (London, British Library).

Welsh Office (1991). *Statistics of Education in Wales: Further and Higher Education 1991 No.5* (Cardiff, Welsh Office).

9

Promoting gender equality in schools

PATRICIA DANIEL

Introduction

Gender stereotyping in schools was formalized almost from the beginning of popular education in the early nineteenth century. Working-class girls learnt needlework and knitting while boys worked on arithmetic. The aim was to produce 'industrious servants' (British and Foreign School Society 1822, 76) who would then be 'wives and mothers of industrious and intelligent mechanics' (British and Foreign School Society 1823, 8). For middle-class girls at Cheltenham Ladies' College the aim was to develop a girl's intellectual powers in order to discharge 'those responsible duties which devolve upon her as wife, mother, mistress and friend, the natural companion and helpmeet for men' (Raikes 1908, cited in Purvis 1991). Old photographs in the Gwynedd Archives of the girls at Bontnewydd County School in the Cookery or the Laundry class indicate that the general emphasis was the same in Wales.

While today there exists for young women the formal right of equal access to education and job opportunities, gender stereotyping continues in schools. There are still, for example, clear sex-role patterns manifested in school students' attitudes towards technology and science. There is still a direct relationship between girls' and boys' choices of school subjects and jobs. These employment patterns also reflect relative wealth, power and status within society – in other words, the pattern is self-perpetuating.

Spender's research (1982) illustrates how the education system remains male-oriented and how girls' experience is radically different from that of boys within mixed-sex schools, for example in the quantity and quality of teacher attention they receive. Stanworth (1983, 7) also notes:

> Girls may follow a similar curriculum to boys and yet emerge from school with the implicit understanding that the world is a man's world, in which women should take second place.

In north Wales, as elsewhere, there are a number of projects attempting to address this issue; one is school-based and another involves initial teacher training. While both these have the potential for changing attitudes they are bound to be limited in their effects because of wider societal influences on sex role stereotyping.

This chapter reviews equal opportunities in education in Wales, focusing on girls' achievements at school in comparison to their destination after school. It discusses a case study of one Local Education Authority's (LEA) response, emphasizing the need for systematic structuring and ongoing monitoring in the promotion of equality. Next, it describes an initiative to raise awareness and establish good practice as regards gender equality among trainee teachers in the Postgraduate Certificate of Education (PGCE) course at the University College of North Wales (UCNW) Bangor. One aspect of this programme involves observation in schools – a means by which students can develop their analytic understanding of the problems, including the very slow rate at which change takes place. The chapter then focuses on an aspect unique to Wales – the promotion of the Welsh language and its inclusion as a core curriculum subject. While traditional relationships still prevail between Welsh as medium of instruction and subject choices made by Welsh-speaking girls, the official standing now enjoyed by the Welsh language has created new opportunities for women to pursue their preferred fields of study and career with enhanced status within Wales. What is the effect of these initiatives to promote gender equality and the enhanced status of Welsh in education on the changing identity of female pupils and teachers in north Wales?

Equal opportunities in education and employment in Wales

Mirroring the situation in the rest of the UK and in Europe as a whole, girls in Wales continue to achieve better results than boys in

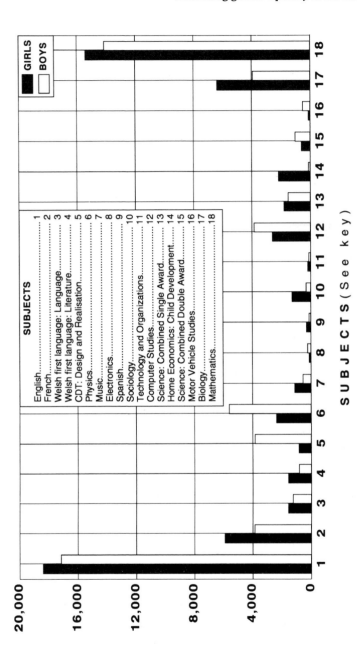

Figure 9.1a. Selected GCSE statistics for Wales, 1991: candidates entered

Source: Phillips, E. (1992, 2–4) 'A comparison of male and female success rates in GCSE subjects' (Cardiff: Welsh Joint Education Committee).

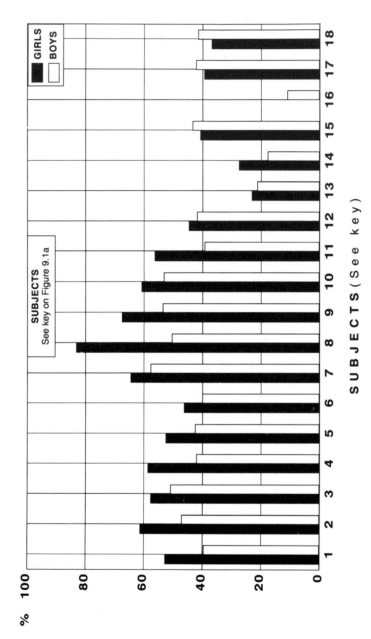

Figure 9.1b. Selected GCSE statistics for Wales, 1991: percentage achieving 'C' or better

Source: Phillips, E. (1992, 2–4) 'A comparison of male and female success rates in GCSE subjects' (Cardiff: Welsh Joint Education Committee).

public examinations and in a wider range of subjects. In 1991, girls in Wales achieved a higher success rate than boys (as measured by grade C or better) in forty-six out of sixty GCSE subjects (Phillips 1992, see Fig. 9.1b). Of those pupils in Gwynedd who go on to 'A' Levels, 54 per cent are girls; of all 'A' Level students who go on to higher education, 57 per cent are girls (Careers Service Gwynedd 1991). However, their post-school experience belies this potential. Girls achieve less well in terms of status and salary in subsequent employment.

With a greater variety of options now available in post-sixteen education, more young people are continuing in schools and colleges. In 1991, 69 per cent of females but only 56 per cent of males opted to remain in full-time education (Careers Service in Wales 1991). Option choices, however, are clearly sex stereotyped. Girls still tend to choose arts subjects at GCSE and at 'A' Level, while boys go into Science and Technology (WJEC 1991), and girls still by far outperform boys in English at GCSE while boys still do somewhat better than girls in Mathematics (Phillips 1992, see Fig. 9.1a). This is despite the fact that at primary school girls do better in Maths and Science than boys, as evidenced by the results of the standard assessment tasks at age seven in Wales (Welsh Office 1992). What is more, if girls do take a non-traditional subject like Physics at examination level, they tend to get higher grades than boys at this stage too. In the 1991 WJEC GCSE results for Physics, 46 per cent of female candidates gained grade C or above compared to 40 per cent of the male candidates (Phillips 1992, see Fig. 9.1b).

This potential is not realized in subsequent employment patterns. Girls leave school with lower career aspirations and expectations than boys, and most girls still enter sex-stereotyped or traditional female areas of employment. Delamont (1990) documents some of the influences on adolescents (particularly peer pressure from both genders) which result in gendered perceptions of appropriate behaviour and acceptable career possibilities. Statistics on destinations for school leavers entering employment or youth training in Wales reflect the general situation in the UK: approximately one quarter of females enter administrative and clerical posts and about a half go into other service employment – caring, catering, hairdressing, retail (Careers Service in Wales 1991). Young women are also less likely to enter employment with

YOUTH TRAINING

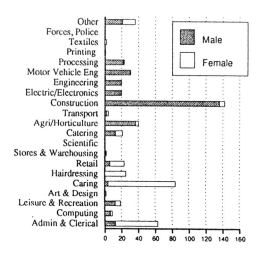

EMPLOYMENT

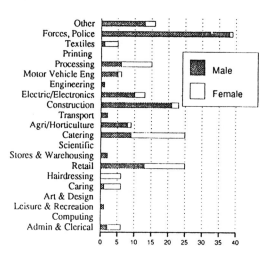

Figure 9.2 Occupational split of year-11 school leavers in Gwynedd, 1991
Source: Careers Service Gwynedd (1991, 9) *Where Did they Go? Gwynedd School Pupil Destinations* (Caernarfon: Gwynedd County Council).

a structured training programme (see Fig. 9.3). Women then earn less than men and tend to remain at lower levels of management (see Rees, this volume).

There is concern in Gwynedd, as in other parts of Wales, over the lack of opportunities for careers in science and technology. Where openings do exist, the number of female entrants is minimal. Even within traditional female careers such as education itself, the pattern of achievement is similarly discouraging. For example, in Gwynedd in 1992, there were two women head teachers at secondary level, and primary male head teachers out-numbered female heads by two to one (Gwynedd Education Office). What could schools be doing, given the situation of high female potential evidenced in education in contrast to their low achievement in employment?

What can schools do?
The challenge for schools is not only to provide equality of *access* to all areas of the curriculum but also to ensure an equal *experience* for girls once within the classroom in order to gain equality of *outcome* (Arnot 1989). Young people of both genders need the skills and confidence to fulfil their potential in adult life. Schools have to counteract social conditioning (both inside and outside school itself) to provide real freedom of choice in terms of subjects to study, skills to develop and careers for which to prepare. There is a need to encourage higher aspirations, to widen girls' horizons and to develop their assertiveness. As Wright (1988) has pointed out, this has to be done without falling into the trap of promoting the male paradigm as the norm or ideal, without devaluing tradi-tional female areas of study and work (these should be promoted so that boys also feel free to choose them) and without expecting girls to be the *same* as boys.

In examining educational changes it is, therefore, useful to bear in mind the distinction made by Weiner (1985), between 'equal opportunities' and 'anti-sexist education'. The former denotes working to help girls achieve within the system as it stands, and the latter working to change the system – in terms of its structures, its relationships and its priorities. Change occurring due to either of these approaches will inevitably influence the other, but they do represent rather different perspectives towards change for women.

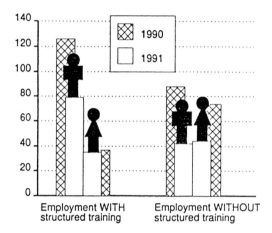

Figure 9.3 Employment with structured training of year-11 school leavers in Gwynedd, 1991
Source: Careers Service Gwynedd (1991,8) *Where Did they Go? Gwynedd School Pupil Destinations* (Caernarfon: Gwynedd County Council).

In what follows I shall be presenting a case study of how one LEA has tried to tackle these issues.

Case study: Clwyd County Council
Clwyd County Council presents a good example of a systematic and serious response to these issues. Countywide, gender equality has had a high profile since 1980 when, in conjunction with the Equal Opportunities Commission (EOC), Clwyd set up an action research project including case studies of three secondary schools (see Clwyd County Council 1983). As well as providing evidence of gender differentiation in subject choices, examination results and career avenues, this project also investigated pupils' perceptions of male and female roles, characteristics and competencies. The replies from the first year pupils to a questionnaire about the family and its activities revealed traditional sex roles:

> The mothers do the shopping (95%) the cooking (94%) the washing (98%) and cleaning (90%) while the fathers mend things which are broken (83%) do the painting and decorating (88%) and fix the car (78%).
>
> (Clwyd County Council 1983, 53)

Teachers' perceptions revealed a similar association of women with a domestic role being held responsible for enhancing males' and impeding females' promotion prospects.

> It is assumed that women teachers are married with small children to attend to and that these responsibilities will take precedence over their jobs and comments by female teachers indicate that they feel that gender is certainly an influence on their promotion hopes ... It appears that women are penalised because they have had children whereas men receive promotion because they have children to support.
>
> (Clwyd County Council 1983, 78)

It was concluded that there was cause for concern on both counts of sex stereotyping and discrimination.

An action plan was carried out on the basis of the recommendations from the research project, starting with the publishing of an Education Department policy statement (Evans 1987). This provides for continuous review and monitoring of progress and promotion of equal opportunities, an in-service education programme and the provision of a countywide Equal Opportunities team with a specialist Advisory Teacher. A similar structure and process was required of individual schools, that is, the establishment of an Equal Opportunities Working Party with a designated co-ordinator to draft out a policy document and to facilitate monitoring throughout the school – a structure which exemplifies good practice in Wales.

Clwyd adopted the *Genderwatch* monitoring schedules (Myers 1987) which were translated into Welsh and made available to all secondary schools in the county. These schedules, initiated by the EOC, comprise a comprehensive set of materials for whole school and departmental review.[1] They include aspects of classroom interaction (who gets the attention and why? who dominates discussion and how?), images of women in textbooks (what kind of role models are conveyed?) and staffing patterns (who has the authority?) as well as school organization (who occupies what space in the playground?). Self-monitoring exercises were carried out with the use of this material and departmental reports and whole-school analyses used for further in-service training.

In-service training has involved awareness raising activities for staff to re-examine their own attitudes. One fairly hard-hitting example entitled 'How sexist are you in the classroom?' is a set of statements about classroom practice for teachers to discuss in pairs. Another, a quiz on 'Women at Work', aims to explode some of the myths; for example; the nuclear family/economic unit – working father, non-working mother and two children under the age of sixteen: how many families in Britain conform to that picture? (Answer: 5 per cent.) Such in-service training also involves consultation and debate on school action plans; that is, which areas should be prioritized next for consideration and change: for example, encouraging women staff to apply for promotion, publishing an equal opportunities booklet for parents' information, or producing materials on sexism for a Year 10 module?

Recognizing that girls may feel inhibited in what appear to be traditionally male areas of the curriculum, girl-only activities have been organized to develop confidence and skills in the use of new technology as well as separate careers visits to local industry. Clwyd also actively promotes other initiatives, for example, the Women in Education group, which organizes cultural events promoting women in the arts, and Women into Management courses, which include job application and interview skills.

While these developments in the school sector are welcome, both local and national experience suggests that, so far, they have not brought about fundamental changes. In the following section, I go on to discuss work in initial teacher training which also raises questions about how much has yet been achieved.

Initial teacher education

While the type of activity established in Clwyd is the means by which attitudes and practice will be influenced among existing teachers, it is clearly essential that the training of new teachers lays a solid foundation for promoting gender equality in schools. One strategy that has been implemented in the PGCE course at UCNW Bangor is that of grassroots research by student teachers during practical placements in local schools. This helps teacher educators to keep in touch with progress in schools and thus to understand the problems facing student teachers.

Equal opportunities in the Postgraduate Certificate of Education
Educational objectives for student teachers in pre-service courses

can be categorized into three domains: the *cognitive domain* involves identification, analysis and evaluation with regard to overt and covert discrimination and good anti-sexist practice; the *affective domain* concerns an awareness of own and others' attitudes, the capacity for self-evaluation and the commitment to work for change; the *practical domain* is concerned with the development of professional skills in order actively to promote equality and counter sexism and to effect change (see Daniel 1991). It is not expected that all teachers in training will achieve all of these objectives nor that in each domain an individual will achieve the same level of development. The categories apply equally to practising teachers and provide a model for assessing professional development over time.

In the one-year PGCE course at Bangor, a developmental approach has been adopted, which means that the issue of gender is revisited at different stages during the course, before and after periods of practical teaching. This means that student teachers have the opportunity to share perceptions and to prepare in more detail for tackling stereotyping in their subject teaching. One example is drawing up a ten-point plan of action : the Technology group 1990–91 included the following points: 'promote skills which require delicacy and sensitivity . . . give positive reinforcement; display both girls' and boys' work'.

In school, student teachers are asked to consider their own practice and reflect on this in their self-assessment:

> I had a tendency at first not to question existing practices within the school, go for a low profile . . . but my conclusion is that a male teacher has to be positive in discrimination to encourage young women into non-traditional areas like Science.
>
> (O'Dowd 1990, 3)

Some student teachers decide to take the issue of gender equality as the focus of academic work in a dissertation which explores it in relation to their subject. Frost (1991), for example, considers the need to raise the status of foreign language learning (traditionally perceived as a field of study for girls and thus implicitly inferior to Maths and Physics) within the current economic context:

> The crucial importance of foreign language skills for success in the increasingly integrated European economy raises the issue of

gender equality in two guises. While it is the main task here to focus on the male/female imbalance in motivation and achievement in foreign language learning, this will inevitably take time to redress . . . The problem is so pressing in economic terms that there must also be a case for saying that the *de facto* female superiority in foreign language skills makes the need to raise the proportion of women working at all levels in industry and commerce yet more urgent. This does not just refer to shipping and export agencies, marketing organisations and the great 'bilingual secretariat' but to directors, executives, sales staff, engineers and designers.

(Frost 1991, 2)

Student teacher research in schools

The research strategy is effective on an individual level for raising awareness and helping students to identify some of the complexities and problems. It can involve a variety of tasks – collecting documentation, observation of classes and general school organization, interviewing staff or pupils as well as students' involvement in their own practical teaching, in coming to grips with some of the problems of classroom interaction (who dominates? who co-operates?) and the materials in use. When the students return to college from their first teaching practice, their information acts as a resource and as fresh evidence in an exchange and discussion with other students. The observations made can also be illuminating for the school itself in the development of a relevant response to its particular situation.

This grassroots research indicates that while progress is being made, change is very slow and that in Wales, as in Scotland, 'there has been an elimination of blatant sexism in education . . . but how massive [is] the challenge in the curriculum, course choice, staff development' (Wojtas 1992).[2] In 1990, investigation tasks carried out by Bangor PGCE student teachers highlighted the continuing limitations of role models for girls in schools: women staff tend to remain subject teachers or take on responsibility for pastoral concerns while male staff dominate in the decision-making hierarchy. The non-teaching staff in the school are predominantly female – employed in secretarial, cleaning and catering jobs – although the caretakers are men (see Lynch 1990). This situation is reflected in pupils' perceptions of men and women. One student teacher of

English looked at the adjectives her pupils regarded as appropriate to male and female teachers:

HUMOROUS: positive and popular in a man; a bit silly in a woman
CONFIDENT: positive in a man; a bit threatening in a woman
AMBITIOUS: positive and proper in a man; a bit threatening
in a woman and maybe a bit manlike?
INTELLIGENT: desirable for a man; a bit threatening for a
woman
DIGNIFIED: proper for a man; not sure for a woman
MOODY: is not associated with men; but it is with women.

(Ostle 1990, 2)

Staff attitudes towards pupils also reinforce stereotypes. Student teachers quoted the following examples among many they had overheard: 'I want two reliable girls to give the books out'; 'that's not ladylike' (Mills 1990, 5). Certain materials are also less than satisfactory, for instance, as observed in a critique of *Physics for You* (Johnson 1978):

In Book 2 there are just two questions which make reference to women; one is about women and diet and the other asks whether a woman should wear horizontal or vertical stripes to make her look slimmer.

(Mills 1990, 1)

Student teachers can identify the accepted norms of interaction within the classroom and explore the difficulties they experience in coping with the situation; for example, in science:

Male pupils dominate, put females down, take the lead in answering questions. I found it extremely difficult to give equal attention to the girls – I found I was always being drawn to the disruptive element in the class (and not going back).

(O'Dowd 1990, 3)

As a strategy for classroom control, some teachers use a boy–girl seating arrangement, the implication behind this apparently being that boys and girls have nothing in common and nothing to say to each other. As pupils seem to accept this, a problem arises when a student teacher expects pupils to carry out groupwork in mixed groups. Segregation between the sexes in some schools extends as far as the staff room: 'our personal tutor said people talked if females joined the male group for too long' (Mills 1990, 8). Small in themselves, these instances can combine to exert a powerful influence against change and student teachers need to develop the confidence to counter them.

It is not only the attitudes of staff and pupils, but also parents' preconceptions which need to be confronted if the opportunities of a broad and balanced curriculum are to be truly realized. Student teachers can observe the effectiveness of strategies which schools are adopting in order to do this. For instance, information for parents about Technology and demonstrations of what boys and girls in early secondary school can actually achieve in this area of the curriculum (boys in textiles and catering, girls in design, computer programming and communications) does help parents to reconsider their children's options (Scholey 1990).

In this section, I have highlighted the usefulness of school-based research as a means to develop student teachers' awareness about gender issues as well as to provide data about the *status quo* in different schools. In the next section, I look more closely at Welsh-medium education and its relationship to sex differentiation.

Welsh language and gender in schools

While the traditional gender divide between arts and science prevails, the additional factor of medium of instruction (Welsh or English) also comes into play. Recent research into the attitudes, aspirations and opportunities for Welsh-speaking sixth-formers (Williams 1989) indicated that girls are more likely to study arts subjects through the medium of Welsh at 'A' Level and to remain in Wales to pursue higher education through the medium of Welsh. In contrast, Welsh-speaking boys are more likely to study Science/ Technology through the medium of English at 'A' Level and to move outside Wales for higher education. The choice of English medium is influenced by the fact that there is no opportunity to follow those subjects further through the medium of Welsh. The report suggests that these young people may lose touch academically and socially with the Welsh language and, therefore, feel less prepared or willing to follow a PGCE course in the medium of Welsh.

One implication of this trend is that it is women teachers in

Wales who are more likely to provide role models of close affiliation with the language, culture and geographical area, while male teachers will continue to reflect the wider experience and opportunities with which 'male' subjects and the English language are associated. Women are more likely anyway to consider teaching as a first career choice and to be able to go into Welsh-medium teacher training. How might this influence the choices female pupils make in the future?

Welsh-medium student teachers
On the PGCE course at UCNW Bangor in 1991–2, the Welsh-medium group attracted thirty-one female student teachers and seven male. While there was still a concentration towards the arts, there was an encouraging number of women in Science, Mathematics and Technology (arts twenty:sciences eleven). Results of a survey carried out among twelve Welsh-medium student teachers at the end of the 1991–2 PGCE course, confirmed to a large extent the trend noted at sixth-form level in terms of the student teachers' own life experience, that is, their opportunities and expectations at school and in higher education. One respondent commented: 'Few girls would risk moving towards sciences as a career.' In their teaching practice schools – particularly in terms of role models and the choice of medium at 'A' Level – the situation has not changed drastically. One student noted:

> Even though there were a lot of women teachers in Science, attitudes and expectations of both female staff and pupils as regards girls' careers remain rather traditional.
>
> (Student respondent quoted in Daniel 1992, 7)

While the student teachers felt there was some truth in the suggestion that the Welsh–English language divide did increase differentiation by gender, in general they were not necessarily convinced that this situation either restricted womens' experience or opportunities or reduced affiliation to the Welsh language for those who studied at higher education level through the medium of English. For example, a woman in the group who had been to an English-medium school and then studied science at an English university had now returned to train through the medium of Welsh. The promotion of Welsh as a medium of instruction under the National Curriculum, accompanied by Welsh Office bursaries to encourage recruitment of Welsh-speaking teachers, has recently provided the opportunity and incentive for both men and women to reaffiliate with the Welsh language.

> There are opportunities for women but we [Welsh] are perhaps more attached to the home and tend to follow a path which will guarantee posts in our own locality.
>
> (Student respondent quoted in Daniel 1992, 7)

The survey also explored how effective the equal opportunities element of the PGCE had been. The students were asked to indicate to what extent they felt they had made progress in each of the three domains using a scale from one (very little) to five (very much). The result averages were as follows:

Development of understanding:	4
Change in attitudes:	3.66
Development of practical skills:	3.66

The student teachers found the research assignment in schools and the integration of gender issues into subject work effective strategies in this development. Working towards putting equal opportunities into operation was quoted in particular: 'experience in the classroom itself is much more useful than sitting talking.' (Respondent quoted in Daniel 1992, 8)

Perspectives from the previous generation
Two of the Welsh-speaking female staff contributing to the PGCE course on a part-time basis were trained as teachers in Bangor in the 1960s.

> In our day there were no openings in Wales – the schools were staffed by English teachers who were there till they retired – so we all had to go away to the big cities in England for work. There were so many of us in Liverpool that they used to put on a special bus on a Friday night so we could get back to north Wales for the weekend. There were flourishing Welsh societies in the major cities and they played an important matchmaking role. A lot of us met our husbands there and our children went to Welsh nursery schools. There was always the plan that eventually we would come back to Wales to settle...but I think it was of benefit for us to get away and experience other parts of Britain. Nowadays there is

more opportunity for people to stay and get jobs in the area – and travelling of course is much easier. What concerns me is that it is the bright ones who leave and don't come back because there isn't sufficient industry and enterprise here to attract them.

(interview with former Head of Special Needs)

In our school Science department there are seven women and two men but both those men teach Physics. But I certainly think this general trend (of girls in Arts) continues and the National Curriculum isn't helping. We're running a Double Science for all to GCSE level as a National Curriculum pilot. This mean that girls have to do aspects of Science that they don't like and they can't do – and they get poor marks for it. Also there's a lot of work to get through so anything they're not very good at just falls by the wayside. All the marks for the twelve modules are added together for the final average. Even girls who get really good grades are dropping Science at 'A' Level because they're so fed up of it. What's quite significant in Year 7 (first year secondary) is the differentiation between boys and girls in basic mechanics – the girls haven't been trained at home or at school to use simple tools or to work on construction activities – and because they find it difficult in comparison with the boys they become demotivated. Gwynedd's new Equal Opportunities Guidelines for Key Stage 1 (Infant classes) is really important in laying the foundation in the early years for developing the range of skills for both boys and girls.

(interview with Head of Science and PGCE Biology Tutor)

The future of Welsh-speaking pupils

The 1992–3 intake of Welsh-speaking student teachers at UCNW, Bangor comprises twenty-four women and twenty-one men with a more traditional divide: on the arts side, seventeen women and four men, while in Science/Maths/Technology only seven women to seventeen men. In terms of developing bilingual education and promoting the Welsh language itself, the steady increase of student teachers training through the medium of Welsh is encouraging. For women, the establishment of Welsh as a core National Curriculum subject and the Department for Education bursaries available for Welsh as a shortage subject have opened up greater opportunities for work within their preferred location and also raised the status of a 'woman's subject'.

While the male–female science–arts English–Welsh trend may well continue, the developments in both initial teacher training and in-service training, in making explicit and countering the factors which condition young people's choices and actions, may mean that, in the future, girls will have a greater freedom to reach their potential in their chosen field.

Conclusion

In this chapter I have highlighted some of the problems facing young women in school, illustrated projects working for change in in-service and pre-service teacher training in north Wales and presented evidence of change beginning to manifest itself, albeit slowly. While schools alone cannot be expected to solve the problems of gender inequality, they can play an important role in working to counteract them. As is stated in Gwynedd's Guidelines for Equal Opportunities at Infant level,

> in offering a variety of experiences within the classroom the teacher can observe what the children choose. The choices will show their priorities and strengths. The teacher's task is to make it possible for them to expand their experience by directing them to alternative choices.
>
> (Gwynedd County Council 1992, 4)

It remains to be seen to what extent initiatives such as those discussed here will contribute to the changing identity of women in the Welsh context and to an increase in the real opportunities open to them. Policy-making and monitoring at regional and school level need to be supported by movement at the grassroots, by individual activity and commitment – and vice versa. Instances of change ought to be nurtured and used as inspiration for further developments. Unfortunately, with recent reforms about to affect LEAs and initial teacher training, the structures for support and stimulus may be drastically reduced.

Notes

[1] This material has now been updated to meet the requirements of the National Curriculum (see Myers 1992).

[2] There have been cases of direct discrimination very recently, however. A formal investigation carried out by the Equal Opportunities Commission between 1986 and 1988 in West Glamorgan found that several primary and

secondary schools were guilty of direct discrimination in connection with access to craft subjects (Equal Opportunities Commission 1988).

References

Arnot, M. (1989). 'Crisis or challenge: equal opportunities and the National Curriculum', *NUT Education Review*, Autumn 1989 Vol. 3, No. 2, 7–13.

British and Foreign School Society (1822). *Seventeenth Report* (London, R. and A. Taylor).

British and Foreign School Society (1823). *Twenty-eighth Report* (London, S. Bagster Jun.).

Careers Services in Wales (1991). *Pupil Destinations. Statistics in Wales* (Camarthen, Careers Service in Wales/BP Chemicals Limited).

Careers Service Gwynedd (1991). *Where Did They Go? Gwynedd School Pupil Destinations* (Caernarfon, Gwynedd County Council).

Central Statistical Office (1990). *Regional Trends 25* (London, HMSO).

Clwyd County Council (1983). *Equal Opportunities and the Secondary Curriculum. Final Report. Joint Action Research with Equal Opportunities Commission* (Mold, Clwyd County Council).

Daniel, P. (1991). *A Teacher Education Strategy for Exploring Equal Opportunities. TVEI in ITT Occasional Paper 7* (Bangor, School of Education, University College of North Wales).

Daniel, P. (1992). 'Welsh Language and Gender in Schools: PGCE Survey' (Bangor, School of Education, University College of North Wales).

Delamont, S. (1990). *Sex Roles and the School* (London, Routledge).

Equal Opportunities Commission (1988). *Formal Investigation Report: West Glamorgan Schools* (Manchester, Equal Opportuniites Commission).

Evans, K. (1987). *Policy Statement Equal Opportunities in the Education Service: Sex Discrimination* (Mold, Clwyd County Council Education Department).

Frost, A. (1991). 'Modern Language Gender Issues in Context' (Bangor, School of Education, University College of North Wales, unpublished PGCE dissertation).

Gwynedd County Council (1992). *Equal Opportunities Guidelines. The Infants' Classroom* (Caernarfon, Education Office, Gwynedd County Council).

Gwynedd Education Office (1992). 'Headteachers and Deputy Headteachers in Schools in Gwynedd' (Caernarfon, Gwynedd Education Office).

Johnson, K. (1978). *Physics for You Book 2* (London, Hutchinson).

Lynch, D. (1990). 'Gender Issues', (Bangor, School of Education, University College of North Wales).

Mills, R. (1990). 'Gender Bias in School' (Bangor, School of Education, University College of North Wales).

Myers, K. (1987). *Genderwatch! self-assessment schedules for use in schools* (London, School Curriculum Development Committee Publications).

Myers, K. (1992). *Genderwatch! After the Educational Reform Act* (Cambridge, Cambridge University Press).

O'Dowd, D. (1990). 'Gender Bias Assignment', (Bangor, School of Education, University College of North Wales).

Ostle, J. (1990). 'Gender Bias', (Bangor, School of Education, University College of North Wales).

Phillips, E. (1992). 'A comparison of male and female success rates in GCSE subjects' (Cardiff, Welsh Joint Education Committee).

Purvis, J. (1991). *A History of Women's Education in England* (Milton Keynes, Open University Press).

Raikes, E. (1908). *Dorothea Beale of Cheltenham* (London, Archibold Constable).

Scholey, A. (1990). 'Gender Bias' (Bangor, School of Education, University College of North Wales).

Spender, D. (1982). *Invisible Women* (London, Readers and Writers Publishing Cooperative).

Stanworth, M. (1983). *Gender and Schooling* (London, Hutchinson).

Weiner, G. (1985). *Just a Bunch of Girls* (Milton Keynes, Open University Press).

Welsh Joint Education Committee (1991). *Statistical Reports on the Summer Examinations* (Cardiff, Welsh Joint Examination Committee).

Welsh Office (1992). *Statistics of Education in Wales: Schools. No. 5 1991* (Cardiff, Welsh Office).

Williams, I. W. (1989). *The Welsh Language in Higher Education. Attitudes and Aspirations of Welsh Speaking Sixth Formers*, Report to the University of Wales Board for Welsh Medium Teaching (Bangor: School of Education, University College of North Wales).

Wojtas, O. (1992). 'Scots plan to widen the equality net', *The Higher*, 4.4.92.

Wright, M. (1988). 'We must change the norm', in *TVEI Developments 2. Equal Opportunities* (Sheffield, Training Agency, 71–5).

ILLUSTRATIONS

by

MARY GILES

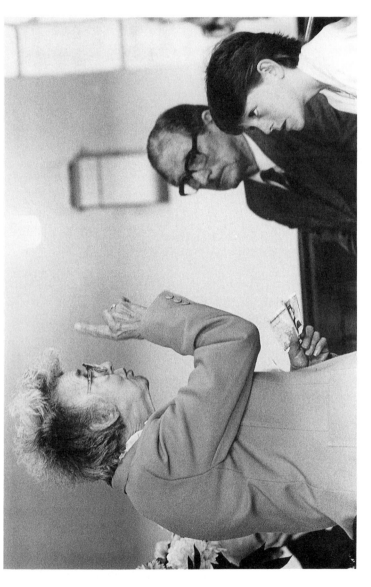

1 *Mair Griffiths, minister at Mount Zion Church, Newport, Gwent, 1985.*

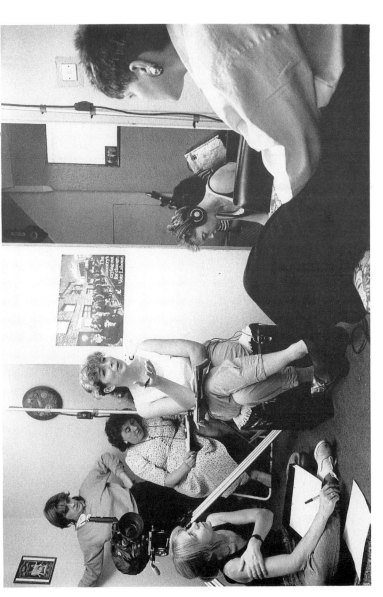

2 *Red Flannel Women's Film Co-operative at work on the film* Mam, *1987.*

3 Women's Aid refuge.

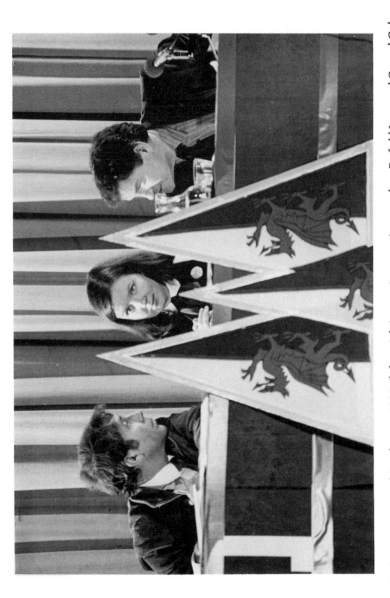

4 Plaid Cymru National Conference, 1984: (left to right) executive commitee members Dafydd Iwan and Carmel Gahan, and General Secretary Dafydd Williams.

5 Binni Jones, hill farmer, Blaenau Ffestiniog, 1985.

6 Clause 28 demonstration, Cardiff, 1988.

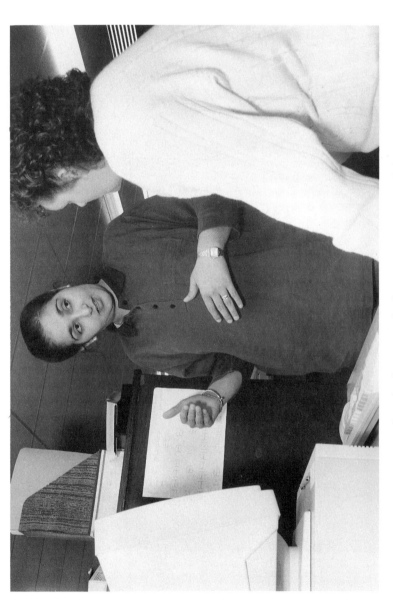

7 *Training in High Technology at South Glamorgan Women's Workshop, 1993.*

8 *Gwenllian Ashley with her Welsh dresser, Aberaeron, 1993.*

9 *Artist Mary Lloyd Jones in her studio at Llandysul, 1993.*

10 *Menna Elfyn calling for a new Welsh Language Act, Cardiff, 1993.*

11 Rally calling for a new Welsh Language Act, 1993.

PART TWO

III. Representing Women: Culture and Politics

10

Finding a voice in two tongues: gender and colonization

JANE AARON

Welsh culture has frequently been represented as one which is particularly repressive of women. The image of the sadistic chapel deacon hounding out from his flock the erring 'fallen woman' has been widely popularized – in such novels as *How Green Was My Valley*, or in Caradoc Evans's short stories – as a characteristically Welsh image. Fear and loathing of uncontained female sexuality, if not outright misogyny, are often assumed to have been of the essence of nineteenth-century Welsh Nonconformity. Yet to view Welsh society as if it was free to develop its own indigenous traits, undisturbed by its close relation to its neighbouring dominant state, can prove misleading: in the nineteenth century in particular no aspect of Welsh affairs was unaffected by English influence, and England at that time was a culture intent upon demarcating, once and for all, the proper role of women. In this chapter I certainly do not wish to propose that Welsh culture has not historically proved itself to be eminently capable of oppressing women of its own accord; women's silence in pre-twentieth-century Wales, as outlined by Delyth George in the introduction to her contribution to this volume, is in itself evidence enough of their secondary status in traditional Welsh ways of life. Rather, what I hope to show is that some of the pressures which have circumscribed Welsh women's lives acquired force not only from processes within Welsh culture itself, but from tensions between Wales and England during the Victorian period.

Feminism is still frequently viewed with suspicion by Welsh-identified communities as an alien and divisive Anglo-American phenomenon. But in the last part of this chapter I argue that its influence has, since the seventies, combined interestingly with a resurgence of confidence in Welshness to produce a new and strong female voice within both the Welsh and English-language cultures of Wales. This voice could be heard not so much as one which threatens traditional Welsh culture with extraneous influences, but as one which rids it of ideas which were themselves introduced into Wales by English interventionism during the nineteenth century. English feminism is currently devoting much of its energies to unpicking the ideological web of gender role polarization constructed during England's imperialistic heyday. A new Welsh feminism, following a parallel route, may not only aid in the construction of a less sexist Wales but also of one more free from the long-term effects of cultural colonization.

Mid-nineteenth-century traumas

Feminist historians have convincingly argued that the rise of the middle class and the growth of industrialism led, in early nineteenth-century English society, to a sharper polarization of gender roles, with women, particularly middle-class women, being confined to the domestic sphere, while the public world of work constituted the male sphere. Leonore Davidoff and Catherine Hall, in their seminal study *Family Fortunes: Men and women of the English middle class 1780–1850*, further suggest that the middle-class gentlewoman's role was also of significance in establishing her class's claims to social leadership. In order to provide an ethical rationale for its growing economic ascendancy, the new middle class laid great store upon what it represented as the superior quality of its moral life; its self-disciplined capacity to maintain 'good order', supported by sound religious principle, marked its distinction from the old aristocracy and the common people, both characterized as hedonistic and profligate by comparison (Davidoff and Hall 1987, 30). In this context the sexual propriety demanded of middle-class women had a double function; female chastity not only ensured the proper passing on, to a rightful son and heir, of the male's capital wealth, but also served as a potent sign of the high moral tone of the new culture. Set apart in the domestic sphere from the cut-throat world of capitalist enterprise and competitiveness, the English 'Angel in the House' served as an iconic symbol of her class's civilized values and its moral right to rule.

The right to rule of the English middle class had, of course, to be established not only over other social groupings in its heartlands, but also over England's rapidly developing colonial empire. In the late 1830s and the first half of the 1840s, however, the orderly government of its oldest colony was proving disquietingly problematic. In Wales, not only had there been a Chartist uprising in Newport in 1839, but from 1839 to 1843 'Rebecca' toll-gate riots were widespread. The language of the Rebecca rioters was Welsh, and this factor had impeded the efforts of the English forces sent in to quell them: there was an obvious need, from the English authorities' point of view, to exert a tighter control over the principality by Anglicizing it further. In 1846, a request by the Welsh – or Anglicized Welsh – Member of Parliament for Coventry, one William Williams, calling for 'an inquiry to be made into the state of education in the Principality, especially into the means afforded to the labouring classes of acquiring a knowledge of the English language' gave them an opportunity to do so. The *Report of the Commissioners of Inquiry into the State of Education in Wales*, when it was finally published in 1847, did not confine itself to commenting upon what was represented as Wales's woefully inadequate educational provisions, but went on to denounce Welsh people as a whole as backward and lawless, as if in an attempt to shame them into rapid Anglicization.

Most shockingly, Welsh women were accused in the *Report* of sexual promiscuity. One of the Commissioners' witnesses, the Reverend William Jones, rector of Nefyn, maintained, for example, that in Wales

> Want of chastity is flagrant. This vice is not confined to the poor.
> In England farmers' daughters are respectable; in Wales they are in
> the constant habit of being courted in bed.
>
> (*Report*, iii, 67–8)

Courting in bed, or 'bundling' as the practice was termed, had been acceptable enough practice in rural England, too, but Victorian middle-class morality was by now demanding changes in sexual behaviour. The licentiousness of Welsh women was proof of the barbarity of the Welsh, and as such helped to establish the ethical right of the English government to intervene in Welsh affairs, and rid the country of an atavistic adherence to a language and a culture which was debarring it from the more civilized values of its English neighbours. The English-language schools established in Wales as a consequence of the *Report*'s findings introduced the notorious 'Welsh Not' system, which required schoolteachers, frequently themselves Welsh-speakers, to cane children caught speaking Welsh.

Like the Reverend Jones, many of the witnesses who bore testimony to the Commissioners about the state of affairs in Wales were Anglican clergymen, much concerned about the growth of Welsh Nonconformity. Fuelled by a number of widespread religious revivals during the eighteenth and early nineteenth centuries, Nonconformity, and in particular Welsh Methodism, had established itself as the pre-eminent religion of Wales; characteristically a religion of the people, it drew its membership largely from those social groups which would in English terms be labelled 'working class', or at most 'lower middle class'. As if in an attempt to debar Welsh Nonconformity from laying any competing claims to moral supremacy, Anglican witnesses quoted in the *Report* took the opportunity to tar Nonconformist sects with the accusation of complicity in Wales's sexual laxity. The Reverend John Price, rector of Bleddfa and a magistrate, claimed that one of the 'chief causes' for the numerous cases of bastardy he had investigated was 'the bad habit of holding meetings at dissenting chapels or farmhouses after night, where the youth of both sexes attend from a distance for the purpose of walking home together' (*Report*, ii, 61). Similarly, the Reverend L. H. Davies, of Troed yr Aur, reported that:

> They [the young people] often meet at evening schools in private houses for the preparation of the *pwnc*, and this tends to immoralities between the young persons of both sexes, who frequently spend the night afterwards in hay-lofts together . . . Morals are generally at a low ebb, but want of chastity is the giant sin of Wales.
>
> (*Report*, ii, 60)

Nonconformist Wales rose up in outrage against these accusations, showing itself more passionate in the defence of its religion than of its language. Ieuan Gwynedd, a Nonconformist minister, published statistics to show that whereas the rate of illegitimacy in Wales was 6.8 per cent , that in England was 6.7 per cent – the difference was only 0.1 per cent. What is more, he showed that certain regions of England had a much higher rate of illegitimacy than prevailed in Wales (Jenkins 1991, 117). But mere facts alone were insufficient to stem the enthusiasm with which English public opinion salaciously seized upon this picture of the Welsh as essentially promiscuous. The English presses of the day reported that 'their habits are those of animals and will not bear description'. The *Morning Chronicle* announced that 'Wales is fast settling down into the most savage barbarism' (quoted in Evans 1991, 95).

Suddenly, after centuries of inconspicuousness, women were under the spotlights in Wales. In order to defend against gross defilement the honour not only of the Welsh as a race but also of their religion, it became of primary concern to the leaders of Welsh Nonconformity to establish beyond all possibility of doubt the purity of their womenfolk. Women's sexual behaviour was to be very heavily policed by Welsh Nonconformity for the rest of the century, and well into the twentieth: any fall from grace resulted in public excommunication from chapel membership. But the indications are that prior to the *Report of the Commissioners* Nonconformist Wales was nothing like as severe in its dealings with sexual delinquents as it was later to become. As late as 1859, twelve years after the publication of the *Report*, a Bangor schoolmistress, Mary Ann Edmunds, whose memoirs were published under the title *Yr Athrawes o Ddifrif* (The Dedicated Teacher), proclaimed herself still frequently mortified by the fact that couples openly 'living in sin' retained their chapel membership, and that her religious brethren were happy to congratulate newly-weds who had 'brought disgrace upon their religion,' as she saw it, by all too evidently having done their courting in bed (Edmunds et al. 1859, 76).

The high moral tone of Mrs Edmunds's memoirs suggest that they were themselves published as part of Nonconformist Wales's campaign both to establish the purity of its women, and to provide exemplary lessons for Welsh women who still needed them in the type of conduct they were now expected to adopt. As such, they formed part of an intensive cultural project. From 1850 to 1851 Ieuan Gwynedd edited the first Welsh-language periodical for women, *Y Gymraes* (The Welshwoman), and used its pages to inculcate the new paradigms for female behaviour. Any appearance of impropriety had to be promptly abandoned in favour of manifest restraint and self-control (see Williams 1991, for a more detailed account of the Welsh women's periodicals). The need to confound the 'lying tales' of the *Report* continued to function as a moral imperative throughout the century: much of the material contributed by women to a later periodical, Y *Frythones* (The British Woman), edited by Cranogwen (Sarah Jane Rees) from 1879 to 1889, demonstrates the writers' burdened sense of their personal responsibility for their nation's good name. In one of Y *Frythones*'s serialized stories, for example, Eveleen, a maid servant in an English household, is surprised one day to discover that a fellow domestic is as Welsh as herself. Lydia explains that she has concealed this fact in order to appear more 'respectable', for 'according to English reckoning' the Welsh are 'low in morals', and she has no desire to share in their shame. Eveleen admonishes her that she should rather have not only acknowledged her race but done all in her power to redeem its reputation: 'is it not our duty,' she says, 'to bear with our own nation, along with doing our best through word and deed, to raise our national character above all insult?' ('onid ein dyledswydd ydyw cyd-ddwyn â'n cenedl ein hunain, yn nghyd a gwneuthur ein goreu drwy air a gweithred, i ddyrchafu ein cymeriad cenedlaethol uwchlaw pob sarhad') (Rees 1880, 362).

The late-nineteenth-century Welsh woman seems, then, to have been presented with three possibilities in terms of choosing an identity. Either she abandoned her Welsh allegiances and adopted the English middle-class model of refined femininity, however inappropriate it may have been to her cultural roots and her social position; or she defensively asserted her Welshness in the face of insult, and, to prove its virtues, clad herself in an armour of strict propriety which would inevitably have entailed self-suppression on a larger scale than mere sexual self-control; or she accepted the English definition of herself as the libidinous hoyden of primitive Wild Wales. None of these possible identities afforded her a voice of her own: the English model was unauthentic and mismatched in terms of class identity, the Welsh 'respectable' model entailed severe curbs on her freedom and self-assertive capacities, and the 'wild' model had no place in civilized society.

Late-twentieth-century rebellions

Charged as a gender with a portentous moral mission, Welsh women who chose to be loyal to their roots seem, for the most part, to have retained the notion that it was their ethnic duty to be strictly 'respectable' long after behaviour patterns had changed in England. The 'New Woman' of the *fin de siècle* period, the 'flapper' of the 1920s, might come – and go – in Anglo-American culture, but as late as 1966 a woman could still die of shame in a Welsh novel because she had all unwittingly had an affair with a married man (Rowlands 1966). In colonized and post-colonized societies this type of conservative retention of repressive behaviour patterns inculcated by the colonizing culture, after that culture has itself abandoned them, is, apparently, a common trait. In Africa, for example, same-sex relations were accepted as part of the normal pattern of affective and domestic arrangements in many pre-colonial communities, but under British rule such practices were labelled as 'homosexual' and illegalized: today, an African pamphlet on AIDS announces with what sounds like moral pride that, unlike in decadent Western communities, 'homosexuality is rare in Africa' (Patton 1992, 226). It is as if the wounds inflicted on racial self-esteem during the colonizing process can only be healed by a continuing repression and denial of behaviour which the imperial culture once castigated as 'barbaric'.

In order to break with this pattern, and shed colonially imposed values, a culture needs a resurgence of confidence in its capacity to define itself. When it is also a matter of women's lives being shaped by male-imposed concepts of correct female behaviour, then, to bring about change, women need to acquire a new confidence in the female right to self-definition. During the second half of the twentieth century, a series of developments, some international and some unique to Wales, combined to bring about a situation in which these two requirements for change in Welsh women's sense of identity were, at last, met.

In 1963, spurred into existence by the recognition that, unless it was fought for, the Welsh language would soon be extinct, Cymdeithas yr Iaith Gymraeg, the Welsh Language Society, commenced its programme of non-violent direct action, to raise the status and promote the use of Welsh in Wales. Such a movement necessarily entails a heightened political awareness of what cultural difference means, and of how a culture's distinctiveness can be established and maintained in the face of the encroaching pressures of the Western world towards uniformity and mass-produced identities. Involvement in the movement inevitably has cultural consciousness-raising effects for the numerous women who take part in and, indeed, in recent years, frequently lead its activities, as Angharad Tomos shows in her contribution to this volume. It can have feminist consciousness-raising consequences too: in her chapter in this book, Menna Elfyn writes of how she went to prison as a Welsh language activist, and came out, no less of a language campaigner, but now a feminist as well. The climate of change in cultural awareness, of which the language movement was a symptom, also led to the establishment of other affirmatively Welsh formations involving women, such as, for example, Merched y Wawr. This Welsh-language version of the Women's Institute, established in 1967, although not strictly speaking either a political or feminist institution, certainly encourages a stronger sense of both Welsh identity and sisterliness amongst its members.

A few women also discovered their literary voices in the urge to proselytize the language movement's cause. Meg Elis's first two novels, *I'r Gad* (To Battle) (1975) and *Carchar* (Prison) (1978), constitute fictional accounts of Cymdeithas activities, based on autobiographical experience. Similarly, Angharad Tomos's first novel *Hen Fyd Hurt* (Stupid Old World) (1982) concerns a young woman's awakening to the need for direct action in the Welsh cause, and her second novel *Yma o Hyd* (Here Still) (1985) is a thinly veiled account of her own prison experiences. Galvanized by the pressing need to prick – or rather put the boot in – the Welsh conscience, these political novels eschew any pretences to either literary or feminine decorum; *I'r Gad* also includes, in passing, what must be about the first graphic accounts of the sexual act by a Welsh woman writer, or at least the first since Gwallter Mechain composed her erotic verses at the end of the fifteenth century – that is, prior to the years of English cultural influence (for an English translation of two of Gwallter Mechain's poems, see Johnston 1991, 36–43). None of these novels have been translated, but in order to give the English-language reader some impression of their iconoclastic style, and of the breakthrough they represent in terms of Welsh women's writing, I translate below a passage from *Yma o Hyd*. The passage describes the narrator, Blodeuwedd's, response to hearing, while in prison, of the arrival of the nuclear warheads at Greenham Common:

> . . . mi ges i f'anfon at y *Governor*. Doedd honno'n methu 'ngweld i

am oes, a disgwyl yn y coridor fues i. 'Radeg yna ar y radio y clywais i'r newyddion – fod y taflegrau wedi cyrraedd Greenham. [. . .] Ddaru mi rioed feddwl y basa'r arfau yn cyrraedd. Dwn i ddim be on i'n ddisgwyl, i rywbeth mawr ddigwydd y funud ola a'u stopio. Ond dydi pethau fel'na byth yn digwydd, wrth gwrs. Daeth y teimlad mwya dychrynllyd o orchfygaeth drosta i. [. . .] Y bomia'n cyrraedd fan'na fel tasa fo'r peth mwya naturiol yn y byd. Affliw o ots fod 'na bobol 'di bod yn protestio'n groch ers dwy flynedd. Affliw o ots bod na griw o ferched diymgeledd 'di bod yn gwersylla ers dwy flynedd yn y gwynt a'r glaw. [. . .] Dim ots o gwbwl. [. . .] Gwlad rydd? Duwcs, ydi, gewch chi ddeud be fynnoch chi. Diawl o neb yn gwrando, ond deudwch be fynnwch chi. Iechyd, ni sy'n llywaeth. Fi – dwi'n llywaeth. Be gebyst dwi'n 'i wneud mewn carchar Sais yn aros yn amyneddgar am gerydd? [. . .] Dwi 'di troi yn sombi. Dwi run fath ag oen bach yn disgwyl tu allan i'r lladd-dy. Dyna sut betha ydan ni'r Cymry bellach. [. . .] Gwnewch rywbeth i mi cyn bellad â bod ddim rhaid i mi sefyll ar fy nhraed fy hun ac ymladd. Hen genedl fasocistaidd ydan ni bellach. Wedi cael ein llyncu'n llwyr. Mam bach, dwi'n rhedag!

A rhedag i ffwrdd wnes i – ffwl sbîd i lawr y coridor. Roedd y giât bellach yn gorad, achos dyma fi ras i lawr ffor'na – i lawr tri set o risiau – a ffwl sbîd i lawr coridor arall. Ew, roedd hi'n grêt cael rhedag achos y funud gychwynnes i mi sylweddolais teimlad mor ffantastig oedd o. Mam bach, don i ddim wedi rhedag ers tair wythnos, 'mond 'di sefyll ac aros a cherdded a sefyll yn stond a gogordroi a sefyll mewn ciw a sefyll yn llonydd. [. . .] dwi'm yn licio i Saeson fy nghadw i mewn caits a finna'n methu dod allan; dwi'm yn licio Cymru'n fy nghadw mewn caits o wlad chwaith, nes dwi'n methu dod allan . . . dyna pam dwi'n rhedag . . . rhedag . . . rhedag . . . rhedag fel y gwynt ymhell i ffwrdd . . . hedfan fel ehedydd achos tra dwi'n rhedag dwi'n rhyddrhyddrhyddrhydd . . .

(Tomos 1985, 107–8)

I was sent to the Governor. She couldn't see me for ages, an' I had to hang about in the corridor. It was at that moment I heard the news on the radio – that the missiles had reached Greenham. [. . .] I never thought the arms would actually arrive. I don't know what I expected, something big happening at the last minute to stop 'em. But that kind of thing never does happen, of course. A most appalling feeling of defeat came over me. [. . .] The bombs arriving there as if it was the most natural thing in the world. Never mind the people who'd been protesting till they were hoarse for two years. Never mind the women campin' out unprotected in the wind an' rain for two years. [. . .] Never mind them at all. [. . .] A free country? Lawks, so it is, you can say what you like. Devil a one listenin', but you say what you like. Heck, it's we who are tame. Me – I'm tame. What on earth am I doing in an Englishman's prison waiting patiently for a punishment? [. . .] I've turned into a zombie. I'm like a lil'le lamb waiting outside a slaughter house. [. . .] That's what we Welsh are like by now. [. . .] Do anything to me so long as I don't have to stand on my own two feet and fight. We've become a nation of masochists. Completely swallowed up. For heaven's sakes, I'm off!

And off I went – full speed down the corridor. The further gate was open, so I went racin' down that way – down three sets of stairs – and full speed down another corridor. Cor, it was great, running, 'cause the minute I started I realized what a fantastic feeling it was. Heaven's sakes, I hadn't run for three weeks, just stood an' waited an' walked an' stopped short an' hung about an' stood in a queue an' stood still. [. . .] I don't like it that the English should keep me in a cage so that I can't get out; I don't like Wales keeping me in a cage of a country either, till I can't get out . . . that's why I'm runnin' . . . runnin' . . . runnin' . . . runnin' like the wind far away . . . flying like a lark 'cause while I'm runnin' I'm freefreefreefree . . .

Characteristics shared by many of the new Welsh women writers, working in both languages, are displayed in this passage: the urge to break out of confining circumstances and protest against them; the refusal to conform any longer to the traditional passive roles into which one is conditioned; the concern with green politics and the resistance to war-mongering, together with a sense of bonding with other women in particular in the face of this threat; frustration at the apparently invincibility of the forces massed against one, and the attempt to shatter their impassivity by speaking, and acting, as directly as possible.

Within English-speaking Wales, the language movement also has its sympathizers as well as its detractors; the growth of Welsh-language schools in largely English-speaking areas since the late sixties is testimony to these communities' sense of a shared Welsh history and culture, which their children should inherit fully, even if they could not. Many a mother learns Welsh at her child's knee, so to speak, in contemporary Wales, and acquires a sharper sense of the difference it makes to be Welsh. Returning to Welshness is a prevalent theme in the work of some of the best known Welsh women poets writing in English. In Gillian Clarke's poem 'The Water-Diviner', for example, the voice of the water 'shouts' through the diviner's hose,

> in the silence
> through fifty feet of rock
> on an afternoon dumb with drought
> . . . . .
> a word we could not say, or spell, or remember,
> something like 'dŵr . . . dŵr'.
>
> (Clarke 1985, 85)

'Dŵr' is the Welsh word for 'water'; the poem encodes a thirst for a lost language and a lost identity, which can yet still be discovered, hidden deep under the accumulated strata of Anglicization. And in the troubled poem 'Second Language', which reverses the 'Welsh Not' attitudes of Victorian education, Christine Evans describes the fears of a teacher of English in a Welsh-speaking area that she may, in helping her pupils to acquire the new tongue, be insidiously alienating them from 'the green depths' of a less barren culture, 'whose language fills the mouth like fruit' (Evans 1989, 60).

Gillian Clarke and Christine Evans are but two representatives of a strong and numerous body of women poets publishing in Wales today. Yet it may be queried whether many of these writers, most of whose publishing careers commenced in the seventies or after, would have gained the high reputations their work deserves, or it may be, in some cases, acquired the confidence to publish at all, were it not for the pervasive social influence of another, more international, movement, the feminist movement. The emergence in 1969 of the first 'Women's Lib' demonstrators may not have been greeted with any great enthusiasm in Wales, but, during the seventies, Wales had its share of the movement's characteristic consciousness-raising groups, a few of them Welsh speaking. The members of these early informal groups went on to set up the diverse range of organizations, pressure groups, companies, training societies and educational networks – some short-lived, others more enduring – which together represent the public face of feminism in contemporary Wales. The activities and histories of many of these – such as, for example, Red Flannel, the south Wales women's film group, or the Welsh local authorities' women's committees – are described in Luana Dee and Katell Keineg's edited volume *Women in Wales* (1987), while Nickie Charles, in her contribution to this present volume gives an account of the longest-enduring and in many ways most effective of them all, Welsh Women's Aid.

In the context of Welsh women 'finding a voice', another organization deserves particular mention. Since the appearance of its first Welsh- and English-language titles in 1987, the Welsh feminist press, Honno, has scored a number of hits with its list of women-only Welsh writers, for all its numerically small output of volumes. Penny Windsor's first volume of poems for Honno, *Dangerous Women*, rapidly sold out; Carol-Ann Courtney's novel *Morphine and Dolly Mixtures*, published by Honno in 1989, was made into a TV film, and its rights sold to Penguin; Catherine Merriman's collection of short stories *Silly Mothers* (1991) was short-listed for the Welsh Book of the Year award. But more significant than these, perhaps, in terms of meeting the Press's feminist aims, is the success of its companion English- and Welsh-language volumes of collected autobiographical writings by women, its two anthologies of women's poetry (*Exchanges*, edited by Jude Brigley, and *O'r Iawn Ryw* edited by Menna Elfyn), and its latest production to date, an English-language collection of women's writings on the Second World War, *Parachutes and Petticoats*, edited by Leigh Verrill-Rhys and Deirdre Beddoe. As well as furthering the public recognition of diverse female talents, such productions also encourage new writers to publish.

But Honno seems to have difficulty in attracting Welsh-language manuscripts: only one such manuscript was offered to them in the year 1991–2. Welsh-language women writers seem more wary of the feminist imprint, or rather, perhaps, they prefer to publish with the more specifically Welsh-language presses. The first contemporary collection of women's poetry, *Hel Dail Gwyrdd*, edited by Menna Elfyn in 1985, came from Gomer Press. That same press had also earlier published a collection of sociological feminist essays, *Asen Adda* (Stephens, 1975), which – along with a special feminist issue of the critical journal *Y Traethodydd*

(Curtis et al., 1986) – still constitutes one of the few resources for Welsh-language students of women's studies. Somewhat unexpectedly, given the macho image of its annual review magazine *Lol*, the Lolfa Press has also succeeded in attracting work from a number of new, radical women writers in recent years. As well as being the publishers of novelists like Meg Elis and Angharad Tomos, it has also brought out, in its 'Cyfres y Beirdd Answyddogol' (Series of the Unofficial Bards), a number of verse collections by strikingly expressive and confident new voices, like those of Elin ap Hywel, Lona Llywelyn Davies (née Walters) and Elin Llwyd Morgan. One characteristic which seems held in common by many of these unofficial female bards is a marked outspokenness when it comes to describing sexual and emotional relations, a characteristic which they also share with some of the English-language poets, like Penny Windsor.

In terms of the break with the nineteenth-century roles for Welsh women which such uninhibited writings represent, we might today be tempted to think that we have already arrived at that 'far country' of female emancipation from which Gillian Clarke wrote her 'letter home from the future'. As Menna Elfyn puts it in her poem 'Byw, benywod, byw' (translated by Elin ap Hywel as 'Live, sisters, live'),

> Cynifer a gân heddiw
> heb ddal eu hanadl
> rhag i'r peswch annifyr
> darfu'r gynulleidfa
> a'r gŵr o'i bulpud.
>
> (Elfyn 1990, 43)

> So many may sing today
> without choking back breath
> in case an incontinent cough
> should pain the congregation
> or draw the man down from the pulpit.
>
> (Meyrick 1989, 51)

But in the poem 'Letter from a far country', Gillian Clarke expresses some anxiety about embarking too easily on a voyage to freedom. For after we have thrown out the hard, stony ballast of the old way of life, what of substance, and of Welshness, is left, with which to resist the seductions of global consumerist culture?

Is it a matter of an unappealing choice between

> A lap full of pebbles and then
> light as a Coca Cola can.
>
> (Clarke 1982, 8)

One movement, referred to already in this chapter, which certainly provided both English- and Welsh-speaking Welsh women with a weight of political ballast with which to ward off the threat of becoming merely the flotsam and jetsam of a dubious New World, was the Greenham Common movement. In September 1981 Anne Pettit, from her smallholding in south Wales, organized a 'Women for Life on Earth' march from Cardiff to RAF Greenham Common to protest against cruise missiles; the marchers, when they got to Newbury, set up a permanent peace picket, to 'be there for as long as it takes' (Jones 1983, 97). Throughout the eighties the peace camp served as a potent symbol for many Welsh women, English- and Welsh-speaking alike, and became a way of life for some. In 1989, Helen Thomas a 23-year-old woman from Castellnewydd Emlyn, and a dedicated proselytizer for the Welsh language cause as well as a peace activist, lost her life at Greenham, after being struck by a police vehicle. References to the peace movement, and to green politics generally, are rife in both Welsh- and English-language women's poetry and prose, and fear at the threat to the fragile balance of natural life is frequently evoked. Concern for the land is central to the poetry of Ruth Bidgood and Nesta Wyn Jones, for example, writers in English and Welsh respectively. An association of this concern with specifically Welsh, or Celtic, values is also frequently stressed. Hilary Llewellyn-Williams draws upon Celtic mythology in her celebrations of the physical world; in such poems as 'The Song of Blodeuwedd on May Morning' she also uses the 'woman of flowers' figure from the Mabinogion as a role model for female sensual delight, in uninhibited accord with life forces (Llewellyn-Williams 1987, 45).

In one of Glenda Beagan's short stories, 'Scream, Scream', a woman 'screams solid', once in every three years, from evening to the next mid-day. Afterwards Mrs Jenkins of Sgubor Fawr is silent and calm, but her screaming, while she lets it rip, seems to express the despairs and frustrations of other women who hear her, as well as her own. Mrs Jenkins belongs to the old Welsh way of life:

> Mrs Jenkins comes from a farm, a farm in the middle of nowhere.

A farm so old it's like a great fungus, an excrescence of the land . . .
Little has changed at Sgubor Fawr since Owain Glyndwr rode by,
swelling his army with the sons of the farm . . . But this is the end of
the line. The very end. This is the scream of the last of the Jenkinses
of Sgubor Fawr, this is.
It's unforgettable.

(Beagan 1992, 32)

Why, the reader wonders, does Mrs Jenkins scream? Is it because
her identity, her Welshness, is threatened with extinction? Or is it
because that identity constituted for her, as a woman, a lifetime of
bitter frustration and imprisonment? Or is it for both reasons at
the same time? Either way, and both ways, her anger finds a less
isolating and more hopeful expression than the wordless scream in
the writings of many of her sisters in contemporary Wales.

References

Beagan, Glenda (1992). *The Medlar Tree* (Bridgend, Seren Books).
Clarke, Gillian (1982). *Letter from a Far Country* (Manchester, Carcanet).
—— (1985). *Selected Poems* (Manchester, Carcanet).
Curtis, Kathryn, Marged Haycock, Elin ap Hywel, a Ceridwen Lloyd-
   Morgan (1986). 'Merched a Llenyddiaeth: Rhifyn Arbennig', Y
   Traethodydd, Ionawr.
Davidoff, Leonore, and Hall, Catherine (1987). *Family Fortunes: Men and
   women of the English middle class 1780–1850* (London, Hutchinson).
Dee, Luana and Keineg, Katell (1987). *Women in Wales: A documentary of
   our recent history* (Cardiff, Womenwrite Press).
Edmunds, J. a Jones, J. W. (1859). *Yr Athrawes o Ddifrif: sef, Lloffion o
   Hanes Bywyd a Marwolaeth Mrs Edmunds [Mary A, Edmunds], Bangor,
   yn nghyda Detholiad o'i Hysgrifeniadau* (Caernarfon, G. Parry).
Elfyn, Menna (1990). *Aderyn bach mewn llaw* (Llandysul, Gwasg Gomer).
Evans, Christine (1989). *Cometary Phases* (Bridgend, Seren Books).
Evans, W. Gareth (1991). 'Y ferch, addysg a moesoldeb: portread y Llyfrau
   Gleision', yn Prys Morgan (gol.), *Brad y Llyfrau Gleision* (Llandysul,
   Gwasg Gomer), 74–100.
Jenkins, Geraint H. (1991). 'Ieuan Gwynedd: Eilun y Genedl', yn Prys
   Morgan (gol.), *Brad y Llyfrau Gleision* (Llandysul, Gwasg Gomer),
   101–124.
Johnston, Dafydd (1991). *Canu Maswedd yr Oesoedd Canol: Medieval
   Welsh Erotic Poetry* (Caerdydd, Tafol).
Jones, Lynne (ed.) (1983). *Keeping the Peace* (London, The Women's Press).
Meyrick, Ceri (ed.) (1989). *The Bloodstream* (Bridgend, Seren Books).

Llewellyn-Williams, Hilary (1987). *The Tree Calendar* (Bridgend, Poetry Wales Press).

Patton, Cindy (1992). 'From Nation to Family: Containing "African AIDS" ', in Andrew Parker, Mary Russo, Doris Sommer and Patricia Yaeger (eds.), *Nationalisms and Sexualities* (New York and London, Routledge), 218–34.

Rees, Anne (1880). 'Eveleen Davies, neu, Gwnaf, am mai felly y dymunai fy mam', *Y Frythones*, ii.

Report of the Commissioners of Inquiry into the State of Education in Wales, 1847.

Rowlands, Mari Puw (1966). *Y Deryn Diarth* (Llandysul, Gwasg Gomer).

Stephens, Ruth (gol.) (1975). *Asen Adda: Ysgrifau am y ferch yn y byd sydd ohoni* (Llandysul, Gwasg Gomer).

Tomos, Angharad (1985). *Yma o Hyd* (Talybont, Y Lolfa).

Williams, Sian Rhiannon (1991). 'The True "Cymraes": Images of Women in Women's Nineteenth-Century Welsh Periodicals', in Angela V. John (ed.), *Our Mothers' Land: Chapters in Welsh Women's History 1830–1939* (Cardiff, University of Wales Press), 69–91.

11

The strains of transition: contemporary Welsh-language novelists

DELYTH GEORGE

Welsh literature before the latter half of the twentieth century is considered to have been something of a male preserve. It was a literature largely dominated by one genre – poetry, and within that genre one poetic form in particular was accorded the highest esteem, that is, 'cynghanedd', or the 'strict metres'. The formal complexities of the strict metres required that they be taught in special bardic schools, or through a close teacher–disciple relation, and such opportunities to learn the craft were not generally made available to women. Although feminist critics like Ceridwen Lloyd-Morgan and Marged Haycock have recently drawn our attention to the fact that a few women did manage, against the odds, to make something of a name for themselves under these adverse conditions, in general they were necessarily few and far between. In an introductory essay to Menna Elfyn's recent edition of women's Welsh-language poetry *O'r Iawn Ryw* (Of the Right Kind/Sex) Ceridwen Lloyd-Morgan points out that of the four thousand or so named bards, whose work was preserved in manuscript collections from the sixteenth century on, only about sixty were women (Lloyd-Morgan 1991, v). What is more, female experience, as the subject of the writer's concern, very rarely featured in the works of these poets. Anthony Conran, in a recent essay on the 'lack of the feminine' in traditional Welsh literature (Conran 1992), points out that whereas on the continent certain poetic genres, such as the French 'Chansons de toile', did concern themselves with the emotional life of women, even though they were written by men, there is no equivalent to these texts in Welsh writing. 'Welsh poetry is overwhelmingly masculine', he argues, and goes on to stress that, before the twentieth century, 'female emotions had not been explored or orchestrated for centuries in Wales, as they had been (often, it is true, by men) in the rest of Western Europe' (Conran 1992, 28, 29).

However, the development of the novel genre in Wales, from its beginnings in the latter half of the nineteenth century, did at last afford women a feasible entry into literary creativity, and one in which they could explore the ramifications of specifically female experience. Best-selling writers like Moelona (1878–1953) demonstrated the popular appeal of women's writing, although it was not until the 1930s or 1940s, with Kate Roberts's growing reputation, that texts primarily concerned with female lives and experiences succeeded in gaining an honoured acceptance into the canon of Welsh literature. Kate Roberts (1891–1985) provided a firm basis for women writers' subsequent development: a prolific writer, the critical and popular success of her numerous novels and many volumes of short stories not only won her the title of 'brenhines ein llên' ('queen of our literature'), but also made her the inspirational literary 'mother' of new generations of female novelists. The names of Elena Puw Morgan (1900–73), Kate Bosse Griffiths (1910–) and others became known during the first half of the twentieth century, and from the late fifties and sixties onwards many more women have turned to novel writing. Jane Edwards (1938–) and Eigra Lewis Roberts (1939–) have been the most productive, and both have been considerably influenced by Kate Roberts. (This is also true of Angharad Tomos of a later generation.) Male writers, such as John Gwilym Jones (1904–89) and others, have also admitted to attempting, at an early stage in their careers, to emulate her style, but without success. Significantly enough, it has been far easier for female writers to do so, as *Tyfu* and *Miriam* (Jane Edwards) and *Si Hei Lwli* (Angharad Tomos), the award-winning work of fiction at the Mold National Eisteddfod in 1991, so obviously show. Does this fact imply that it is far easier for women writers to learn from female predecessors, and male writers from men? Is literature influenced to such a considerable extent by gender?

Undoubtedly, this is often the case. Since the lives and experiences of men and women differ in many respects, it would be surprising if such differences were not reflected to some degree in the literary compositions of the two sexes. According to the

conventionally accepted generalizations regarding sexual difference in writing, while male-orientated traits can be found in the
novels of women who have been largely influenced by the values of
a male-dominated society, more often than not, works produced
by women offer a specifically female perspective and display a
greater diversity of female experiences and roles. Additionally, the
background, compass, emphasis and style chosen by male and
female writers vary, with female writers such as Kate Roberts con-
centrating on the domestic sphere and excelling in fine detail and
psychological precision, while male writers such as T. Rowland
Hughes (1903–49) and Islwyn Ffowc Elis (1924–) tend to experiment more with background, writing on a larger social canvas, in a
less intense emotional manner.

While some of these generalizations ring true, others betray a
derogatory tone, implying, for example, that women writers are
unable to handle abstract thought, that their work is excessively
emotional, and lacks a political analytic perspective. Traditional
literary criticism seems to have over-emphasized certain differences
between male and female writing, with the female traits being
looked upon less favourably. We are not often enough reminded
that generalizations such as these can be overruled. In recent
Welsh literature, Aled Islwyn is a good example of a male author
who has found his inspiration in the terrain of female emotions
and experiences. There are also female writers who have written
extensively on political themes, for example, Angharad Tomos and
Meg Elis.

Only over the past thirty odd years or so have readers been
made aware of these gender issues, due to the growth of feminism.
Feminism is a term which is becoming increasingly difficult to
define, owing to its rapid development, encompassing a great
diversity of viewpoints. However, to simplify, one can claim that
feminism has roughly two aspects:

> First, it identifies inequalities and injustices in the way girls and
> women are treated in a particular society, and the disabilities and
> disadvantages which result from these . . .
>
> (Sherry 1988, 14)

It aims to eliminate these inequalities and injustices through political action. Secondly,

... it asserts the value, and the values, of women – the human dignity and worth of each individual woman and also the distinctive contributions that women make to their culture.

(Sherry 1988, 15)

It seeks to enhance women's self-awareness and to aid them in finding their true identity, rather than one which has been bestowed upon them by patriarchal or chauvinistic influences.

Literature and literary criticism has a vital role to play in this quest for identity and assertion of women's value. Women's writing offers insight into female consciousness, and feminist literary criticism ensures that this voice receives critical acclaim. This feminine voice is often not an overtly militant one; it does not aim primarily to identify 'the wrongs of women' (to use Mary Wollstonecraft's phrase), and deliberately to work to bring about social and political change. However, most women writers tend to draw attention to injustices suffered by women, on some level or other, even if they do not, or can not, offer a positive way forward. The critic Ruth Sherry goes as far as to suggest 'that the mere fact of devoting one's energy to writing about women is an implicit acknowledgement of the value of women' (Sherry 1988, 16).

When exploring works by Welsh-language women writers, one will soon discover that self-proclaimed feminist writers are hard to come by. And yet a number of these writers have drawn attention to the plight of female fictional characters, both in a historical and a contemporary setting. Kate Roberts, under the influence of her time and age, is fairly conservative, from a contemporary point of view, a writer claiming no radical economic and political reforms for society or for the role played by women in its very structure. Significantly enough, however, her characteristically strong-willed female protagonists betray traits which could be regarded as unconventional and unfeminine, by virtue of their resistant strengths. Alongside them, her male characters appear to be weak-willed and insufficient, fading into the family background. Her men are often either of little importance, or of downright iniquity, bringing shame or suffering to their hard-working wives. And yet, even though these strong women of hers are economically dependent on their weak men, on no occasion does she question the social structure of which the institution of marriage is so vital an ingredient. But her compliance with the rules, her desire to uphold conventional attitudes, is somehow not in keeping with her unromantic view of love and marriage. She concentrates on the individual's essential loneliness within a relationship, within the family, and within society. This loneliness is something which, in her novels, everyone has to, and is able to, come to terms with, without despair. Her emphasis is on inner strength and a will to survive against all odds – her women being the obvious survivors.

It may be true of most writers that their texts tend to be influenced more by the prevailing tastes and conventions of their times than by any extraordinary experience of their own, but this seems more true than usual of Kate Roberts. Herself a professional writer, a teacher, and the owner of a publishing press, she chose to write mainly of servants, dressmakers, housewives and mothers, all traditional female roles. Consequently, she placed extraordinary female characters (similar to herself in many ways) in extremely ordinary circumstances. Creating these strong independent women, with their feet set firmly in chains which they do not try to break, certainly enhances the pathos of her work. If she belonged to a later generation, her views might well have been different. As things stand, one cannot but sense within her work a disciplined frustration with life, as if she has had to persuade herself (and is in her work persuading others) to accept a confined space/situation in life, on a personal and on a political level. Her attitude was, perhaps, influenced by her mentor John Morris Jones's theory that literature should not in any way propagate political propaganda for social change. Such an attitude, of course, merely underlines and upholds the status quo.

In his essay 'The Lack of the Feminine', Anthony Conran suggests that it was the absence of female predecessors, as much as her acquired notions as to what was appropriate for her art, which accounted for Kate Roberts's characteristically restrained tone: 'the austerity of feeling in [her] stories comes', he argues, from her isolated position as a woman writer, 'from a lack of tradition as much as her own deliberate artistry' (Conran 1992, 29). The women writers who followed her were spared, by her own example predominantly, from the unique strain of being first in the field. From the fifties onwards there was a renewal of interest in the novel form in Welsh writing, and many of the new novelists were women – Catrin Lloyd Rowlands, Beti Hughes, Hazel Charles Evans, Dyddgu Owen, Ennis Evans, Marged Pritchard, Eirwen Gwynn,

Irma Chilton, and the historical novelists Marion Eames and Rhiannon Davies-Jones, to list but a few. A third generation of women novelists, whose writing career began in the seventies and eighties, has since appeared. This latest generation is to all appearances unhindered by any notion of a necessary literary decorum which would restrict a novelist's, and particularly a woman novelist's, potential to create overtly protesting and political texts. As I indicated above, Angharad Tomos and Meg Elis, two award-winning representatives of the latest wave of women writers, write straightforwardly political works: in both cases, the primary object of their political allegiance and concern is the Welsh language movement, but in such texts as Meg Elis's *Cyn Daw'r Gaeaf* (Before Winter Comes) (1985), a novel in journal form recording some months in the life of a Greenham Common protester, feminist preoccupations are also uninhibitedly explored.

It would appear, then, that the women writers of the second generation, whose careers began in the fifties and early sixties, mark a transitional point in Welsh women's writing. Having gained a sense of the possibilities from Kate Roberts's success, they can be said as a group to have established, self-consciously and unequivocally, within Welsh literary traditions, the suitability, and justifiability, of female as much as male experience as the subject of art. However, their work does evince, to a greater or lesser extent, the unavoidable strain and ambivalence of a state of transition, between the continuing influence of traditional, repressive social attitudes and new feminist thought. My aim, for the rest of this chapter, is to explore the shifts and slides in the development of this new aesthetic through a detailed investigation of the work of two representatives from this generation of women writers, Eigra Lewis Roberts and Jane Edwards. I will concentrate particularly on their exploration of gender relations and of women's social roles, within a changing society. Given that I cannot assume that my English-language readers will be familiar with their novels, none of which have been translated into English, I am afraid that this project will necessarily involve a good deal of plot synopses, for which I must ask the reader's (and particularly the Welsh-language reader's) patience.

Both Eigra Lewis Roberts and Jane Edwards initially gained prominence through winning the main prize for fiction at National Eisteddfodau. Eigra Lewis Roberts was merely nineteen years old when her first novel, *Brynhyfryd*, was published in 1959, delineating life in a row of rural houses during one turbulent summer. In keeping with a wave of cynicism which swept Welsh literature at the end of the fifties and early sixties, both *Brynhyfryd* and *Tŷ ar y Graig* (House on the Rock) (1966), her second novel, deal with the restlessness of youth and the individual's sense of isolation and alienation within a family and social context. Whilst most of her characters in *Brynhyfryd* come to terms with their situation, providing a happy ending, no satisfactory solution is offered to Enid, the central character in *Tŷ ar y Graig*, in her plight. Eigra Lewis Roberts concentrates her exploration of human weakness and instability mainly on her female characters, but this by no means implies that her male characters do not betray the same insecurities. Solutions are brought about through co-operation and trust, both male and female characters gaining inner strength by helping each other.

This theme is further explored in her third novel, *Digon i'r Diwrnod* (Enough Unto the Day) (1974). Here, Alis Watkins, the main protagonist, reaches a crossroads in her life, and finds herself unable to choose which way to go. She is separated from her first husband, Ifor, a weak character who still lives under the shadow of his dead mother. Both had married each other for the wrong reasons, as a means of escape from a state of insecurity. Alis is attracted to Jac, but cannot commit herself because she feels bound to return to Ifor who will not divorce her. Her puritanical, strong-willed mother, and the conservative attitudes of a closely knit community, are also presented as repressive forces she has to contend with. However, during the course of the novel, Alis manages to conquer her fears, and ventures to create a new life for herself with Jac. Here, Eigra Lewis Roberts presents a positive outcome following from the failure of a first marriage, in which the marriage institution itself, and the false security that it offered, had taken precedence over mutual trust and understanding. Significantly enough, Alis is helped to recognize her plight and free herself from her unhappy situation by reading Simone de Beauvoir. Though she had relinquished her post as a teacher at the beginning of her married life to comply with Ifor's wishes, Alis can now identify herself politically with the average afflicted housewife, confined and isolated in the home, her life left in the hands of others. Evidently, therefore, this text reflects a positive change in the female perspective: a willingness to recognize, and break free from, constraints. If a marriage is restricting the growth of an individual's development, then its chains should be broken.

However, with *Mis o Fehefin* (A Month of June) (1980), Eigra Lewis Roberts's best-known novel, a more cynical, bleaker view of life emerges; here the female characters are cast as helpless victims in a male-dominated working-class environment. They seem to be boxed in by their situations, living boring humdrum existences, oblivious to any influences from outside their narrow-minded community. The novel focuses on the crises faced by its characters during one turbulent month of June. They are all hounded by failure, or fear of failure. Even the widow Mati Huws, apparently the most stable element in the community, has great difficulty in coming to terms with her past, which involved a poverty-stricken childhood, and a father hospitalized for mental illness. Grieving for Arthur, her dead husband, she dwells on the negative elements in her life, and becomes preoccupied by the breakdown of relations between herself and her children. This portrait of Mati seems to be a complete reversal of the traditional Welsh matriarchal figure, deeply loved and highly respected by her children, who plays such a central role in Kate Roberts's work.

Lena Powell, Mati's daughter, is another woebegone character, who has spent the best years of her life in an unhappy marriage with Richard Powell, who married her because she was carrying his child, and now, eighteen years later, has finally deserted her. Lena is depicted as cold and unfeeling, but even so, Richard Powell proves to be far more selfish and calculating; he returns only to abandon her again when she becomes terminally ill, leaving all the responsibility to Mati. Powell is also shown in an unfavourable light in his dealings with Eunice Murphy; his offers to help her and her husband, Brian Murphy, who is seriously ill with tuberculosis, are motivated only by his desire to take advantage of Eunice's vulnerable situation, and step into Brian's shoes as soon as he is sent to hospital. Eunice's portrayal as victim is twofold; on the one hand she must support a weak-willed and terminally ill husband, and, on the other, do her utmost to resist Richard Powells's insincere concern and charm. Lena and Richard's daughter Gwyneth is the only character in the novel to have ties with a world beyond the immediate locality; her student life brings her into contact with the outside influence of university and language politics. Her political stance and beliefs form a striking contrast to the uneventful lives of the other characters. In the sequel to *Mis o Fehefin, Ha' Bach* (1985), however, Gwyneth too is relegated to the domestic sphere as an unmarried mother.

In a neighbouring house, Pat Owens, the victim of a wife-beating husband, Leslie, loses all capacity to love due to her loss of self-respect, openly admitting resentment towards her baby son. Made to feel a failure both as wife and mother, her life is a sheer misery. Rejected and dismissed by nearly all her acquaintances, she spends a period in a mental hospital, and in the sequel attempts suicide. Her neighbour Madge Parry is another character who has her feet firmly set in chains, following the birth of her handi-capped, illegitimate child, Os. She has chosen to shut herself off from her community and devote all her time to her son. Dei Ellis, the father of Madge's child, has never faced his responsibility. Over the years, Madge has gained strength from battling alone, and when, in the sequel, Dei wants her to abandon their child and move away with him, she chooses to stay with Os. Dei is left to patch up his disastrous marriage with Gwen, the village gossip who has turned poison-pen writer, punishing others for their sins. Ironically, she is totally oblivious to her own husband's adultery.

Evidently, Eigra Lewis Roberts has no wish to portray an idyllic picture of people living happy family lives. She is more than pre-pared to explore the crises incurred in marital life which can ultimately lead to its breakdown. More importantly, from a femi-nist point of view, she also points out how detrimental the institution of conventional marriage can be to personal fulfilment. Her representation of the conventionally macho roles played by Dei Ellis, Richard Powell, and Leslie Owens are a harsh condemna-tion of such conduct; clearly their insensitive and disrespectful behaviour leads to the breakdown in communication with their wives. Significantly enough, the gamble of marriage has paid off for hardly any of these Minafon characters (apart from Mati). On the other hand, however, Eigra Lewis Roberts is quick to condemn those who are not brave enough to gamble for fear of failure. A firm commitment to the idea that people have to make decisions, and live with the consequences, forms the basis of her work.

In particular, of course, as these synopses have, I hope, indi-cated, her concern is with the decisions women have to make, when faced with changing social structures which allow for greater flexibility in female life choices, particularly with regard to marriage and divorce, but which can lead to an increase of disillusionment and bitterness when raised expectations are not met. Her contemporary, Jane Edwards, explores similar aspects of contemporary female experience, though, whereas Eigra Lewis Roberts concentrates mainly on the problems which beset women in working-class communities, Jane Edwards, particularly in her later novels, is more concerned with the frustrations of middle-class women. Perhaps because of the middle-class context, her characters are also portrayed as having a greater awareness of feminist influences than those of Eigra Lewis Roberts, and as being more conscious of the political significance of their trapped lives.

Her first two novels, however, both published well before the late 1960s women's movement began to have social significance, delineate the changes brought about in young women's lives as a result of the sexual revolution rather than the feminist one. In *Dechrau Gofidiau* (The Commencement of Sorrows) (1962) two sisters face the consequences of their rebellion against the sexual mores of their working-class background; when one of them has an illegitimate child, both are regarded with suspicion by their community. Before the novel's close, however, their sisterly solidarity triumphs over the emotional conflicts created by their social rejection. In Jane Edwards's second novel, *Byd o Gysgodion* (World of Shadows) (1964), sexual experimentation does not result in a happy ending for at least one of the two main female characters, however. When Aurien, a schoolteacher, has an affair with one of her sixth-form pupils, her inability to commit herself wholeheartedly to him leads to his suicide, and she is left to endure alone her resultant grief and guilt. Her friend, Mair, a secretary, also embarks on an illicit relation, with her unhappily married boss. But in Mair's case, for all the confused Aurien's hypocritical disapproval of her behaviour, the affair ends satisfactorily, with a divorce and a second marriage. At this early stage in her writing, Jane Edwards's texts seem to reflect conventional romantic attitudes: a wholehearted passionate commitment, however illicit the affair from the point of view of traditional morality, leads to happiness for the woman involved, but ambivalence, and an inability to give oneself entirely to an emotional relationship, ends in loneliness and despair.

By the time she came to write her third novel, *Bara Seguryd*

(Bread of Idleness) (1969), however, marital disillusionment had become her central theme. All three of the main female protagonists in this text are entrapped in destructive marriages. Carys attempts to break free by having an affair, but through her failure to distinguish between fantasy and reality, she finds herself as disappointed in her lover as she was in her married life; she attempts suicide and is admitted to mental hospital. Her friend, Einir, after a short-lived period of independence in Cardiff, returns to her natal community to enter into a joyless marriage, frightened by the bogey of possible spinsterhood. In this novel, women's roles as mothers are presented in as bleak a light as their prospects as wives. Lena, isolated and lonely mother of three, is determined to go against her unsupportive husband's wishes and avoid at all costs a fourth child. But when her secret cache of contraceptive pills is found and swallowed by her son Huw, she allows herself, traumatized by the incident, to be pressurized into yet another pregnancy. By now, all traces of romanticism have disappeared from Jane Edwards's work; the burdens of women's lives are depicted as by far outweighing any possible joy or fulfilment. Her female characters are given centre stage to air their grievances, but no answers are offered. *Bara Seguryd* ends abruptly, its fragmentary narrative structure (much information is supplied through letters, thoughts and conversations) seeming representative of the anchorless world it portrays.

The growing unrest which beset the lives of the women in *Bara Seguryd* is again present in *Epil Cam* (Crooked Offspring) (1972), her fourth novel. The three women characters who play central roles are Catrina Puw, an unstable minister's wife, who, like Carys, has attempted suicide; Rhosfair, a housewife expecting her second child; and Kate, a part-time dentist, mother of twins, and second wife of James, a middle-aged English doctor. Language politics now come to the forefront of Jane Edwards's work, for Kate is torn between her husband's influence and the magnetism of an active and prominent language campaigner, Pryderi. However, the author's main interest lies not with policies and campaigns, but with the effect political aims have upon private lives. Great tension is once again displayed between husbands and wives, Kate having married James to gain status and security, only to be frustrated by the fact that he will not allow her to return to full-time practice. Rhosfair also suffers a crisis of identity, feeling that she is losing herself and becoming part of her husband's personality, a fear increased by his family's insistence that the couple should move locality and join the family business. Similarly, Catrina's life is made difficult by the clash between her own unconventional way of living and the rigid expectations of her husband's congregation. Motherhood offers no possible escape from such frustrations for her, for, fearing to lose her sanity in childbirth like other women in her family, she has aborted her child.

Abortion forms the main theme of *Dros Fryniau Bro Afallon* (Over the Hills of Avalon) (1976), Jane Edwards's fifth novel, which shows a greater degree of feminist awareness on the part of the characters than was apparent in her previous novels. Menna Morgan, a disillusioned and depressed middle-aged married radio producer, has decided to abort her child in order to protect her independence and career. When faced with the disapproval of a doctor who is a firm believer in family values, she quotes Doris Lessing:

> The family is a dreadful tyranny, a doomed institution, a kind of mechanism for destroying everyone – the family is a source of neurosis.
>
> (Edwards 1976, 12)

The doctor responds by telling her that a wife's place is in the home and that her body was made to bear children. She withstands both his pressure and the values of her puritanical background, and goes ahead with a private abortion. Consequently, however, even though adamant in her decision, she does suffer psychological as well as physical pain, and the rift between herself and her politically aspiring self-centred husband Huw is further widened. Both Huw and Ieuan Puw, who seeks an affair with her, are unfavourably portrayed as selfish and hypocritical characters. Male unreliability becomes even more of an issue when Menna discovers that Huw has been having an affair with her friend's daughter. The fact that the affair coincided with her own crisis of identity, and quest for freedom and fulfilment, leads to Menna's decision to leave her husband, not for another man, but for independence. Her act is neither condoned nor condemned by the author, but the choice in itself undermines the marital institution which forms the basis of our social structure.

Cadno Rhos-y-Ffin (The Fox of Rhos-y-Ffin) (1984) shows an interesting development in Jane Edwards's treatment of gender relations. Here, we are presented with a reversal of conventional sex roles: Arfon, a television producer, is married to Elsbeth, an aspiring politician who is an almost exact copy of Huw in *Dros Fryniau Bro Afallon*. Perceiving himself as deprived of Elsbeth's love and attention, Arfon is attracted to Magi, a working-class wife and mother, whose satirical attitudes offer a striking contrast to the pretentious and hypocritical lives of the middle-class characters. Magi's brother Robin, another colourful character, embarks on an affair with Hannah, a middle-aged housewife, dissatisfied and disillusioned, on both personal and political levels, and driven to drink. As in Jane Edwards's other middle-class novels, the familiar theme of unhappy, unfulfilling marriages and illicit affairs yet again forms the basis of the work. Hannah, however, unlike Menna, has disconnected herself from feminism, freedom for her meaning abandonment of all ambition. She is critical of women who exhaust themselves through the struggle to cope with both families and careers. When her brief affair ends, she reverts to self-pity.

Y Bwthyn Cu (The Beloved Cottage), Jane Edwards's latest novel to date, again concentrates on a woman's mid-life crisis. Mari Morgan, reminiscing about her lost youth, regrets the fact that she has allowed herself to be moulded by her husband, and feels that her children have taken up her time and taxed her energy. Bored with life, and anxious to assert herself, she takes up a challenge to write a play, and accepts the use of a summer cottage in Llŷn. Alone and cut off in the countryside, she dwells on old romances and is visited by old flames, a device used to show how she has been, and is still being, exploited by men. One old friend rapes her, another tries to blackmail her emotionally into a relationship by reminding her of her loss of youth. She is deceived by them and by Ifan, the object of her romantic fantasies, and used to political ends. Finally her husband decides to divorce her.

Mari, like many other female characters portrayed by Jane Edwards, is fundamentally frustrated by life, having existed under her partner's shadow and consequently felt unfulfilled. Throughout her work, Jane Edwards has consistently drawn attention to women's discontent and suffering. Her awareness of the difficulties facing contemporary women has become so acute that it is perhaps time for her to go one step further and create new role models, portraying female figures who manage to conquer their fears, find a way of getting to grips with their problems, and achieve their desires. As well as criticizing the grim reality of many women's lives, a feminist text needs also to create female protagonists whose 'outlook and behaviour will presage a new social order that integrates the best aspects of "female culture" with selected "male" values' (Morgan 1972, 183). However, in perhaps her finest and most touching novel to date, Jane Edwards forbears to present us with her usual bleak scenarios of female disillusionment. *Miriam* (1977) deals with a young girl's attempt to come to terms with the loss of her mother and her father's subsequent remarriage. But Beth, her new stepmother, manages to conquer her initial depressive reactions; she refuses to be overwhelmed by the circumstances and the novel ends on a positive note.

It is tempting to underline the similarities in the works of Eigra Lewis Roberts and Jane Edwards, for both have dealt extensively with basic issues which have traditionally affected women's lives – relationships, marriage, children – and the vulnerability, fear, negativity and hysteria which follow years of dependence and male dominance. However, it would be a mistake to overlook the differences in their approach, in an attempt to construct a spurious impression of an universal female perspective. The crises faced by women torn between the various expectations and demands made upon them by a rapidly changing social order are represented differently by both authors. In their cases, the differing class context of their most characteristic work may account, in part, for these dissimilarities. But, of course, women's writing is no more one homogenous mass than men's writing: it represents a variety of conflicting positions, and, as women authors grow in confidence, the variety of viewpoints is likely to increase rather than diminish. As we have noted, the youngest generation of Welsh women novelists are less concerned with the difficulties for women in breaking free from the old gender pattern, and convey through their female characters a sense of greater social and political freedom: their women are not emotionally crippled by their rebellion against the still prevalent norms. But the increase in confidence apparent in these most recent writers' work may in part be due to the achievement of their immediate predecessors. For all that, in the novels of writers like Jane Edwards and Eigra Lewis Roberts, the emotional strain and tension involved in coping with radically changing roles remain the key notes, the realism of their portrayal of women, and the wholeheartedness of their concern with female predicaments, cannot but have helped to raise the consciousness of Welshwomen. The first step towards positive change must always be a pressing sense of need for it, and the multiple and various dissatisfactions of the frustrated characters who dominate the texts I have described at the very least emphasize the need for continuing progressive change with regard to gender relations in contemporary Wales.

References

Conran, Anthony (1992). 'The Lack of the Feminine', *New Welsh Review*, 17, Summer 1992, 28–31.

Edwards, Jane (1976). *Dros Fryniau Bro Afallon* (Llandysul, Gomer).

Lloyd-Morgan, Ceridwen (1991). 'Rhagymadrodd Hanesyddol', in Menna Elfyn (ed.), *O'r Iawn Ryw* (Honno, Welsh Women's Press).

Morgan, Ellen (1972). 'Human-becoming: Form and Focus in the Neo-Feminist Novel', in Susan K. Cornillon (ed.), *Images of Women in Fiction: Feminist Perspectives* (Bowling Green, Ohio, Bowling Green University Popular Press, 1972).

Sherry, Ruth (1988). *Studying Women's Writing: An Introduction* (London, Arnold).

12

The cost of community: women in Raymond Williams's fiction

GWYNETH ROBERTS

In his first successful book, *Culture and Society*, Raymond Williams argued that

> A good community, a living culture, will . . . not only make room for but actively encourage all and any who can contribute to the advance in consciousness which is the common need.
>
> (Williams 1958, 320)

The concept of community is central to all of Williams's work, representing, for him, the best and most creative of social structures. In this chapter, however, I will show that, for Williams, 'community' as portrayed in his novels is a gender-specific concept, in that it rests upon the twin pillars of masculine work and close involvement in socialist politics. Women, by being effectively excluded from both these traditions are also denied the right to play a full part in the community. As a result, Williams's definition of communal life as being advantageous to all its members does not apply to the women who appear in his own novels.

Applying a consciously feminist critical approach to Williams's work seems particularly necessary in the Welsh context, where his writings are held in very high esteem and are being looked to for models of how Welsh culture can develop in the future. Just as Williams insisted upon the validity of class and, later, nationality in criticism, so too must Welsh feminists insist upon a close reading of his texts from a committed gender position. However, it may well be that what is to be learned from the novels will pose uncomfortable questions to those for whom it has become an article of faith that Williams's concept of the 'knowable community' represents the best possible future for Wales.

For the purposes of this chapter I have chosen to concentrate on the three novels which make up the *Welsh Trilogy*: *Border Country*, *Second Generation* and *The Fight for Manod*. Their publication, spanning the period 1960 to 1979, is contemporaneous with the emergence of feminism as an active political and cultural force, a phenomenon which one might expect to see reflected in the novels of a writer so determinedly wedded to the realist tradition. In fact the *Welsh Trilogy* shows Williams's attitude toward gender issues to be ambivalent at best, and arguably even at times regressive in nature. It is true that in *Second Generation*, it is possible to detect an embryonic attempt at representing the burgeoning conflict between the needs of the community and the needs of individual women, but Williams the novelist seems more concerned to quash this emerging conflict than to explore it. This is illustrated by the third novel within the trilogy, *The Fight for Manod*, in which he offers a fictional projection of the future which effectively ignores the changing nature of women's lives, and places them firmly in a domestic context. In the fictional mode, at least, his model of community continues to draw upon the experience of his childhood, as depicted in *Border Country*, in which women are seen as peripheral to the main action of the novel.

At a very fundamental level *Border Country* functions as an examination of patriarchy, concerned as it is with the interaction between father and son, and the transmission through the generations of a masculine sense of belonging. Like most women of her time, Matthew Price's mother, Ellen, sees her role as responding to the needs of her husband and son; and even when she does very occasionally manage to distinguish and express her own wishes they are largely ignored. She is, in fact, a character who is defined by her silence. Williams devotes very little time to a physical description of Ellen. The sketchy reference to her hair and eyes contrast with the care he takes in establishing her husband Harry's considerable physical presence. The initial impression Williams creates is of a frightened and immature girl. Indeed, throughout the novel, he continually attaches the adjective 'frightened' to descriptions of Ellen; in later life she seems nervous and ill at ease, even with her own son.

Those parts of the novel in which we do glimpse Ellen as an autonomous character are also the areas which illustrate the tensions not only between mother and son but also between the masculine and feminine concepts of community. When his father's illness brings him back to Glynmawr, Matthew is angered to find that his mother has shared news about his life with the neighbours. He also resents the constant stream of visitors, mostly women, who call on his mother and allow her to go through the story of her husband's collapse again and again:

> 'What is this an illness or a tea party? You can't be kept running upstairs and at the same time have a whole stream of them in the kitchen. Not just asking how he is, mind, but settling down in the chair for every detail, and then going on to whatever interests them, just a good general gossip.'
>
> (Williams 1960, 81)

Ellen's reaction to her son's aggression suggests that, although the neighbours' visits are a strain, they are also supportive and give her the kind of sympathetic understanding which Matthew seems unable to provide. Ironically, it could be argued that here Ellen is functioning within a pattern of mutuality which is at the heart of community life, particularly that informal and unstructured social network which revolves around women and children. But Matthew seems to perceive the relationship between his mother and her women friends as a threat because it is grounded in emotional intimacy rather than the male-bonding experiences of work and political belief towards which he is so respectful.

His hostility toward female friendship can be seen more clearly in his encounter with his childhood sweetheart, Eira. The daughter of his father's friend and colleague Morgan Rosser, Eira is now married to the doctor who is treating Harry Price. Matthew's reaction to this seemingly innocuous coincidence is extraordinary, particularly when he learns that Eira and his mother have remained friends:

> 'The fact is that for years you've been keeping up a completely false relationship with my mother. False on both sides. I'd say you've both kept it up as a sort of lien on me. You don't get anywhere, but it's there, as a perpetual criticism. I can't understand you meeting and talking about me, exchanging your photographs. I find it disgusting.'
>
> (Williams 1960, 272)

Since the novel provides us with excellent reasons why Eira should remain friends with a woman who helped look after her from the age of nine weeks and who, furthermore, is married to her father's best friend, Matthew's reaction seems excessively petulant.

But Matthew's anger also highlights an important difference in the manner in which Williams interprets the experience of social mobility for men and women. As the wife of the local doctor, Eira has also made a class transition, although Williams has been careful to give her husband a suitably proletarian background; he actually identifies much more strongly with her husband, 'the boy from Llanelly' (Williams 1960, 268), than with Eira's experience of social mobility. This in turn points up an area of tension between Matthew and his mother since, like Eira, Ellen is unable to grasp the nature of his inner conflict at having left his natal class. It seems probable that Williams, together with other male writers from the working class, defines the experience of class transition in terms of exclusively masculine angst. As Carolyn Steedman points out women are, in that sense,

> without class, because the cut and fall of a skirt and good leather shoes can take you across the river and to the other side: the fairy-tales tell you that goose-girls may marry kings.
>
> (Steedman 1986, 15–16)

In terms of Steedman's argument it is interesting to note that, in making Eira a nurse who marries a doctor, Williams has used a characteristic plot device from romantic fiction. In this way the experience of female social mobility through marriage is seen to be wholly desirable and untroubled by the sense of loss which haunts his male protagonists.

One of the problems Williams faces in attempting to portray the female community is that of language. The glimpses we have of Ellen's world – the chatting with neighbours, the swapping of family gossip – show it to be part of what Deborah Jones calls the 'speech community' of women. Jones further argues that

> Gossip, a language of female secrets, is one of women's strengths and, like all our strengths, it is both discounted and attacked.
>
> (Jones 1990, 245)

Jones describes gossip as a 'language of intimacy' (Jones 1990, 224), and this is precisely the reason why Williams distrusts it and attempts to exclude it. The power of intimacy can seriously distort the balance between individual and social reality, which is the exact area that Williams seeks to negotiate in his novels. Despite the richness of the communal female language, it is one which has grown up outside the parameters of the political and social dialectic through which Harry and Matthew Price explore their relationship. Therefore, by the terms of the agenda which Williams has set himself as a novelist, it must be excluded. This, in effect, silences the women of *Border Country* by devaluing the importance of their bonding when seen in relation to the patriarchal traditions of the male working class.

Women's struggle to find an appropriate language in which to articulate their lives, and Williams's suspicion of their motives, forms an important part of the second novel in the *Welsh Trilogy*, *Second Generation*. Kate Owen, the principal female character, has been described as a proto-feminist, and Williams himself felt that the novel explored gender issues more fully than the rest of his work. But whilst Kate certainly has much in common with the angry and disaffected women who formed the staple ingredient of much early feminist fiction, Williams does not identify the source of her frustration as arising directly from her gender; instead, he attributes her anger to the failures of trade-union based socialism. There is no indication, at this stage, that Williams is aware of the anomaly of Kate's situation, in that she works tirelessly for a cause which twenty years later he would describe as having 'excluded the reality of women and families' (Williams 1989, 242). Yet trade unions are precisely the kind of organizations that Williams values as being amongst the finest creative achievements of working-class life. So that, although in raising the question of Kate's dissatisfaction he shows a degree of sensitivity to her situation, he also sees her rebellion as a betrayal of those masculine Welsh working-class values which he reveres. If her anger was fully articulated, then Williams would be forced to confront the flaws in his own core beliefs. Thus Williams undercuts Kate's very pertinent political criticisms by linking them to her sexuality and to the threat posed to the collective aims of socialism by the assertion of individual desire.

However, Kate's affair with Arthur Dean, the cynical middle-class intellectual who represents almost the antithesis of her husband Harold's fundamentalist trade-union socialism, cannot simply be read as political metaphor, since her attitude to her own sexuality provides us with much information concerning Williams's views of women. Before Kate actually consummates her affair with Dean, she tries to work through her reasons in a dialogue with her sister-in-law, Myra. Myra is a curiously hybrid character; for all that Williams paints her as an earth-mother we are also meant to see her as a deeply sensual woman who has repressed her sexuality because of guilt. She became pregnant before marriage, and later confesses to her daughter that she breached the moral code out of pure sexual desire, But, in her exchange with Kate, Myra strenuously denies that she felt any real desire, and insists that it is improper for a woman to enter a sexual relationship in order to secure her own pleasure.

This is an argument which is reproduced in various forms throughout the novel, as Williams explores the tension between private and public morality. In this context, however, it allows Kate to approach some of the central arguments of feminism, albeit from a rather oblique angle. She accuses Myra of teaching her daughter to feel guilty about her sexuality, seeing it as a crime shared by all mothers, 'twisting and crippling their daughters because of their own guilt' (Williams, 1964, 122). Kate recognizes that this is linked with society's demand that girls remain chaste until marriage whilst at the same time using the promise of their sexual favours as a way of catching a man:

> 'The woman's never there as a woman, as herself. She's just a bit of portable property, that he's going to take possession of. But of course, since she is property, she's got to bargain. She doesn't make herself cheap, because it wouldn't do to make property cheap. Let her sell herself dear, because selling is all it can be.'
> (Williams 1964, 123)

Implicit in Kate's argument is the idea that, because women are not permitted to express sexual desire, an honest relationship is prohibited. Myra, on the other hand, believes that the controlling of women's sexuality 'keeps a woman to her home' (Williams 1964, 124). Kate takes Myra's point, but instead of continuing the argument in terms of its implications for women she uses it against her own sex:

> 'Look what it does to her, look what it does to her children. This empty, narrow sort of half-life we've got here, and we deserve it.

Does it look, walking round here, like living at all? And we've broken the men, taken the heart out of them with our narrowness. They go to work just expecting to be bored and cheated, and they don't know anything more they could really get.'

(Williams 1964, 123–4)

This speech effectively reverses Kate's earlier distinctly feminist analysis of female subordination and places the responsibility for their plight squarely on women themselves, blaming the powerless for inhibiting the powerful. By this means Williams directs the force of the narrative away from Kate's plight as a woman and back into the debate about the decline of the working-class man. She is shown as being aware of her anger but she cannot articulate her distress through a gender-specific argument. Instead, she is forced to use the only language available to her, which is rooted in the tradition of male oppression by the capitalist system.

Arguably it is the presence of Kate's anger which shows that Williams was sensitive to the emergence of dissent amongst women at a stage when it was barely beginning to be articulated within society. His portrayal of Kate is certainly of a different order to his depiction of the timid Ellen Price in *Border Country*. However, to see this as any real advance in Williams's desire to explore feminist issues is to ignore the harsh way in which Kate is punished for expressing her discontent. Williams does not question the source of the frustration which drove her into adultery, he merely returns her, at the close of the novel to the close confinement of her marriage – a marriage which he has previously depicted in very bleak terms as lacking in any emotional or sexual compatibility. In fact his portrayal of this arid relationship is so effective that Kate's eventual recommitment increasingly appears as a false resolution imposed by Williams in an attempt to demonstrate his belief in the unassailable unity of the working-class family.

At a deeper level, however, Kate Owen appears to function as a vehicle for Williams's own growing sense of alienation from the working class, thus enabling him to act out a psycho-drama based upon the feelings of guilt aroused by such thoughts. As a woman within a male-dominated movement, she is both marginalized and powerless: the ideal scapegoat. By raising the spectre of untrammelled female desire and its effect upon the moral values of the community, Williams is drawing upon the most primitive of male fears. It is so powerful that he can use it to mask the very real justice behind many of Kate's statements.

Williams's subconscious fears in relation to female sexuality surface very clearly in his depiction of the relationship between Peter Owen, Kate's son, and Rose Swinburne. Rose's sexual boldness is frightening to Peter; he perceives it as predatory and controlling, describing their love-making in language which is redolent with resentment and self-disgust:

> 'She wasn't involved . . . I can remember that now. At the end she laughed, because she was stronger. My skin was burning, but she was quite cool. Yes, I enjoyed her, but as a treat, a present. I was back like a child on her body. She was quite beyond me, and it was as if nothing had happened, though to me it had happened.'
>
> (Williams 1964, 239)

The phrase 'like a child on her body' clearly links the relationship with his struggles against his mother, and reproduces the classic dilemma of the male child who must reconcile the state of being in thrall to the all-powerful mother with his growing perception of himself as the superior gender.

Whilst Peter is threatened by the power of Rose's sexuality, he is comforted and sustained by the almost aggressive virginity paraded by Myra's daughter Beth, whom he later marries. The consummation of their affair is presented as sacramental and transfiguring; Peter proclaims:

> 'I won't leave you, I want to give you my life.'
> 'Yes love, give it to me.'
> 'I've wanted to feel my own life, to feel where it grows. And it will only grow if I give it to you.'
> 'I want to grow with you, Peter.'
> 'It will feel like your life. It will feel so to me.'
>
> (Williams 1964, 325)

This is an embarrassing exchange, both in language and meaning. If we are meant to assume that such a commitment represents all that Williams feels a relationship should be, then we can perhaps see why he found it difficult to integrate feminism into his system of beliefs.

Beth's absolute commitment to her husband seems to be the only approved option for the women in Williams's novels. After her brief bid for greater fulfilment, Kate is forced to realize that she can only be of service to her class if she repudiates her personal growth and returns to the community which oppresses her. That is not the choice which is presented to either Matthew Price or Peter Owen. The difference arises because female characters like Kate do not have the vocational justification of 'work' to sponsor their need to move beyond the boundaries of their natal class. Instead, as Kate realizes, they can only change their lives vicariously by attachment to a man through whom they can have access to greater intellectual development. Women in Williams's novels exist in isolation, excluded from the cultural institutions which represent the aspirations of their class and without access to a sense of their history within it. *Second Generation* sees the surfacing of Williams's political and social loyalties because he sees that they are shaped by forces other than those of male-bonding through work. True, none of Williams's heroes are permitted to choose individual intellectual fulfilment to the exclusion of their affiliation to the working class, but it does emerge as a 'reward' for their struggles. Only the women in his fiction are consistently denied the right to willed class mobility. For them the cost of community is shown to be tangible, in that it requires that they demonstrate their loyalty by a total subjugation of their intellectual and sexual energies. Kate Owen's rebellion against this fate does not herald an initiative on Williams's part to question the validity of this sacrifice; instead, it seems to renew his desire to return women to the silence he attempted to impose on them in *Border Country*.

This is certainly the case in his futurist novel *The Fight for Manod*. This final novel in the trilogy was first published in 1979, fifteen years after *Second Generation*, during which period the feminist debate grew in intensity. By this later date, to essay any kind of futurist novel which did not include even the most elementary discussion of women's rights and demands implies that the author is deliberately excluding such issues, or that he is stubbornly blind to their significance. Williams's reputation as a political thinker, and his own infrequent declarations of support for feminism, makes it hard to excuse him on the grounds of ignorance, thereby suggesting that he found his vision of the regenerated community to be incompatible with the changing role of women.

In fact, the actual realization of a town like Manod would probably have involved women on a far greater scale than Williams was prepared to admit. As the traditional heavy industries of Wales have declined their place has been taken by the service industries, administration, and the new technology. In the novel, Manod is finally envisaged as 'a city built primarily to demonstrate the new energy and communications technology' (Williams 1979, 191), with its major industries centring upon the manufacture of those new technologies – industries which, in practice, draw heavily upon women workers.

It is clear from the novel that Williams sees Manod as a way of reconciling the industrially depressed south with the depopulated heartlands of Wales, thereby restoring a sense of common culture. But, since Williams's definition of Welsh culture rests very much on the male-dominated movements of trade unionism and socialist politics, it is likely that his vision of an ideal future would include the resurgence of such entities. Since women have been quite deliberately excluded from such organizations, the implication must be that Williams was happy to reproduce the old patterns of male oppression in a modern setting. It is not difficult to see why Williams's hopes for the resurgence of a self-confident and homogenous working-class culture rested upon the recreation of male patterns of employment and not upon the shoulders of under-paid, under-skilled and over-burdened women. To have acknowledged this fact openly and to have explored its implications would have meant relinquishing his attachment to the male-centred culture of *Border Country*, and confronting the problems posed by gender as well as class divisions. In practice it seems to have been less painful for Williams to continue to exclude women than to attempt to integrate their needs with his vision of the new Wales.

The Fight for Manod operates upon two levels. There is the male community which has access to money, information and varying degrees of power, and the female, or sub-community, which operates in a state of powerlessness and ignorance. Within that community Williams shows the effects of change upon two women in particular: Gwen Vaughan and Modlen Jenkins can both be seen as representative of an economic system which is founded upon the exploitation of women and families. By the end of the novel each of them has apparently benefited from the breakdown of the old social and economic structures, but in practice it is only Gwen Vaughan who really achieves independence.

Gwen's life can be seen as a paradigm of conflict between the community and the individual woman. By taking care of the family on the death of her mother and rejecting a competitive career as a showjumper, she fulfils the community's expectations of her as a woman. However, her subsequent rejection of marriage renders her without status or function within that same community, which now requires that she 'disappear' in order to permit her brother to marry. The complex inheritance system which governs the land means that Gwen has no control over the farm on which she has spent her life; instead she is humiliatingly dependent upon the actions of her younger brother, to whom she has been a surrogate mother. The fact that he now addresses her as 'girl' only points up her ambivalent status.

At first Gwen is appalled at how easily her brother sells his land, and asks Matthew Price to help her stop what she sees as the corruption of local values by outside money. But soon she realizes that within such change lies the potential for her to make a fresh start. With her small share of the capital, she is able to make a business from her life-long love of horses. Having no place in what Williams later described as 'the movement of the country: the movement of difficult land through the network of marriages and children' (Williams 1979, 162), she is uniquely placed to take advantage of the possibilities offered by the gradual disintegration of the traditional rural economy. It is through the breaking up of that old land-based, patriarchal community that Gwen can secure her own life.

Modlen Jenkins also benefits when property deals which seek to cash in on the Manod project make it possible for her husband Trevor to have his own farm. But unlike Gwen Vaughan, who at least had a capital stake in the land and can use it to buy herself autonomy, Modlen and Trevor are placed entirely at the mercy of property speculators. The reader knows, as Modlen and Trevor do not, that their new security no longer depends upon local, family connections but upon the vagaries of international capitalism.

For both Modlen and Gwen the undermining of the traditional land-based community offers an opportunity for personal regeneration: they thrive at the community's expense. Yet there is a chilling sense of impermanence about their achievements because they remain excluded from the real centres of power. There may have been some breakdown of the directly patriarchal system of land-holding but it has been replaced by the facelessness of international capitalism. Modlen and Gwen are still denied the right to make informed decisions because they have no real status and no access to information. They build new lives upon the basis of fundamental ignorance.

The Fight for Manod has an especial interest because it contains a portrait of Matthew Price's wife, Susan, although she appears only as a mother and wife, as if her own personality has dissolved into that of her husband. Little is made, for example, of the fact that Susan is not Welsh, but actually comes from Cumberland. The narrative drive in both *Border Country* and *The Fight For Manod* centres around Matthew's need to reconcile himself first with his natal community and, in the later novel, with Wales as a whole. Susan, however, is presented as being without a community; she has received one, by default, as she supports Matthew in his career. In the end, then, the Price marriage is utterly conventional and reproduces, albeit in a mutually respectful form, the familiar patterns of male domination.

Their experiences in Manod also resolve along gender lines, as Susan becomes involved in the illness and death of their elderly neighbour, Mrs Lewis. In Mrs Lewis she sees an image of her own loneliness:

> She stared down at the worn counterpane, thinking of Harry and Jack. She had felt old herself, her effective life finished, as her boys grew up into men. Now she saw this again, past Mrs Lewis lying there: a generation further on: a single frail life, on beyond her family.
>
> (Williams 1979, 101)

This is, in part, a recognition of her own mortality, but it can also be seen as the acceptance of her own invisibility without the defining role of 'mother'. The phrase 'her effective life finished' is a marked contrast to Matthew's post-family experience in finding a new cause to which to dedicate himself. Susan's judgement of her own worth is very like that of Kate Owen in *Second Generation*, who considers that at forty-one she is of 'the age to be a grandmother' (Williams 1964, 270) Her lover, Arthur Dean, argues that she is a victim of class expectations:

'There's been no worse slavery than this, Kate. At an age when most middle-class women are settling down to enjoy life, most working-class women are expected to write themselves off.'

(Williams 1964, 271)

But buried within this seemingly positive statement is a veiled judgement on the relevance of women's lives. In Raymond Williams's novels no one 'enjoys' life except for politically apathetic characters like Gwyn Owen, or the elderly and roguish Jack Price; worthy and 'approved' characters suffer and are broken in the fight for socialism. In this context Dean's injunction that Kate should enjoy life is as much of an insult to her capabilities as is Susan Price's belief that her life is effectively finished.

Another scene from *The Fight for Manod*, in which Susan Price takes tea with two of her Manod neighbours, confirms that although, as a novelist, Williams was at ease with the idea of women as wives and mothers, he showed considerable unease when dealing with them in other roles. When the novels require him to extend the fictional community to include other female characters, he relies heavily upon stereotypes. Thus we have the beautiful but paranoid and anorexic Juliet Dance sharing her tea-table with Mary Pearson, an embittered sex-obsessed divorcee, both of whom are viewed with horror by Susan Price. Yet, as we have seen, Susan's own life now lacks any meaning beyond a vicarious identification with her husband's work. All three women have been diminished through their varying experiences of marriage, although Susan has at least been compensated by what is obviously a loving relationship with Matthew.

Williams's treatment of the women in his fiction seems to suggest that the ideal community, as he saw it, relied upon the continuation of existing gender inequalities. His political and cultural writings make it clear that he saw the family and the working-class community as being threatened by the encroachments of capitalism, but only in the novels does it become evident that he also saw women as a threat to those same institutions. Whilst not accusing Williams of misogyny, or of any conscious opposition to women's rights, I am suggesting that at a sub-textual level the novels express a fear that for historical and cultural reasons women were unlikely to share his wholehearted commitment to what he defined as the values of Welsh working-class life.

References

Jones, Deborah (1990). 'Gossip: Notes on Women's Oral Culture', in Deborah Cameron (ed.), *The Feminist Critique of Language: A Reader* (London, Routledge).

Steedman, Carolyn (1986). *Landscape for a Good Woman; A Story of Two Lives* (London, Virago).

Williams, Raymond (1958). *Culture and Society 1780–1950* (Harmondsworth, Penguin, 1963 ed.).

—— (1960). *Border Country* (London, Hogarth Press, 1988 ed.).

—— (1964). *Second Generation* (London, Hogarth Press, 1988 ed).

—— (1979). *The Fight for Manod* (London, Hogarth Press, 1988 ed.).

—— (1989). *Resources of Hope*, ed. Robin Gable (London, Verso).

13

Artefact and identity: the Welsh dresser as domestic display and cultural symbol

MOIRA VINCENTELLI

In Aberystwyth Public Library there are a number of scrap-books made by members from local branches of the Women's Institute in 1965. In the scrap-book from Llanbadarn Fawr, a small but historic village on the outskirts of the town, we find the following statement:

> Generally 1965 saw many changes in style of interior decoration in the village, setting the trend for years to come. Llanbadarn is 'with it' to use a modern phrase.
>
> The furniture inside our homes provides an interesting contrast – the older and true natives of Llanbadarn nearly always possess a genuine Welsh dresser, handed down to them by previous generations. These dressers are rightly cherished, being beautifully made and standing high and wide against the wall. Placed on the shelves are various coloured plates and jugs – all sizes – and all valuable, as is obvious from the offers made by visiting antique dealers.

On the surface, this statement is an innocent representation of generation difference but it raises a number of significant points. The writers want to emphasize that they possess up-to-date tastes in interior decoration to dispel any notion that, living in a small town on the west coast of Britain, they may be trapped in a provincial backwater, but they go on, nevertheless, to affirm their historic roots – the sign of the 'true native' is to possess a 'genuine Welsh dresser'. The necessary compliment of plates and jugs are further validated by their financial value within the (dominant) outside culture as represented by 'visiting antique dealers'.

In this chapter I want to trace the development of symbolic meaning around the Welsh dresser and to examine the tradition of collecting and displaying china, considering to what extent this tradition is still alive and in what way it functions.

The Welsh dresser appears to operate not merely as a piece of furniture for domestic storage and display but as a focus for the establishment of social meanings associated with gender, domestic well-being and national identity. To explore this, I have drawn on the work of a number of writers on material culture who examine the way that artefacts function in the production of meaning, in particular, Pierre Bourdieu, Henry Glassie, Adrian Forty, and Daniel Miller: Miller has argued that much recent cultural theory bases its arguments on the centrality of language as a means of constructing social realities, overlooking the ways that material culture can be used to construct social meanings and identities (Miller 1987, 102). In the twentieth century the Welsh dresser is by definition a piece of antique furniture which has become a highly prized object in many Welsh homes. As a domestic object the dresser and its contents are largely associated with the female sphere and, furthermore, the collecting of china as domestic decoration is usually a female activity although the particular ways that men may become involved will be addressed briefly. My research is principally based on evidence from interviews conducted with women and some men, and draws on individual accounts of dressers and the objects their owners put on, and in, them. Although it would be inappropriate to generalize from a few individual accounts, it is important to recognize how individuals appropriate meanings for their own needs within a broad social and historical context.

In all societies people are surrounded by material goods but in contemporary society, dominated by consumerism, this has become increasingly significant. The things that we own or choose to buy help us to create our own identities. In turn, we read appearances: our goods and chattels signify to other people what we stand for, our origins, class, status and gender. But these readings are made through relativities and assemblies of information. Objects in themselves have no single meaning but are sites around which meanings can be constructed. The Welsh novelist Kate Roberts provides a fictional example of this process in her short story 'The Quilt'. In this tale Ffebi Wiliams and her husband face bankruptcy, but as the receivers move in to remove everything from the house, she rescues a precious quilt, which she had bought in spite of their dwindling fortunes, and sits on the bed wrapped in it as the house is cleared. She remembers the day she was first tempted by the quilt when she saw it on display in a local show:

Cwilt a dynnai ddŵr o ddannedd pawb. Gafaelai pob gwraig ynddo a'i fodio wrth fyned heibio a thaflu golwg hiraethlon arno wrth ei adael. Cwilt o wlanen wen dew ydoedd, a rhesi ar hyd-ddo – rhesi o bob lliwiau, glas a gwyrdd, melyn a choch . . . Daeth awydd ar Ffebi ei brynu, a pho fywyaf yr ystyriai ei thlodi, mwyaf yn y byd y cynyddai ei hawydd.

(Roberts 1937, 22)

A quilt that made you catch your breath; that brought every woman there to finger it and look longingly at it as she walked away. A quilt of thick white Welsh flannel, with wavy stripes, green and blue, yellow and red . . . She wanted to buy it, and the more she thought of her poverty, the greater grew her desire.

(Roberts 1946, 52)

Here, the quilt, an object that has particular associations with Wales, has become a symbol of resistance to her fate, an object that would make her the envy of her friends/peers. This story also suggests the way that artefacts can be a source of pleasure and comfort.

It is often claimed by commentators on Welsh culture, including Welsh commentators, that Wales has an oral, literary and musical culture but lacks a visual culture. At face value, such claims are hard to deny but they must be interrogated. They are the product of a colonizing and colonized mentality. Peter Lord in *Aesthetics of Relevance* has proposed that Wales has 'an unrecognised visual culture', and that it is a lack of confidence that prevents the Welsh from taking their own culture seriously. Patronage and critical writing, the essential tools which have to be deployed to establish a sense of tradition, have not been mobilized. The failure to recognize a Welsh visual culture has meant that there is no foundation on which to build. Furthermore, the values of fine art and high culture that have been so strongly associated with 'civilization' continue to exert a powerful effect on people's perceptions of what is valuable, and in turn marginalize other things. Within feminist discourse this process has long been recognized. If judgements about visual art are based only on the hierarchical framework of the European academic tradition then the contribution of women as artists or as patrons is overlooked (see Parker and Pollock 1981).

But women have always bought domestic items and in a consumer society women are the major audience for advertising campaigns for domestic goods. And such women have power (see Attfield and Kirkham 1989). As buyers and collectors of china women are patrons. The pottery on Welsh dressers was, for the most part, not made in Wales but in Staffordshire, but much of it was made for the Welsh market. Lustre jugs were popular in Wales as nowhere else in Britain, and the brightly coloured china known as Swansea Cottage or Gaudy Welsh (albeit in the latter case suggesting negative connotations) is clearly named after its market. Welsh women were patrons of a form of visual culture that was suited to their modest means.

It has to be recognized that the opportunities for visual enrichment in nineteenth-century Wales were limited. This is one reason why, I would argue, the tradition of the Welsh dresser has taken on such a central place within the visual culture in Wales. In a modest interior and a grey climate, colourful and shiny ceramic surfaces are a welcome contrast. In many parts of the non-industrial world imported plates are used as decoration, sometimes even set into the wall (Courtney-Clarke 1990). Dressers or their equivalent, that is, display storage for domestic utensils, were used widely in Europe, America and throughout Britain in the eighteenth and nineteenth centuries, but for a number of reasons they have become particularly associated with Wales, to the extent that many people in England who have such an item of furniture will call it a Welsh dresser although often they have no historical reason to suppose it came from Wales.

With the colonization of large parts of the world in the nineteenth century the need to create depoliticized and unthreatening images of national identity increased. This process is examined in the seminal volume edited by E. J. Hobsbaum and T. Ranger, *The Invention of Tradition*. In the chapter on Wales, Prys Morgan traces the changing forms of 'Welshness' from the early nineteenth-century romantic version of an ancient bardic past to the more modern versions of the second half of the century created by 'fresh myth-makers and creators of traditions, those of radical and non-conformist Wales' (Hobsbaum and Ranger 1983, 100). In the latter part of the nineteenth century the Welsh, by and large, adopted the mores of the English bourgeoisie and were encouraged, or compelled, to speak English in school and in the workplace, but in response new picturesque symbols of Welshness were acceptable and indeed were increasing. The consolidation of the dresser as a symbol of Welshness began to develop at this time.

The Welsh dresser is normally written about by furniture historians who are interested in classifying and identifying early examples and are less interested in modern variations: the older versions are seen as more genuinely Welsh and 'authentic', which implies a false notion of an unchanging past untainted by outside culture (Miller 1987, 10); the more modern versions are seen as influenced by the wider culture of Britain, through pattern books and furniture catalogues from wholesalers and shops. Pre-nineteenth-century dressers are perhaps the most prized. This was a time when the accommodation of the rural peasantry was very rudimentary and only the affluent could think of owning a major piece of furniture. Hence dressers were produced by highly specialized craftsmen who served a prosperous client. It was only in the nineteenth century that rural farmers and workers could begin to aspire to furniture of this kind. The resultant expanding market meant that local carpenters were offered the opportunity to extend their skills. In the early years of the century most dressers were still made to a particular local pattern with, for example, a closed base with cupboards and drawers in north Wales, and an open base, or pot board, in south Wales. By the end of the century the dresser became less regionally distinctive and many clients preferred to have it with glass fronted cupboards on either side. These smaller cupboards displayed delicate china and tea-sets protecting them from dust, while jugs continued to be hung in the open centre part. Soft woods, often stained to look like mahogany, were increasingly used rather than oak. Such dressers would be more likely to be bought from furniture stores rather than custom-made for the client.

By the early twentieth century the new-style dresser had rendered the older ones old fashioned but as the dresser itself became old fashioned with the introduction, at least for middle-class families, of the new-style fitted kitchens in the 1930s, the older ones began to gather the status of family heirlooms. In many households the dresser ceased to have a central role as a place for storing crockery in everyday use, although already in the nineteenth century much of the ceramics on dressers was for display rather than use. Mostly, the things on the dresser were hardly used at all.

It was moved out of the kitchen/living room and into the dining room, the parlour or the hall way. The dresser was increasingly a symbolic piece of furniture: it came to stand for family history and a disappearing Welshness, perhaps of a rural past.

But the pressure to adopt new fashions was limited, and the money with which to indulge such tastes was in short supply in the 1930s and the war years; it was only in the post-war period that large sections of the population could consider buying new furniture, building modern houses and following the latest trends. As the new bungalows went up, the old furniture was sold off or consigned to the barn. Wales became a happy hunting ground for dealers and the antique trade. However, the great increase in the monetary value of old Welsh furniture soon alerted people to what was happening: there was, for example, an increase from £100 to £1000 for an old dresser in the space of a decade in the 1960s.

The 1960s was also of course the decade that saw a burgeoning awareness of Welsh culture, with the language movement gathering momentum and the youth culture of the late 1960s manifesting strong nationalist tendencies in Wales. The idealization of rural life was further confirmed by the movement of young people from outside settling in rural Wales in the search for an 'alternate' lifestyle. The growth of the tourist industry was another vital factor which stimulated the creation of cultural symbols. The woollen mills also saw a revival and Welsh 'tapestry' cloth became hugely popular for the indigenous population as well as the tourist, along with Welsh crafts such as lovespoons and, indeed, the making of miniature Welsh dressers. This renewed focus on cultural identity and national pride provided the background for an increasing awareness of the dresser as a Welsh artefact. But what of the objects that go on the dresser?

The extensive use of ceramics for eating began in the eighteenth century but mainly for the gentry. Although pewter was still widely used in the early nineteenth century ordinary folk used wooden bowls and had a few big dishes of metal or ceramic (china or earthenware). Wooden bowls and utensils were retained for a long time, especially in rural Wales.

The industrial production of china immediately offered a form of collectable house decoration or 'value' available to country people of modest means. In the nineteenth century, a period of social mobility, the need to express changes in social status was important and manifested itself in dress, behaviour, social mores, house design and house decoration. Collecting ceramics became a means of expressing a certain well-being and standing. In this way popular culture emulated the aristocratic taste for collecting fine porcelain.

The nineteenth century was also a period when gender roles became more sharply distinguished. China was now relatively inexpensive and its modest price and association with domestic activity brought it into the domain of women. The ceramics that normally appear on nineteenth-century dressers include blue and white plates, copper lustre jugs and Staffordshire dogs. Already much of this was show material, not functional. The collecting of tea-sets became increasingly important towards the end of the century and has continued to be significant up to the present day. Collecting china is not, of course, exclusive to Welsh women, but precisely because of their relative poverty in relation to other parts of Britain, along with the Nonconformist mentality which distrusted visual display, the collecting of relatively cheap and 'apparently' functional objects could offer an acceptable outlet for the need to demonstrate industrious femininity and conspicuous consumption. A well-polished dresser with rows of gleaming jugs signified domestic well-being and the prowess of the woman who maintained it.

There is further evidence for a particular conjunction of Welsh women and china. Around the beginning of the century representations of Welsh women often associated them with china, usually in the form of a tea-party in which ladies in tall hats sit by a table set with cups and saucers and sometimes a teapot. This image seems to have emerged in the last decades of the nineteenth century and can be seen in photographs, prints and decorations on tea-sets, mugs, and glassware. It was a popular stereotype but it could hardly be said to have reflected any lived reality. It is an image that emulates paintings and photographs of the leisured classes picnicking or taking tea in the garden. The Welsh costume is intended to represent the clothes of peasants or ordinary (rural) people but the activity was associated with people of a higher class. The 'Welsh Tea-party' is an image of tamed and gentrified Welshness (Jenkins 1992, 13). The need to prove the respectability of Welsh women was a burning issue in the mid-nineteenth century after the publication of the Education Report of 1847 (the 'Blue Books') which had accused the Welsh of immorality, singling out particularly the social practice of 'bundling' (courtship on beds at night). It was, of course, the women who were accused of being 'unchaste' and this was seen as especially dangerous because of their role as mothers of the next generation (John 1991, 70). The image of women drinking tea could also be read as one that reinforced the Temperance ideals that held such sway in Nonconformist culture in the latter part of the century, particularly among women. The image presents women drinking tea usually in the open air, at the cottage door, and might be contrasted with male beer drinking in the dark interior of the public house. In the image of the 'Welsh tea-party' china cups become symbols of dutiful femininity alongside other supposed female accoutrements such as spinning wheels, or knitting. Cultural symbols may be based on stereotypes but they have an important social function. In the conjunction of ideas around women, dressers and china there appears to be a continuing potential to generate social meanings which can be explored through the use of contemporary oral evidence.

In the eighteenth and nineteenth century most dressers were probably commissioned around the time of a marriage by one or other set of parents or by the groom himself. Along with the *cwpwrdd deuddarn* or *tridarn* (two-part or three-part cupboards), which might also be acquired at the same time, they were the most significant pieces of furniture in the house. Thereafter, in rural communities, the dresser was often seen as part of the house: hence the person (usually the son) who inherited the farm would also keep the dresser.

But the dresser could represent a more specific marker of status than the house itself. One interviewee recalled, for example, that when her family built a new farmhouse in the 1960s they moved into the new house with the furniture, including the dresser. But when the son of the family grew up, married, and took the lead in the farm, the young couple took over the new house and the parents moved back into the old house. The dresser, however, was left in the new house because it was now seen as the main family settlement. The dresser, then, could be read as an affirmation of the status of the son's position as he began to take the lead in the family farm.

Yet its particular significance for women may not have been affected by such ownership rights. Recently, at any rate, when I was introduced to one couple where the wife collected china enthusiastically, her husband made it clear that the dresser was not hers but his, as it was inherited along with the farm through his family. But when his wife was asked how she related to the dresser that she had inherited on moving into her husband's home when they married, her husband responded first with: 'She took it over immediately.' She replied:

> I dust it once a month and take the plates down and I just cross my fingers and hope I don't break one. I haven't done yet.

This seems to suggest that the dresser and, in this case, the things on it are clearly situated in the female domain, although the female role may be largely custodial, caring for it on behalf of future generations.

Since dressers are very large pieces of furniture, understandably they often remain in the houses for which they were first made, or are only moved to the branch of the family living nearest. The objects on the dresser are sometimes seen as inseparable from it, but usually these become more associated with the women of each generation who acquire new pieces. This, then, allows for redistributions of plates, jugs and tea-sets when daughters marry, when someone dies, or as small gifts for favourite grandchildren. Two interviewees had very vivid memories of having first become interested in collecting china when their grandmothers had given them little pieces from their dressers.

In another case an English woman, who had always been a passionate collector of china, recounted how she had decided to buy a dresser as soon as she moved to live in west Wales. The acquisition of a dresser seemed to be a symbol of her adoption of a new environment/country, a place where her past and her present could be brought together in a harmonious relationship:

> We didn't have much money but we were determined to have a dresser when we came. Although we could only afford one new piece of furniture. I don't want it to sound all yuppieish, 'We had to have a dresser'. But because . . . I have moved a lot in my life . . . little bits that I pick up have got to be in the house wherever I go. I suppose my dresser is a bit like an altar.

The latter part of that statement is a testament to the power of objects to give pleasure, to comfort and to soothe. Many collectors of china would recognize that sentiment.

The care and cleaning of the dresser is almost always a female activity, but it is often talked about as a pleasurable activity rather than a household chore. In this example, the activity itself is one which links the present with the past:

> Often when I polish I wonder how they felt. I wonder what kind of life they had doing this . . . I expect Aunt Sarah used to do it every time she visited the cottage and her mother polished it before that. It gives me pleasure because it is a link with my aunt Sarah who was such a lovely person . . . and so kind to me.

Another older woman remembered how as a girl one of her household tasks was to wash and polish the dresser every Friday night. In her case it was a chore, perhaps even seen as part of her education in domestic management. Most people did not seem to handle the objects on the dresser as often as that, but the times when they took everything down and washed them and put them back, were noted as 'big' jobs, carried out as part of spring cleaning or before Christmas.

During times when the storage in the house was quite limited, dressers were wonderful pieces of furniture for storing small or important items. One interviewee recalled how 'the needle for stitching the sacks was always in the second jug on the left'. Important papers, insurance policies, bank savings books, birth certificates were often kept in one of the dresser drawers, and keys could be hung on its hooks. Obviously many people kept cutlery and table linen in the drawers but it was very common for different members of the family to have different drawers for their own special things. In that sense men too certainly used the dresser as storage.

Some of the people I interviewed had very clear notions of how to decorate the dresser at Christmas time while others held it was absolutely inappropriate to decorate the dresser. Similar distinguishing notions of what is or is not appropriate on a dresser were very specific. For example, two of my interviewees talked in a disapproving manner about the way their daughters-in-law kept their dressers. One claimed that her daughter-in-law's jugs were too spaced out, and seemed to attribute this to an Anglicized south-Walian lack of knowledge of the 'proper' tradition: 'she doesn't really understand – she's from south Wales, you see'.

Another area where interviewees were divided was on whether it was appropriate to put photographs on dressers. Most people did, but some felt it was quite wrong. This difference appeared to rest on whether the dresser was seen as an historical object which had to be preserved in some kind of 'authentic' form, or whether it could be adapted for present-day needs. Assumptions were frequently made that I would espouse the former position; they would say to me, for example, 'Oh well, that shouldn't be there, of course', lifting off the telephone, or a trinket brought to them by a grandchild. Or they would point out items apologetically, saying, 'that's just modern'. It is as if the owners had a set of rules in their head about how a dresser should look, but they rarely adhered to them. The dresser and its display is a visual language or communication; parallel to a spoken language, it constantly evolves against a basic structure.

Things on the dresser act as a repository of family history, as objects which can carry people through time. In this story, even in its very telling, there is the ring of an oft-repeated tale:

> My great-grandmother, when she was a little girl – under fifteen – her mother's sister lived in Ireland and she was taken ill there and the doctor said she must go home to her native air. As she had a household of children my great-grandmother as a girl had to go over to look after the children to let the mother come home. To get over to Ireland, her father had to walk with her from Fishguard to Milford Haven, about twenty-five miles, to get the ship over to Ireland, and one of the sailors on the ship gave her that cow creamer jug. So she kept it, brought it back and it is still here. She was born in the early 1800s, and was ninety-six when she died in 1911. So that cow is at the latest 1830. She was the first person who had the dresser.

The concept of 'sentimental value' is clearly applicable to many objects that find their way on to dressers. In some cases these may then also acquire other values more 'real', as antiques and objects of financial value. In reassessing these different kinds of values and their respective status it is important to bear in mind that the financial value of antiques and works of art is no more real than the value of a share and as likely to fluctuate. In a capitalist world a high financial value will inevitably be transmuted into a sign of ultimate or universal value (Buck and Dodd 1991). If it is recognized that all values are constructed in some social and historical context then the personal, even the sentimental, are just as valid as the financial. Objects on the dresser are often valued because of the personal memories that they embody:

> This little lustre jug I bought in a jumble sale and gave it to my mother when I was fifteen or sixteen. It was broken but it went with everything on the dresser. It was only about sixpence.

Of course one of the great pleasures of collecting is the knowledge that things have increased in value. The excitement of the chase, finding a bargain or buying in advance of the market is an important part of collecting. There are gendered aspects to this activity: men are more likely to be involved in collecting ceramics that have financial values and the higher the value the more marked the gender division (Vincentelli 1992, 14). Men still command more personal expendable income. However, the adrenalin flow of the auction sale can be experienced at any level, as expressed by this female collector as she described her china:

> Well, they were all bought at local sales. I can remember the delight of taking home these wonderful transfer jugs . . . That second one is a Llanelly seaweed pattern and that one at the end. I remember the delight of taking it home.

Knowledge is power. There is ample evidence to suggest that the kind of people who collect china are privy to an area of specialized knowledge. They can recognize an old jug, or a Llanelly pattern, or a good quality piece of gilding. In discussion with a group of old people, most had memories about dressers and china display and readily expressed their views, but it was apparent that certain members of the group felt they had more specialized knowledge, which they expressed with authority and which gave them a certain status, at that moment at least, among their peers.

A young woman in her twenties who came from a family with a strong sense of Welsh identity was very self-conscious when she decided to buy an old pine dresser. At the same time she was determined that it should be a functional piece of furniture and not an object of mere domestic display:

> I was wondering what my mother and father would say about it really because it is used – that is the crockery we use. It's not displayed . . . This is totally practical.

She expected her parents, as she put it, to 'think it was sacrilege' and was pleasantly surprised when they accepted it. She then went on to note her own surprise at how much she was influenced by her own family tradition:

> The way I have the dishes on the dresser is reminiscent of how my mother has them, you know, the two saucers with two cups in each other – that's exactly how my mother has the cups and plates . . .
> The interesting thing is I take great pleasure in putting the dishes on the dresser again. Moving them around is big part of it, really . . .

Pleasure is an important factor, whether in the visual appeal of the display or, as in this case, in the actual handling of china and the pleasure of arranging and rearranging. The interviewee was using this piece of furniture, and the rituals associated with it, both as a way of expressing her own identity and separation from her family and as a way of maintaining her links with it.

To conclude, domestic display in the form of the dresser and the objects put on it has been a vehicle around which cultural meanings have formed, a process particularly important in Wales because the dresser's history and development have coincided with moments when there has been a need to affirm Welsh identity. Its potential as a functional object was quickly overlaid by its symbolic value and, although Welsh dressers have long been classified as antiques, that does not exclude them from playing an active role within their contemporary social setting. From the interviews conducted I would suggest that their symbolic potential is still capable of development, and available as a site of new meanings. In general, it seems that the domestic associations of this piece of furniture, of food preparation and consumption, have meant that these meanings have largely been the prerogative of women though not exclusively so. Welsh dressers and their panoply of displayed objects deserve to be recognized as a form of popular art central to any concept of Welsh visual culture and tradition.

References

Appadurai, A. (ed.) (1986). *The Social Life of Things, Commodities in Cultural Perspective* (Cambridge, Cambridge University Press).

Attfield, J. and Kirkham, P. (1989). *View from the Interior: Feminism, Women and Design* (London, Women's Press).

Buck, L. and Dodd, P. (1991). *Relative Values* (London, BBC Publications).

Bourdieu, P. (1979). *Distinction: a Social Critique of the Judgement of Taste* (Paris, London, Routledge & Kegan Paul, 1986 ed.).

Cooper, E. (1992). *Bringing it all Back Home* (Aberystwyth, Arts Centre exhibition catalogue).

Courtney-Clarke, M. (1990). *African Canvas: The Art of West African Women* (New York, Rizzoli).

Davies, A. (1992). *The Welsh Dresser* (Cardiff, University of Wales Press).

Hobsbaum, E. J. and Ranger, T. (1983). *The Invention of Tradition* (Cambridge, Cambridge University Press).

Forty, A. (1987). *Objects of Desire: Design and Society 1750–1980* (London, Thames and Hudson).

Glassie, H. (1982). *Passing the Time in Ballymenone: Folklore and History of an Ulster Community* (Dublin, O'Brien Press).

Jenkins, J. G. (1992). *Getting Yesterday Right: Interpreting the Heritage of Wales* (Cardiff, University of Wales Press).

John, A. (ed.) (1992). *Our Mothers' Land: Chapters in Welsh Women's History 1830–1939* (Cardiff, University of Wales Press).

Jones, C. M. (1992). 'A Study of the Cultural, Social and Economic Significance of the Welsh Dresser since the Middle Ages', BA dissertation, University of Wales, Aberystwyth.

Lord, P. (1992). *The Aesthetics of Relevance* (Llandysul, Gomer Press).

Newton, C. and Putnam, T. (1990). *Household Choices* (London: Futures Publications).

Miller, D. (1987). *Material Culture and Mass Consumption* (Oxford, Blackwell).

Parker, R. and Pollock, G. (1981). *Old Mistresses: Women, Art and Ideology* (London, Routledge & Kegan Paul).

Roberts, K. (1937). *Ffair Gaeaf a Storiau Eraill* (Dinbych: Gwasg Gee).

Roberts, K. (1946). *A Summer Day and Other Stories* (trans. by various hands) (Cardiff, Penmark Press).

Vincentelli, M. (1992). *Talking Pots: Ceramics in Wales* (Aberystwyth, Arts Centre exhibition catalogue).

14

Women, nationalism and feminism

CHARLOTTE AULL DAVIES

Women have historically had a dual role in their relationship with nationalist movements, as political activists and as nurturers of the nation. Women contribute to nationalist politics through their participation in the organizations and activities that constitute individual movements. And they have also been seen as crucial for the reproduction of the nation, both materially, by giving birth to the next generation of nationalists, and ideologically, by transmitting to them those cultural understandings central to the maintenance of their national identity. These two roles are not necessarily complementary and indeed may be seen as conflicting. The comment – variously attributed to the Irish nationalist Patrick Pearse and to American civil rights activist and black nationalist Stokeley Carmichael (and doubtless to others) – that the only position for women in their movements was prone is a crude illustration of precisely this point.

Both of these roles have been in evidence in the relationship between women and nationalism in Wales in the twentieth century, and in this chapter I will examine each of them and the ways in which they have interacted. In so doing, it is important to note that women's experience in the nationalist movement has not been a unitary one but rather has varied according to their class, age, family circumstances, and linguistic background.

A recent review of the volume on Welsh women's history, *Our Mothers' Land*, regrets 'the lack of research into women and Welshness, nationalism, and identity' (Edwards 1992, 14), and the editor of that volume also notes that 'the historical relationship between women and nationalism in Wales is a subject which would merit research by feminist historians' (John 1991, 11). Clearly, a short chapter of this nature cannot fill this gap. What it can do is to look at what is known about women and nationalism in Wales from available studies of the history of the nationalist movement. In preparing the chapter, I have also drawn on unpublished materials from my own research on contemporary Welsh nationalism (Davies 1989), which I began in the mid-1970s, and have undertaken some additional interviewing among women activists in Plaid Cymru (the party of Wales, until 1945 called the Welsh Nationalist Party).

Founding mothers

Interviewed in 1976, Gwynfor Evans, then Welsh nationalist MP for Carmarthen and president of Plaid Cymru since 1945, said that women had not taken a leading role in the party. He could point to only one woman parliamentary candidate for Plaid Cymru, out of the 36 Welsh seats contested in the 1974 General Election, but noted that the newly appointed party organizer for Anglesey was a woman. Nevertheless, although not highly visible in either the official (Williams 1990) or 'folk' versions of party history, a number of women did play important parts as founding mothers of the Welsh Nationalist Party in the 1920s and 1930s.

Mai Roberts, who was private secretary to the Liberal nationalist MP E. T. John, was a prime mover in arranging the 1925 meeting between the two nationalist groups whose merger created the Welsh Nationalist Party. The first of these, the Home Rule Army, was based in Roberts's home area around Caernarfon. She learned of a group with similar aims in south Wales from one of its members (Ambrose Bebb) whom she met while attending a conference in Paris with John. Saunders Lewis, the prime mover behind this second group, Y Mudiad Cymreig, intended it to remain a secret movement, but Roberts nevertheless helped H. R. Jones of the north Wales movement to make contact with them. At a meeting in Pwllheli in 1925, representatives of the two movements created the Welsh Nationalist Party (later simply called Plaid Cymru) which was to become the political nucleus of the nationalist movement in Wales. The six men who attended that meeting are regarded as the founders of Plaid Cymru. Yet in a 1976 interview Prissy Roberts maintained that her sister Mai should have been among them, having arrived just as the meeting was breaking up, due to a delay *en route*; in spite of missing this opportunity to be numbered officially among the party's founders, she took pride in the fact that she was the first to pay her membership fee and was subsequently quite active in the party.

Kate Roberts, the novelist, has been named, along with four men, in the comprehensive history of the Welsh Nationalist Party's first two decades, as forming 'a body of socialist support' attracted to the new party in the 1920s (Davies 1983, 99). Far from being among its founders, she initially expressed great scepticism about the party's purpose:

> I really cannot see myself any nearer to joining the Blaid after reading it [the first issue of the party newspaper, *Y Ddraig Goch*]. I can see Mr Saunders Lewis's point of view as I love literature, but as I am a Socialist I really cannot reconcile myself with his ideas. Personally I see no difference between doffing one's cap to an English merchant and doffing one's cap to our old Welsh princes.
>
> (quoted in Davies 1983, 124).

However, she joined shortly thereafter and was a leading figure in one of the party's most effective and politicized branches – at Tonypandy in the Rhondda Fawr – through the 1930s. She was reported in 1931 as resisting the introduction of English into party literature; again in 1936 she was writing in *Y Ddraig Goch* to chastise members for their unwillingness to contest elections. Indeed the party had managed to put forward candidates in only two electoral campaigns in that year, but of these two one was led by yet another woman, Cathrin Huws, then a student in Cardiff. That her political activities were valued by the party is attested by the fact that she had been contacted in 1934 by J. E. Jones, the national secretary, for advice on canvassing methods.

Finally, Lady Mallt Williams, who had been active prior to the establishment of the Welsh Nationalist Party in promoting various efforts on behalf of the Welsh language, provided essential financial support for the new movement. Her gifts of £100 on several occasions in the 1920s and 1930s literally kept the party in existence.

These four do not exhaust the list of women who made significant contributions to Plaid Cymru in its first two decades. Nevertheless, their stories suggest a few general points about women in the party in that period. In the first place, their contributions were highly individualistic. They were not involved in the Nationalist Party primarily as women, nor did they share a common outlook. Differences in attitudes about the party's basic goals have already been mentioned. And there were women who were prominent on both sides of the debate in the 1930s about the use of English in the party, with Noëlle Davies (the Irish wife of party activist D. J. Davies) campaigning to increase its use, and Kate Roberts resisting its introduction into party publications. Although a Women's Section (with Kate Roberts as Chair and Mai Roberts as Secretary) was established as part of the party organization in its Inaugural Summer School in 1926, it 'never became a prominent feature of party organisation' (Davies 1983, 70). It did not develop a coherent position on women's issues nor was it a focus for the activity of those women who were prominent in the party. The fact that these women were all middle-class, well-educated and (with the exception of Noëlle Davies) Welsh-speaking tells us that they were collectively of similar composition to the men who made up the party in its early days. Additionally, they tended to be women who had a career or some independent means of support. Most were unmarried; those who married and remained active in the party did not have children. Several of them, in particular Kate Roberts, Mai Roberts and Cassie Davies (a lecturer at Barry College), were on the Pwyllgor Gwaith, the party's central executive committee, during this period. However, their experience did not match that of rank-and-file women. According to Prissy Roberts, the role of the majority of women in the party, and certainly the main purpose of the Women's Section, was organizing fund-raising activities like jumble sales and coffee mornings. It is difficult to say how many women members the party had during this period. Photographic evidence (Davies 1983, 65, 191) suggests that the proportion of women members considerably exceeded their representation among the leadership. A formal photograph of those in attendance at the Inaugural Summer School held in Machynlleth in 1926 showed 26 per cent women of the fifty-three adults in the picture. By the 1932 Summer School this had risen to 57 per cent, of a total of fifty-eight present, although the fact that this photograph was taken during a social outing probably increased the number of women present.

A woman's place

The Women's Section seems to have disappeared, along with most of the party's local organization, during the difficult years of the Second World War. Several women whom I interviewed in 1976 and 1977 recalled it as dating from the mid-1940s when the party began to experience a revival and growth in its membership. The late 1940s and 1950s apparently saw women's committees established in association with most of the local branches of the party. In this period these committees, as well as the central Women's Section, appeared to be even more focused on supportive activities than formerly. The local women's committees were primarily intended to serve as fund-raising groups. The Women's Section was reported as helping at the Annual Conventions, not actually organizing them, but taking charge of auxiliary services. The women I interviewed who were active in the Women's Section in the mid-1970s explicitly denied that the Women's Section was in any way influenced by the women's movement. Phyllis Ellis, then the only woman on the Pwyllgor Gwaith, described their activities as follows:

> [T]he women's committees are mostly concerned with social and financial matters – raising money for the movement and helping at local level, e.g., voluntary work such as Citizen Advice, hospital work and helping the elderly.
> We have an annual rally with discussions on topical problems. Last year we dealt with local government. Other subjects have been the Common Market, the penal system and the legal system with especial emphasis on women's problems.
> We are keenly interested in women's role in the community and in helping them to secure their rights but have never been connected in any way with the 'Women's Movement'.
>
> [personal communication, 13 April 1977]

Most of the relatively few women who were active in mainstream political pursuits within Plaid Cymru tended to be very critical of the Women's Section, one describing it as an irrelevance which attempted to confine women to their own separate, poorly defined sphere and to prevent them taking part in the running of the party.

There appear to have been fewer women who attained any sort of prominence in the party in the decades of the fifties and sixties than there had been in the era before the Second World War, a fact that was drawn to my attention by Olwen Jones, the wife of J. E. Jones, the party's General Secretary from 1930 to 1962. Certainly, women were not at all in evidence in the Plaid Cymru Annual Conference in 1976. There were no women on the platform during working sessions; during the formal session, two women appeared on the platform, one of whom, Nans Jones, was being recognized on her retirement as secretary in the national office. No more than half-a-dozen women spoke at the Conference and women's issues were not on the agenda.

The women's movement and Plaid Cymru

On the other hand, there were clear indications that some women in the party were beginning to reject the helpmate role that had hitherto characterized the activities of the Women's Section and of most individual women within the party. Of the handful of women who did speak at the 1976 Conference, the two who were most visible were both from urban areas in south-east Wales. One of the two, Phyllis Cox, spoke in favour of an amendment calling for a reorganization of the party's decision-making apparatus and pointed out that the national executive had been guilty of ignoring the wishes of the Conference of the previous year in not acting on a motion to look at the problem of women within the party structure.

The first straightforwardly feminist motion to reach the Conference came in 1978 when the party adopted a stance in favour of women's rights. Of more immediate significance to women trying to assume more active roles in party politics was a motion calling for the provision of a crèche at party meetings and annual conferences. After the 1979 defeat in a referendum of the Labour Party's proposals for a Welsh Assembly, followed by a poor showing by Plaid Cymru in the subsequent general election, the party was in considerable disarray. However, these experiences did leave it rather more open to new ideas and a possible change of direction. One of the consequences was a more explicit socialist commitment than had ever been made before. A second was increased pressure from women to be given more power within the party organization.

This pressure resulted, in 1981, in yet another general motion expressing good intentions regarding the position of women in society, saying that Plaid Cymru supported equal status for women in education, work and family reponsibilities. However, the same conference passed a constitutional amendment that provided that the Women's Section be allowed five representatives to the Pwyllgor Gwaith (instead of the single representative given to all other special sections) for a period of five years, in order to encourage more women to become active in the party. Working from this greatly strengthened position, first the Women's Section and then the Pwyllgor Gwaith, in the 1982 and 1983 Conferences, proposed constitutional amendments to force equal representation for women on both the Pwyllgor Gwaith and the National Council. These motions met with rather more resistance, and, although both times they received majority support, they did not have the two-thirds majority required for constitutional changes. By 1984, women had abandoned this approach and concentrated on introducing motions on issues of particular concern to women, such as one concerned with women as carers. In the 1985 Conference one more unsuccessful attempt was made to secure positive discrimination for women. But in 1986, upon completion of the five-year trial period of extra representation for the Women's Section, the party decided that this form of positive action for women had served its purpose and the Section returned to a single representative. There were by then three women officers on the Pwyllgor Gwaith, along with five other women representatives from the Women's Section, which meant that women made up one third of its members, the largest proportion before or since.

During this period, from 1976 to 1982 approximately, the Women's Section itself had been transformed. One woman interviewed a decade later reported it as having become defunct in the late 1970s and then been reformed. In any case, it consciously rejected the role it had previously filled as fund-raiser and provider of various support services (such as catering, making banners and providing clerical assistance) and assumed the responsibility of representing women's interests, both within the party by facilitating more women's participation in mainstream political activities and in society in general by raising issues of particular concern to women. This transformation involved a change of personnel in the Women's Section. Following the retirement in 1976 of Nans Jones, who as secretary in the national office had been responsible for the Women's Section and had tended to maintain its traditional orientation, women from urban south-east Wales began to gain control of the Section. These women were influenced by the women's movement which, as a movement essentially of urban, middle-class and well-educated women, had arrived earlier and had a greater impact in the south-east than in most other parts of Wales. This change in the nature of the Women's Section was symbolized by the gradual shift in its Welsh title from Adran y Merched to Adran y Menywod. One meaning of *merched* is 'daughters' and it carries the connotation 'girls', whereas *menywod* means, unambiguously, 'women', and has been used consistently by Welsh Women's Aid (Cymorth i Fenywod). As these new women gained control of the Women's Section they began also to alter its activities. Instead of an Annual Meeting in which women came together to listen to an address by 'the great man', they held training sessions to teach women political skills, especially public speaking. In order to increase women's active participation in the party, they arranged pre-conference meetings at which individual women were chosen to speak on selected issues at the Annual Conference.

The period 1981–6 of extra representation for women on the Pwyllgor Gwaith appears to be unique in Plaid history as the only time when some women chose to become active in Plaid Cymru primarily as feminists rather than as nationalists. Helen Jones, active in the Women's Section and Gwent Talaith representative to the Pwyllgor Gwaith in 1992, explained that 'for a short time in the mid-1980s Plaid Cymru was perceived as being more woman-friendly than the Labour Party'. Another long-term member of the Women's Section criticized these women for coming on the Pwyllgor Gwaith knowing almost nothing about Plaid Cymru or about nationalism and argued that the extra representation for women had been counter-productive as a result.

Indeed few women whose nationalism was in any sense secondary to their feminism remained very active within Plaid Cymru through the 1980s. A few of the women activists in the party in the early 1990s had initially been attracted to the party through involvement in more stereotypically women's concerns, in particular the peace movement, or were primarily involved with such issues as domestic violence and were active in Women's Aid. Most, however, had become nationalists before they were feminists and had subsequently tried to bring feminist concerns into the party.

They either viewed their nationalism as of greater importance to them than their feminism or refused to choose between the two.

Nevertheless, the legacy of this period of high feminist activity remained in evidence in several respects. In the first place, women's representation in the party hierarchy, while not as high as during the five years of positive discrimination, was significantly improved, with six women, 24 per cent of members, on the Pwyllgor Gwaith in 1992. And women's representation continued to be an issue; for example, 1991 revisions to the constitution required that there be at least one woman on the shortlist for any contested internal party post, although some women activists criticized this measure as tokenism. In the 1992 General Election, there were seven women nationalist candidates and the party was careful to ensure high visibility for women during the campaign by having at least one woman candidate present at national press conferences. On the other hand, both constituencies regarded as winnable (Carmarthen and Ceredigion and North Penfro) were contested by men; and the only time the party has put forward a woman as candidate in a by-election was when Janet Davies stood in Brecon and Radnor in 1985, without the wholehearted support of many in her own party who felt they should not have contested such a hopeless election. Furthermore, women who have attained positions of leadership, both in Plaid Cymru and through electoral success, continued to maintain that, although more women do speak at conference, they are not normally called for the 'glamour issues' when the media, especially television, are present.

Leaders of the Women's Section also argued that equal representation for women should have become a priority for the party organization as a whole and not simply the responsibility of the Section. One reason for their concern in this respect was that many of them had been brought into the party leadership structure and as a result had found they did not have time to act as watchdog to ensure that women were represented in every context. While their new responsibilities were to some degree a reflection of the success of their previous campaign, there did not appear to be adequate numbers of politicized women to maintain the pressure for equality. In fact, the takeover of the leadership of the Women's Section by women with strong feminist concerns in the 1980s had not healed the split among women in the party so much as relocated it. In the late 1970s, Plaid Cymru contained a group of women political activists who felt disaffected from a Women's Section which was limited to a supportive role in party activities. In the 1980s, as the Women's Section, under new leadership, took on board a feminist perspective and began to put forward political initiatives, it unintentionally distanced itself from large numbers of women members of Plaid Cymru. The annual meetings of the new Women's Section were not as well attended as had been those of the previous decade. Some of the leaders of the section felt that many women nationalists regarded feminism as something foreign, English or American, and destructive of the ideals of Welsh nationalism, an outlook common to most nationalist ideologies and one to which I shall return shortly.

Women, nationalism and nationalist ideology

The position of women in the Welsh nationalist movement, as represented by the Welsh Nationalist Party, has in its broad outline followed the trends of women's social position in the societies of western Europe and north America in the twentieth century. As such, it is not surprising that it is broadly similar to the history of women's involvement in other British political parties, in particular the Labour Party. In the decades between the two world wars, having achieved formal political equality through enfranchisement, individual women were able to attain access to new spheres of endeavour, party politics being one of these, and to enjoy considerable influence, and some power, in these areas. They were probably assisted in these ambitions by the demographic fact that large numbers of young men of their generation had been killed in the First World War. Nevertheless, these new opportunities were primarily open only to women of broadly middle-class background, and the women who took advantage of them usually found it necessary to restrict their life-style in other respects, specifically marriage and children.

In the two decades following the Second World War, the roles of housewife and mother were strongly projected as cultural ideals for women. At the same time, increasing numbers of women were entering paid employment, although they were concentrated in poorly paid service-sector jobs and part-time work. In a parallel process, in Plaid Cymru, even fewer women attained any degree of prominence during this period than in the pre-war years, and the party's Women's Section fulfilled a stereotypically female role by providing supportive services for the political party dominated by men and by masculine concerns. The late 1960s also saw the creation of a new women's organization Merched y Wawr, a Welsh version of the Women's Institute. The linguistic nationalism of this highly successful organisation doubtless absorbed the political energies of many women in this period, particularly those from Welsh-speaking areas.

However, by the mid-1970s, as described earlier in this chapter, the women's movement began to affect the attitudes and expectations of some women in the nationalist movement, and a split developed between women who accepted the traditional role played by the women's committees as well as by the national Women's Section and those who resisted this marginalizing of women within the party. This latter group was concentrated in the urban industrial areas of south-east Wales where the women's movement was strongest. In the early 1980s they took control of the Women's Section and transformed it into a political unit which worked to secure equal rights for women within Plaid Cymru. A few of the women involved in this transformation were primarily pursuing feminist goals within a nationalist context. However, most of the women who remained active in Plaid Cymru beyond the period of positive discrimination in favour of the Women's Section placed their nationalism on a par with, or ahead of, their feminism.

Thus, the question of the relationship between feminism and nationalism has not received much attention or stimulated debate in the same way as did that of the relationship between socialism and nationalism, particularly in the early 1980s. Even so, at the beginning of the 1990s, with the prospect for a Welsh parliament more promising than it had been for over a decade, some women in Plaid Cymru were beginning to argue that such a body must not be a replica of Westminster. If women were to be treated fairly under the new constitutional arrangements then changes such as flexibility of working hours, provision of childcare and an end to the confrontational style of debate would be necessary. The question then naturally arises as to whether women nationalists should give first priority to securing a Welsh parliament unless such a body incorporated changes that would make it equally accessible and responsible to women and men.

Most nationalist ideologies have responded to such dilemmas by maintaining that their principal aim is to win freedom for the 'nation'. Other inequalities will be readily resolved within the context of native national institutions once national liberation is secured. Indeed, inequalities within the nation are often attributed to the presence of an external oppressor in national life. One study of women and Irish nationalism noted just such a position in Republican idealization of the egalitarian traditions of Gaelic Ireland:

> If the subjection of Irish women was directly related to the foreign conquest of Ireland, then Irishmen, who had also suffered from foreign domination, could not be blamed for what had occurred over the intervening centuries. As they were fighting for freedom, in some unexpressed manner it was always assumed that they must also be fighting for the freedom of women. In Republican mythology, Irish men used to be non-oppressive and this dubious proposition somehow becomes transmuted into an assurance that they will automatically become so again – as soon as the contaminating effects of 'foreign influence' are removed.
>
> (Ward 1983, 254–5)

In the Welsh version of this proposition, much is made of the fairer treatment of women under the medieval laws of Hywel Dda, with the underlying assumption that this is somehow relevant for women's oppression in a twentieth-century post-industrial society.

Another aspect of the relationship between feminism and nationalism derives from the stress placed by most nationalist ideologies on women's responsibility for the material and cultural reproduction of the nation. Clearly, by insisting on a more active participation in the political nationalist movement, women are rejecting the notion that their primary purpose and utility to the nation is in reproduction. Bearing children for the cause may be more salient in nationalist movements involved in armed struggles (see, for example, Yuval-Davis 1989; Afshar 1989), but it is not without its advocates in other contexts. For example, a mid-1970s study of the Welsh language and its prospects noted, 'The Welsh reservoir is small, and in areas where Welsh speakers are half or less of the population, only a birth rate far in excess of that of English speakers could tilt the balance back' (Betts 1976, 27–8).

When a separate language is a prominent feature of the identity of a national group, the role of women as reproducers of the cultural heritage is also likely to receive considerable attention, given the close connection between language and the rearing of young children primarily by women. Indeed, in the language movement, material and cultural reproduction often seem to merge. In this chapter I have been concerned principally with the political nationalist movement. However, I should note that young women played an important part in the campaigns of Cymdeithas yr Iaith Gymraeg (the Welsh Language Society) from the 1960s onwards. They represented a large proportion of activists and many went to prison for their beliefs. At the same time, it was assumed that their careers as language activists would naturally culminate in a marriage that would produce several Welsh-speaking children. One of Welsh folk-singer Dafydd Iwan's ballads of the mid-1970s, 'Baled yr Hogan Eithafol' ('The Ballad of the Girl Extremist'), relates one young woman's exploits for the Welsh language – painting signs, climbing television masts, occupying holiday homes – then, in the final verse, describes how she marries, has three or four children and disappears from the struggle, although she would remain a rebel all her life. Given this presumed career structure for women, it is not surprising that Cymdeithas yr Iaith did not have a woman as chair through the 1960s and 1970s. During the 1980s, several women were elected chair, a development that appears to be related to the less restricted career expectations of educated women influenced by the women's movement.

The second major arena of the Welsh language movement, that of campaigns for Welsh-medium schools, has allowed for rather different experiences for some women who managed to invert the process whereby women were consigned to concentrate on childcare in order to ensure the survival of their national language. These women, non-Welsh-speaking themselves, wanted to ensure that their children acquired fluency in the language. Clearly they could not secure this end by confining their activities to childcare and the domestic sphere. Instead they had to become involved in the public realm in the campaign for Welsh-medium education. And many women, particularly from south-east Wales, managed to build an active public career on such campaigning.

Thus, in summary, while nationalist ideologies are not normally encouraging of women's active involvement in national movements, nationalist organizations may be rather more accessible to feminist ideas and campaigns. As the women's movement raised the expectations of many women and increased general awareness of the issue of women's participation in public life, women Welsh nationalists (both political and linguistic) transformed their roles within individual organizations and movements. While relatively few have addressed the tensions at the level of ideology between their identities as nationalists and as feminists, most have succeeded in resolving such tensions (if perhaps temporarily and *ad hoc*) at the level of practical political activity.

References

Afshar, Haleh (1989). 'Women and reproduction in Iran', in N. Yuval-Davis and F. Anthias (eds.), *Woman-Nation-State* (London, Macmillan), 110–25.

Betts, C. (1976). *Culture in Crisis: The Future of the Welsh Language* (Wirral, Merseyside, The Ffynnon Press).

Davies, C. A. (1989). *Welsh Nationalism in the Twentieth Century: The Ethnic Option and the Modern State* (New York, Praeger).

Davies, D. H. (1983). *The Welsh Nationalist Party 1925–1945: A Call to Nationhood* (Cardiff, University of Wales Press).

Edwards, S. (1991–2). 'Land of our mothers', *The New Welsh Review* Vol. 4, No. 3, 11–14.

John, Angela V. (1991). 'Introduction', in A. V. John (ed.), *Our Mothers' Land: Chapters in Welsh Women's History 1830–1939* (Cardiff, University of Wales Press), 1–16.

Ward, M. (1983). *Unmanageable Revolutionaries: Women and Irish Nationalism* (London, Pluto Press).

Williams, D. (1990). *The Story of Plaid Cymru: The Party of Wales* (Aberystwyth, Plaid Cymru).

Yuval-Davis, Nira (1989). 'National reproduction and "the demographic race" in Israel', in N. Yuval-Davis and F. Anthias (eds.), *Woman-Nation-State* (London, Macmillan), 92–109.

IV. Personal Voices: The Politics of Identity

15

A Welsh lady

ANGHARAD TOMOS

The police grabbed our arms and shouted, 'Slags', 'Lesbians'. We were pushed into a police van and taken to the nearest police station. 'One male, four females,' shouted the constable. His colleague frowned: four females? That meant an extra cell. It meant calling a WPC out. Not only were they Welsh language freaks, they were women as well. Why did they have to be women? Crime is a man's world. Having four female burglars the same night was unusual.

Two of us were put into one cell and two in the other. Huw was put in a cell at the far end. We were awakened for questioning, then for having our photographs taken, and then for formal interviews. Before being released, fingerprints had to be taken. By three o'clock the following day, a warm comradeship had been formed between us. You can't fail to be drawn to one another when sharing the same cell for twelve hours or more.

It is these kind of circumstances that bring members of Cymdeithas yr Iaith together. We're only actually segregated by our sex when it comes to police cells and prisons. Otherwise, we are inseparable. When someone actually asks me specifically about the role of women in Cymdeithas yr Iaith, I've got to sit back and think 'Which are the women?' because they don't stand out as a separate or a peripheral group in Cymdeithas. They *are* the group. Take the women from Cymdeithas, and it wouldn't be the same movement at all. That's why, come to think of it, we've never had a 'women's section' in Cymdeithas. Because if we did form such a group, what would you call the rest?

Being brought up in a family of five sisters and no brothers is good training ground, I suppose, for learning that there's nothing beyond a woman's reach. This faith in my sex comes naturally, therefore, and it was not challenged when I became a member of Cymdeithas.

In a relatively small movement that believes in direct action, you learn to appreciate everyone's contribution. From the beginning, when it was decided on that February afternoon in 1963 to form a blockade on Trefechan Bridge in Aberystwyth to protest about the lack of Welsh in public life, no one segregated the men from the women. Everyone who was willing to risk being arrested was in. There was no shortage of women. Among the first to be jailed was Gwyneth Wiliam. It is true that up to the late seventies, it was men who were given the roles of chairperson, vice chairperson and similar duties, but the ratio of men to women on the ruling body of Cymdeithas has always been quite balanced. In the direct action record, men and women have served on an equal basis. It is unusual to have a sexist approach such as was seen on the cover of the movement's monthly in the early seventies. It printed the names of a dozen women and said, 'The women acted – what about you?'

When 'Women in Cymdeithas' is mentioned, faces come to my mind. Many faces, of different ages, but of similar natures. Over the years, they've all been very close friends of mine.

The first is Teresa, a brave and bold creature who feared no one and nothing. I still have the note, written in her artistic handwriting, that drove shivers down my back when I received it, an eager eighteen-year-old who had said so many times that I wanted to take part in direct action: 'There are plans to occupy holiday homes Friday night. If you're coming, be at my place at nine. Tell no one, – and *burn this note.*' I turned up, and so did one other girl. It meant three. How the heck were we going to gain an entry into this house? The only man to turn up was the one who drove the car there – and away. Under the moonlight, I watched fascinated as Teresa undid her shoelaces. 'Stand back!' she warned us, before hurling her shoe through the window. In an instant we were inside. In an instant, I had been taught the basics of direct action.

That shoe often came in handy. On several occasions it was used to gain an entry – to holiday homes, Government offices, and once into a television transmitter. One could not have asked for a better training than the one I had under Teresa. There was a determination in her that conquered all odds. There were two of us, and with that amazing figure, nothing was impossible. If more were needed, you asked everyone until someone gave in. If no target was suitable, you'd find another one. If no lift was available, you hitched, or you found the cheek from somewhere to knock on someone's door at two in the morning and persuade them to drive you to London. It was a 100-foot mast. We'd never been to Crystal Palace before in our lives. It was five in the morning, and pitch dark. I was scared. If you went too high, you risked being radiated, or so we'd been told. Teresa went up. I followed. Hours later, we were in front of some magistrate or other on a charge of disturbing the peace. 'Whatever you do, don't agree to be bound over,' warned Teresa. I took her advice – and was given a five-day prison sentence. It was then I panicked. 'Where are they taking us?' I asked, wondering what my parents' reaction would be, they having sent me to college only two weeks earlier. 'You're on your way to jail', said Teresa, before giving me the most practical advice on how to survive Her Majesty's accommodation. 'Keep your head down, do your time, and don't get into trouble.'

Teresa spent more time inside Risley Remand Centre one year than out. Then she fell in love, and got her lover out of the Army. Then she got married, with a Cymdeithas badge on her wedding gown. She's not married now. I see her every now and then. And comes a time when I'm in trouble, a card or a phone call comes – from Teresa.

Ifanwy comes from the same village as Teresa. Older, quieter, but with the same will of steel. Ifanwy worked as a shop assistant. When she was nineteen, the manager told her not to speak Welsh in front of English customers. She gave in her notice. Ifanwy and I were given a one-month prison sentence, and were placed in the same cell at Risley. When you're locked up with someone for twenty-four hours a day, sleeping, waking, working, eating in each other's company, it can be a strain on any friendship. It cemented ours. While there are women of Ifanwy's calibre, Wales will always be different from England.

I can still recall the stench of that cell, the small table, the frosted glass on the window with one pane missing. Over the plastic mugs of bitter tea, we talked and shared. She could conjure up images of that land that seemed so far away, She told me stories, dreadful, spine-chilling stories of her father who was an undertaker. She would share her letters, she would share her meagre meal with the sparrow on the window ledge, she could be as stubborn as a mule. One day, the visiting magistrate came to the prison. On that day the standard of our diet changed dramatically; on that day, our shirts in the workroom were stacked away, and we were given soft toys to sew. Ifanwy could not bear such hypocrisy.

'Rise, girls!' said the screw, when the visiting magistrate came in. Everyone got to their feet except Ifanwy. 'Rise!' said the screw again, with a warning look. Ifanwy did not budge. She was punished for it, right enough. But her hatred of prison, of its servants, and of what it did to people, would not allow her to stand up in respect for its magistrates.

When the name 'Meinir' is mentioned, the colour of gold comes to my mind. There is a golden quality about her, and it's not only the effect of her hair. I did not know her when she was a student, when she worked full-time for Cymdeithas, when she was often jailed, and when she made history by jumping over the gallery at Mold Crown Court. I knew her, at the time, as a name in newspapers, where she was generally referred to as the daughter of former Plaid Cymru MP, Gwynfor Evans, and wife of veteran campaigner, Ffred Ffransis. A loving daughter, a joyous wife, a dedicated mother she may well be, but she is also a person in her own right. When I came to know her first, she had two small children and was running a Welsh crafts business with her husband, but still devoted much of her energy to Cymdeithas yr Iaith. The work she does day in, day out, is not glamorous. It's not the stuff that headlines are made of. Yet, I cannot think of a more dedicated woman. I think it's Meinir's serenity that warms my heart. Bearing a burden is one thing, bearing it with a smile is another. A mother of seven by now, with the business still frail, she uses none of these factors as excuses for stepping back from the heat of the campaign. Come rain, come shine, Meinir will always be there.

Along with Meinir's comes Enfys's name, which aptly means 'rainbow'. People have come and gone from Cymdeithas ranks and many have returned. Enfys is one who never left. From the time she was a student twenty years ago, through more than her share of personal tragedies, Enfys is a survivor. I've sometimes been tempted to concede from time to time, to tire, to give in. Then I think of Enfys. On more than one occasion, she has taught me that a person's strength lies in her belief, rather than in stature or in position. In an instant, she can bare a soul of all its pomp and deceit. Many have been left naked, others have been forced to face her quiet challenge. The children who have the honour of having Enfys as a teacher are not likely to forget her. When Meinir and Enfys were imprisoned in Holloway, the prison staff – in their ignorance – gave them psychiatric tests to try and find what was wrong with them. Why should two accomplished women want to break into an office and cause damage? Meinir and Enfys were deeply insulted and, in protest, went on hunger strike. The officials never did find out what the root of their malady was.

Why anyone should volunteer to take on such a fight will remain a mystery to many people. If you can avoid conflict, they reason, why not take the easy way out? Helen was not born into a Welsh family. Her English parents lived in Anglesey, and it was at school that Helen learnt Welsh. By the time her brothers were at school, there were enough English children to make it unnecessary for them to learn the language. But Helen had learned more than a language. She felt strongly and deeply for the survival of that language and for its country. She was still at school when she joined Cymdeithas yr Iaith. By the time she was at college, she had spent Christmas in jail. There is in Helen a resoluteness and devotion to Cymdeithas that has yet to be surpassed. In the mid-eighties, she became the society's full-time official and stayed in the post for several years. She is the kind of person that most movements would give their right arm for: she worked late, on weekends, early, overtime, any time that was needed. She changed the administration of the Central Office from a casual one to a totally professional one. Usually, one has to have a group to do that and some kind of reasonable budget: Helen was a one-woman band. When her partner could not get work in Aberystwyth, Helen had to face the most difficult decision of her life – she had to put someone else before the needs of Cymdeithas. In the end she left, but she left a legacy behind her. She still does voluntary work for Cymdeithas, and she now gives the same unfailing commitment to the work of teaching Welsh to nursery school children in Gwent.

I could not talk about women in Cymdeithas yr Iaith without mentioning Jên. Jên is a warm tea-cosy of a person. She worked in the society's office in Aberystwyth. Coming from a rural farming background, Jên is Welshness personified. She is fun-loving, talkative, mischievous and able, and she brought light-heartedness to a job that is so often tedious and daunting. If the society's phone bills increased when Jên was employed, it was money well spent.

Jên was a person to whom you became attached, and joining Cymdeithas with Jên was more a result of a long and friendly chat about what was instinctively right rather than an impersonal talk before filling in a membership form. Jên is now married with two young children: although her husband did not speak Welsh when they married, a couple of months listening to Jên was the quickest Ulpan course he could wish for!

And then there's Siân. Siân has taught me so much about life, that I feel deeply indebted to her. She became the first north Wales organizer for Cymdeithas. Not a person who is easy to get to know at first: there is a mysterious side to her. She can be a very private person who does not suffer fools gladly. When she began working, she had no office, no typewriter, no phone, no staff, just her inner resources. She had just finished a research thesis on 'Niclas y Glais', the communist – and Christian – poet, and this was her first job. She took it in her stride. Siân is herself a committed Christian and she taught me what it really means to live out your faith in the world. She taught me to be grateful for small blessings. In a movement like Cymdeithas, one is totally dependent on voluntary workers. You can't demand anything, only thank those who are willing to sacrifice their money, work, or time. I'm continually exasperated at the slow speed of change. Siân has a faith that things are slowly changing. Countless times, I've seen her organizing a rally, preparing for a court case, ordering direct action or arranging a deputation, with a style that is quite unique to her. She gets to know a person, she spends time with them, builds their inner faith and radiates a quiet confidence, and a determination that things will work out. She is acknowledged as one of the most gifted public speakers Cymdeithas has. She will start quietly, shyly, unassumingly. Then something within her is lighted: she speaks up and glows with inner conviction. She was chairperson for one year only, but now, a year later, and married, her conviction has not been daunted. In a demanding job as a social worker, she still gives priority in her spare time to Cymdeithas work.

While Siân was an organizer, she drew a certain Branwen to the ranks, and Cymdeithas yr Iaith hasn't been quite the same since. Branwen is the kind of person who cannot help but leave her mark on the communities with which she comes into contact, be that school, university or prison. She's been sung about, praised, abused by the media, been the subject of poems, been the butt of scorn.

She's been likened to a meteor. Branwen possesses those rare qualities that cause her either to be loved passionately or despised. She lives life at twice the speed of others. If the language issue means anything to Branwen, it's a matter of deep emotion. She devoted her life while at college to Cymdeithas, daubing walls, occupying offices and houses, marching, writing, organizing, spending time in courts and prisons. After leaving college, she became co-ordinator of Cymdeithas in north Wales. Because of the damage she caused to Tory offices whilst protesting against the Anglicizing effects of their housing policies, she was imprisoned after a much publicized trial, and became a household name, a contemporary Welsh Maud Gonne kind of figure. It can't be easy being such a public character, and she's had to pay a price. But come what may, nothing will daunt Branwen's spirit. If that day of Wales's death ever comes, it will be Branwen's company I'll need. Her spirit is that of Cymdeithas. As the poet Waldo Williams said, in another context, 'she'll be as young as ever, as full of mischief'.

There are many more faces I could mention. The faithful face of Dawn. On how many occasions have I come out of a police cell after a rally to be welcomed by Dawn, pram and all, tired perhaps and blue with cold, but cheerful as ever. Lyn in Cardiff, a member of Côr Cochion, swaying to the radical swing of a protest song, one you know who'll never give up. Jessie, in that lonely group of sixty plus, a cheerful battle ram who went to jail – despite her ill-health – rather than pay a fine. Eileen – who started it all in the fifties – an ordinary mother of two who had had enough of receiving English-only bills from Llanelli Council, and who refused to pay them, and had to watch the bailiffs take her belongings away. Kate, a bubbly nineteen-year-old who helps in the office at present, ever willing to be on call with a welcoming cup of tea and a smile, although she has to work in a refuse tip. Gill, mother of four, with a will of iron, who works in the office in Cardiff, and who has continued the fight for so long in the face of much apathy, to ensure that the capital of Wales shows some respect for its language. Lleucu, daughter of veteran campaigners Ffred and Meinir Ffransis, seventeen years of age, awaiting her first court case and belonging to yet another generation of fighters. Beryl, a late beginner, who found herself at thirty-three in court for the first time on a charge of daubing a slogan, and her three children are proud of her. Ffion, my own sister, who sparkles with enthusiasm and gets me going on the darkest of days.

All these are my sisters, the ones that make the fight such an inspiring and worthwhile cause. For what is the fight for the Welsh language, if it's not for a smile between friends, a hug after a policeman's fist, a shared cry before a trial, a dance in the face of violence? There's such a deep level of commitment and trust between us – men and women alike – that I can confidently say that our day will come.

I was given reassurance of that on the day the five of us whom I mentioned at the outset were facing trial. We had travelled all the way to Cardiff, only to be told, after a two-and-a-half-hour wait, that our case was not going to be heard because there was no translator. We entered the dock and demanded a Welsh hearing. The court was emptied, and they spent an hour trying to persuade us. There were guidelines to adhere to, didn't we understand? All we understood was that the niceties of courts always have priority over the needs of defendants, especially Welsh-speaking ones: 'We want our case heard in Welsh, and we want it now.' In the end, we did get it. As lunch-time approached, it somehow became easier to sidestep the guidelines. As they became hungry, the difficulties became easier to solve. As they tired of arguing, they remembered that they just might have enough Welsh to understand us.

'Why bother?' some may ask. When life is hard enough as it is, why go to all this trouble? The answer is simple. I'm a Welsh lady, and I want to be heard. If you won't listen, I'm very sorry, but I'm afraid I'll have to use my shoe.

16

Identity and religion

ENID MORGAN

I was brought up in a Welsh Baptist chapel. There is much glib talk these days of chapels and guilt; there is less that acknowledges the warmth of the chapel community, the love and concern for individuals, the way in which young people were nurtured, valued and affirmed. They loved me and I loved them. At the age of seventeen I was baptized, just a year before I went to St Anne's College, Oxford, where I read English. I 'went up' like many Welsh youngsters before me from what one principal of Jesus College Oxford called a 'ragamuffin Welsh Grammar School'. Like them I found the experience traumatic, exhilarating, disorientating. Mine was a co-ed grammar school in which the science provision for girls was (in restrospect) grossly discriminatory and sexist. But at least the girls who tackled 'A' Levels did so with a confidence born of experience that boys might be exciting, but that they were noisy, grubby, bossy and certainly showed no signs of being superior. Leaving school, however, we entered a different world. It was 1958. In the 'Freshers Fair' I made enquiries of OUDS, the Oxford University Dramatic Society, but, sorry, girls couldn't belong. Yes, they were invited along when women were needed. 'Of course, you're Welsh, aren't you . . . ' I got the strong feeling I was inferior on two counts!

There was no point in trying to join the Oxford Union itself. There were still a few years to go before women were allowed in as members and not just decorative guests on the gallery (at least there wasn't a screen as in synagogues . . .). More important to me was the fact the the Oxford Welsh Society, Cymdeithas Dafydd ap Gwilym, also rejected women. I didn't expect to be accepted by the posh English of Eton and Balliol, but to face a smirkingly shut door from my contemporaries from Ammanford and Swansea and

Bangor was humiliating. I 'knew' rejection. There remained two places in which I could meet my Welsh contemporaries. One was an ephemeral but lively group that called itself 'Welsh Forum', and the other was the Welsh chapel which welcomed Welsh students on Sunday afternoon and gave us tea. Oxford was where I discovered that English Nonconformity was oddly alien. It lacked the intimacy of home; its formality lacked the structure and aesthetic which I discovered in Anglicanism. I was gradually discovering the richness of Catholic liturgy.

Being thus uprooted at eighteen made me turn to the ultimate question of identity, the question the Welsh poet Waldo Williams calls 'Gwaelod pob gofyn' ('the baseline of all questioning'): who am I? The answer at the age of eighteen had to do with relatedness, *perthyn*. At eighteen I had related primarily to family, school, chapel community – the issue of Welshness I had to a considerable extent avoided. Thrust into confident, English, Anglican Oxford, I had a lot of decisions to make about myself – what to do, where to go. It was the call of Welshness that was first decided – despite the exclusion from the *Dafydd*. For being Welsh, speaking Welsh, worshipping in Welsh, had been as natural and inevitable to me as breathing and sleeping. I had to think about it, start learning fast, make decisions about work, and home. The decision about returning to Wales to work still left in the air the issue of religious identity. It appears from the outside such a little side-step. But at the time to become Anglican seemed like becoming a turncoat; it involved betraying not just childhood, family, but religious community, even Welshness. I had to discover liturgy in a Welsh context before choosing 'church' rather than 'chapel' became possible.

A few years later I was struggling with more explicitly feminist issues. It was 1968. I was married with two small children. Where we lived was determined by my husband's work. The question of 'Who am I?' resounded ever more insistently, less now in social terms (that is, in terms of national and religious identity) than in the demands made upon me in the roles I had to play. I was a wife and mother. I had rebelled against following my parents into teaching and had worked as a journalist. I was able to continue writing and editing as a freelance when the children were little. Such work gave me interests and satisfaction beyond the purely domestic, even if very little in the way of money and status! So the issue of 'Who am I?' became ever more important as I struggled to care for people who depended on me, while I didn't know who I was. I am told that it didn't look like that from the outside. I was broadcasting, writing, a member of the County Council, editing a church magazine and then a weekly paper, as well as caring for three small children.

Strangely, the work of editing the paper helped. I had been confirmed, and writing for *Y Llan*, which was then a weekly Welsh paper for the Church in Wales, meant getting to know the institution and its people. It meant taking its faith and assumptions seriously. It became clear that I had to sort out who I was in spiritual, not merely domestic, cultural, political and economic terms. So for me discovering identity had to do with religious conversion and commitment, a discovery of salvation from the chaos of inner demands for fulfilment, achievement, success, status; salvation from failure, guilt, hollowness, self-justification and self-centredness. I discovered, though it is only now, much later, that I can express it in this way, that the 'I' that is myself, is not a mask for the world and society around me, but a simple reality deep in the ground of my being. It is the 'I' who says yes to the 'Thou' of God; it is myself, hearing the voice of Christ in the garden, a voice asking 'Who are you looking for?'

That outline of my personal story is what lies behind my present unlikely situation, working as a Deacon-in-Charge of four churches. I struggle with the issues of feminist theology, compromise on inclusive language and tolerate the intolerable. I write at a time when, according to the media, the Church of England is tearing itself apart on the issue of women priests. The General Synod in England and the Governing Body of the Church in Wales are nerving themselves for a decision. There are in the Church in Wales some fifty women deacons. The word 'deacon' conveys something rather different to those brought up in the Welsh Nonconformist tradition where a deacon is a lay person (usually male) who bears particular responsibility in the church community, and who sits in the *sêt fawr*, the wide deacons' pew in the front of the chapel. My father was a Baptist deacon.

As an Anglican deacon, however, I am a Clerk in Holy Orders, and belong to the first, humblest order, the diaconate. In other provinces of the Anglican church, including Hong Kong, Kenya, and Ireland, the second order – the priesthood – is open to women.

The third order, the episcopate is open to women in the United States and in New Zealand. Many have yet to recover from the ecclesiastical shock of a woman wearing a mitre. One priest told me, in all seriousness, that he disliked seeing women in cassocks because they were an essentially male garment! He clearly had lost the lay perception of clergy as men in skirts. Here in Wales we wait for a decision on the priesthood, a decision which may come in Spring 1994.

Thus, ordained women, in various parts of Wales, are doing the vicar's job, but are not given by the Church the authority to celebrate the central ritual, the Eucharist, which is, *par excellence*, the sign that gives meaning to the church community. Meanwhile, the Church struggles with its indecision, and provides ways of circumventing the difficulty. Thus, as a 'Deacon-in-Charge' (the term is, strictly, a contradiction in terms) I have for six years ministered to, loved, taught, prayed, preached, baptized, prepared for confirmation, married and buried the people of four parishes in Cardiganshire. I am not allowed, however, to say the words of consecration over the elements of bread and wine, I am not to proclaim the words of the absolution nor the words of the Apostolic blessing – simply because I am female not male. Again the pain of rejection. But because I am still surprised to have got even this far in such a slow-moving system, so resistant to change, most of the time I cope without too much agitation. Friends and supporters, amazed observers from the outside, can often allow their sympathy more vigorous expression.

What does the religious system, to which I have chosen freely and gladly to belong, do to my identity? How do I perceive my identity in a historical system about which many Welsh people feel ambivalent if not downright hostile? God is concerned with the potentialities and wholeness of every single person, female and male, but because we are all in some measure damaged and distorted, religions and religious structures can actually reinforce the damage and distortion produced by cultural stereotypes. As a result the Anglican church is struggling with the results of a faith which conformed to the patriarchal systems of the world and then exalted it to a dogma of so-called 'natural' order. Some women have felt it right to abandon ship, to ditch, not only the ecclesiastical structure, but the content of the faith itself. Others, like me, still feel that our identity, our meaning as individuals is still nurtured by God within the Christian tradition, even if the fathers in the Christian family have denied to 'mother' Church the right to extend to her daughters the same value as her sons.

In trying to make sense of the variety of experience of religion by very different temperaments I have found it very useful to use the classification devised by Baron von Hügel, the Roman Catholic writer of the earlier part of this century. He recognized three kinds of attitude to religion. Firstly, there are those for whom the institution of the community of faith is tremendously important. It provides security and rules, continuity and certainty, a framework as unchanging as possible. There are such in most Christian denominations, even those which call themselves Nonconformist! Secondly, there are the critics – those who reject church structures as unnecessary and even harmful, who can only find meaning through individual conscience in total freedom. Fortunately they too are found in most traditions. Lastly, there are the mystical, those for whom experience of the divine, spiritual dimension, whether experienced individually or in community, is the most important thing. Von Hügel linked these categories with stages in psychological development. He saw the need for security as an infant stage, the need to criticize and reject as adolescent, and the mystical as adult and mature. Elements of these attitudes coexist in most people, just as the infant, adolescent and adult coexist in mature individuals. Such an understanding of religious people and their experiences (including my own) at least enables me to cope with the temptations of submission and rebellion. The church structure is unjust and repressive, and it has devalued women and made a virtue of it, but none the less it still contains within it a community of women and men searching for wholeness, aware of their weakness and struggling to grow. Ditching it does not seem to be the right way forward!

To analyse my experience from a feminist point of view is a painful challenge since, for the thoroughgoing feminist, staying within the Church, let alone seeking to play a part in its structure, would appear to be collaboration with the enemy and a betrayal both of my own identity and of women in general. To those who feel like that I can only say that as I understand the human – as well as the female – predicament, patriarchy, sexism, the obvious inability of women and men to grow and work together for their own and each other's wholeness and fulfilment before God, is one manifestation, perhaps indeed the most obvious, of the radical dis-orientation of humanity within creation. It is still a symptom not a cause. Sexism and sin are not coterminous! Women as well as men are sinners and to discover our identity as women is not totally distinct from the journey on which men are engaged. We actually do belong together. And we discover that, gloriously, in God.

17

Between two worlds

MARY LLOYD JONES

During my five years at Cardiff College of Art in the early fifties I only ever encountered two or three other students who could speak Welsh. Most of my fellow students came from the industrial valleys, a large proportion commuting each day and disappearing on the weekend. I therefore became accustomed very quickly to being a member of a minority. In my own capital city, I was in fact a foreigner. My background in a tiny, scattered village in the uplands of Cardiganshire was totally different to that of the other students who only knew of urban living. The journey from Devil's Bridge to Cardiff on the Western Welsh bus took all day, and during those ten hours I had time to orientate myself, so that I could slide with ease between two worlds.

The benefits of industrialization in the form of mains electricity and mains water did not arrive in Devil's Bridge until the mid-fifties. What at the time seemed to be a distinct disadvantage did give me the benefit of experiences associated with rural peasant life lost to all who have lived only in cities. Today I realize that I am one of a very tiny and privileged minority who spent formative years in a pattern of living that has remained virtually unchanged for thousands of years. Who can know the assault on the senses of the inky cold black of a winter's night in the country if they are only accustomed to street lights?

Very few children lived within playing distance, so I spent much time on my own. I grew to know intimately the square mile around my home. Long days were spent scrambling the deep valley sides around Devil's Bridge, covering territory that was quite dangerous, but I grew to know the chasms and waterfalls and could navigate the terrain in safety. This extensive knowledge of a particular place now informs my work, and images set in the experiences of this time now emerge with a life of their own in my paintings.

My father never missed the weather forecast even in old age, a habit, I believe, inherited from generations of forefathers whose existence depended on responding to the weather. My father also inherited the ancient art of the *cyfarwydd* (story-teller). Neighbours would gather on winter nights to listen to his endless repertoire of tales from the recent past of minor catastrophes, comic characters and amusing incidents. Some of these stories dealt with darker material, tales of corpse candles associated with particular places and the astonishing skills of the *cwnjer* (conjurer) who could undo spells and curses and cure burns at great distances. Through these stories I glimpsed an older world that was mysterious and irrational. These tales cemented a permanent relationship and sense of belonging to the village and its environs.

To this day I cannot explain what gave me the idea that I would be an artist. I had no role models, not within the family, the school, or the community. Indeed, I did not meet a real live artist before entering college. During my school years in Aberystwyth I only remember seeing one exhibition of contemporary art which was at the National Library, in those days the only venue in west Wales which had an art gallery. But drawing and reading were constant activities and gradually the need to enter that place created by my own marks became an essential part of me.

Embarking on a career as an artist living in Wales in the early sixties was fraught with difficulties. In 1961 after three years in London my husband and I returned with our two small daughters to live in Aberaeron. In later years I have learnt that all who embark on a life-style that is radically different to that of parents and family are exposed to severe stress frequently leading to illness and breakdown. My 'squiggles' and ambitions were incomprehensible to my parents and to most members of the community in which I was living. The specific difficulties that all women face in breaking into any profession have been extensively documented and it is well known that the world of fine arts is one of the most male-dominated fields. Combining motherhood with ambitions to be an artist in a culture which did not appear to value the work required a supportive partner and a stubborn streak.

The traditional fine art media of painting and sculpture need the patronage of the middle and upper classes or the state or, more recently, big business in order to flourish. It is understandable that the Welsh, who mainly lived in rural peasant communities, should have no tradition in these arts. But the fact that there appeared to be no folk art tradition of decorating domestic furniture and artifacts puzzled me for many years until I realized that a Welsh visual tradition lay in women's textile arts. Discovering my great-grandmother's splendid log cabin quilt gave me the foundation and background on which to develop my own language, safe in the knowledge that my work was linked with that of previous generations. Remembering rag rugs from childhood and reading about the personal meanings stitched into the intricate designs produced by professional quilters gave me the confidence to experiment and create works that combined painting and textile techniques. These enabled me to make the transition from my great-grandmother's quilt to my present work which employs the full range of expression which I feel is only possible with oil paints, currently my preferred medium.

It became clear that the decision to stay and exist as an artist in Wales in the early sixties meant that energy must be directed into changing the climate for the visual arts. Over three decades I have been involved in numerous projects aimed at increasing public understanding of my subject, in particular within the Welsh-speaking community. For example, over the years, many groups of Merched y Wawr (the Welsh equivalent of the Women's Institute) have visited my studios. I began to collect old quilts, woven *carthenni* (bed covers) and other traditional textile articles, as I felt that by our looking together at the Welsh textile tradition I could use these artifacts as an introduction to a visual language.

To understand the nature and character of the Welsh temperament it is necessary to reflect on how centuries of life lived in the shadow of a stronger culture has shaped the character of a people. Margaret Atwood's work on the impact of colonization in her book *Survival* was a revelation to me, as the difficulties facing Canadian artists and writers are in many ways identical to those encountered by the Welsh. One of the most damaging results of colonization is the feeling that real culture is something that happens elsewhere. I certainly felt at times that to succeed as an artist I was the wrong sex, living in the wrong place at the wrong time. Miraculously, of all the Celtic languages Welsh alone is still spoken by a substantial number of people. Nevertheless, centuries of colonization and exploitation have left the Welsh with a damaged psyche. Lack of autonomy has drained away self-confidence with tragic results. All the difficulties faced by disadvantaged groups are compounded for members of those groups who happen to be female. Typically a member of a colonized people feels herself to be a victim. But an artist must feel empowered in order to work. The answer, according to Margaret Atwood, is for aspiring artists from a colonized people to become creative non-victims using the experience of their place and time in their art, and to reject the idea that significant work can only be that of dead foreigners (male, white and middle class, of course).

Whilst opportunities for exhibiting and employment in residencies and various education programmes have created a more supportive environment for artists in Wales over the last twenty-five years, difficulties continue to exist for indigenous artists. Of the 1,500 artists working in Wales at present, only a minority will be from a Welsh background. The image of the archaic peasant clings to the Welsh artist in spite of the improved support system provided by Gweled (Association of Welsh-speaking Artists). Imported artists from Birmingham or Hackney frequently appear to fare better in Wales than the home-grown product.

The development of galleries and art centres over the last twenty-five years has seen a growth in the profession of art administrator. I personally have received constant encouragement from Aberystwyth Arts Centre. Without the opportunities given me to show work at regular intervals the gradual emergence of my own style would have been impossible. However, almost all the gallery directors and exhibition officers in Wales are from elsewhere and unfortunately this does little to change the natives' perception of the visual arts as being alien to Welsh culture. Arts administration is a comparatively new profession. Grasping opportunities in a new area of activity requires an enterprising spirit, a quality I feel is not often found in Welsh persons for reasons already described.

Eastern philosophy tells us that everything in life has a duality. So Welshness can be viewed from negative and positive perspective. On the one hand one encounters bigotry and ignorance. Chapel culture has left a legacy of passivity. There is a tendency to allow newcomers to take over the decision-making positions. Key posts in national institutions are increasingly filled by *bobl dwad* (newcomers). One cannot imagine this happening in Scotland. The

Welsh story is a tragic story. The people of a country provided with enormous natural resources and mineral wealth have not benefited from these but have been the victims of continuing exploitation and many to this day suffer from inadequate housing and poor health.

A power group always needs another group with whom comparisons can be made to endorse feelings of superiority. It is much too dangerous for the English to ridicule the Irish and the Scots but a scapegoat must be found and indignities are piled on to the Welsh. It was depressing to read that Neil Kinnock's failure in the 1992 election was blamed on his Welshness. In the midst of a recession, business activity and investment in Wales is deflected by the subtle means of introducing huge toll charges for entry into the country over the Severn Bridge.

Aspiring artists who belong to a disadvantaged group can, according to Margaret Atwood, stay in the culture and be crippled as an artist – or escape into nothing. Circumstances and my need to be within reach of wide open spaces dictated my decision to stay and work in Wales.

Wales is special because of its size. With today's mobility it is possible to get to know it all reasonably well. Where else in the world can one encounter such variety of landscape within manageable distances. The geology of Wales is on a human scale, it is never boring as vast tracts of France or America can be. After all my travels I return to Wales and I find the beauty of this land to be astonishing. This is my place, it is the starting point for all my paintings and two lifetimes would not exhaust the possibilities of what I can see.

Being Welsh means belonging to an enormous extended family. Conversing in Welsh with a total stranger means instant and unquestioning acceptance. Membership of a large family can have a claustrophobic and inhibiting effect, but the confirmation of identity that it gives is priceless. Its absence goes with the anonymity of much urban living in our time and can even make people mentally ill.

The artist needs roots. The raw material for the artist is what she knows well, and the indelible marks of early experiences are what must be mined for later creations. After the early years of relative isolation I now feel myself to be a member of a community of artists. From Anglesey to Cardiff, from Clwyd to Pembrokeshire I am in contact with fellow artists. I may not see these individuals regularly but the fact that they are there is an affirmation of one's endeavours.

As the years advance one goes through the process of eliminating what is irrelevant. Reflecting on the art of this century most of it can be described as an art that has grown out of urban experience. Today, for me, there is only one issue – our relationship with the natural world. This is the subject of my painting and my early years seem to be especially designed with this in mind.

All art is a process of self-discovery. I am conscious of the fact that my ancestors were the first inhabitants of these islands. Britain's aborigines are the Welsh. The untranslatable word *hiraeth* describes the longing which the Welsh have for a particular place. This special relationship with the land is of the same nature as that of the American Indians and the Australian Aborigine. Today, after these cultures have been virtually destroyed it has been realized that we need to understand and learn how these peoples lived in sustainable harmony with their environment.

My paintings are a celebration of mountains and wilderness, an attempt to draw attention to the natural world. I am conscious of the need to reveal the underlying energies, that which one feels but cannot see. Within a painting, decisions taken are intuitive, and if things are going well, the painting almost seems to paint itself. My painting, however, is also informed by reading, and my efforts to understand the underlying order of the building blocks of matter. I eagerly read books which attempt to make today's physics understandable to a lay person.

Living in Wales one cannot but be aware of ancient history. Certain areas are littered with standing stones circles and hill forts. The oldest rocks in the world are called Pre-Cambrian and not surprisingly some of these can be found in Wales. I am fascinated by the cryptic markings made by our ancestors such as those known as 'cup and ring'. No one knows what they mean but they suggest the beginnings of language. Painting is essentially a building up of marks with fingers or brushes. A painting can be multilayered in its reference and sometimes the simplification of forms in my paintings can echo these ancient primeval marks. None of these devices can be contrived, but must arrive uninvited in the solution of a painting.

Whilst I have exhibited regularly both in Wales and further

afield since 1966, it is only in the last three and half years that I have been able to devote all my time to being a painter. I place my faith in the processes of my own work. I am encouraged to see around me growing numbers of young artists from a Welsh background. Outside Wales, however, Welsh art remains invisible. Our funded galleries could reverse the present direction of art traffic to take art from Wales beyond Offa's Dyke and into Europe. The improved self-image and resulting empowerment could benefit all sections of Welsh life.

18

Writing is a bird in hand

MENNA ELFYN

One of my first recollections of poetry is of thumbing through a hymn book (Y *Caniedydd*) and reading all the hymns of that remarkable woman Ann Griffiths. When one considers that she is the only woman included in the *Oxford Book of Welsh Verse* (ed. Thomas Parry) it is likely that this early discovery was a significant contact. I remember wondering what she could have been like, to have been able to write hymns that became the vehicle of a congregation's enthusiasm and passion. Ann must have fired my imagination in those early days because when given the chance at primary school to dress up as one of our heroes (*sic*!) I decided to be Ann, clutching a Bible and a hymn book firmly in both hands.

At twelve years of age, poetry remained for me a source of mystery and wonder. I spent fruitless nights trying to write and despairing over my petty efforts. When we moved to live on the outskirts of Carmarthen I held on to poetry as a means of keeping sane, as I felt hostage to an oppressively English system of education. There, we were only allowed to study Welsh as one subject; the medium of our education in general was English, and yet Welsh was the medium of my perception of the world. Simple acts of oppression appeared both minimal and yet far reaching at the same time. One example will suffice. Whenever I returned to school, after a period of illness, my mother's notes of explanation in Welsh would always enrage the teachers. I was told countless times to inform her not to write again in 'that language'. Needless to say, I never carried the messages home as I knew my mother would courteously yield to their demand. Those small struggles built within me an inner strength, both arrogant and passionate for the rights of a people to breathe their language with dignity.

This was the beginning of my need to write, and of my need to feel free in the use of my own language. During those early sixties I could see 'Free Wales' daubed on walls, or 'Cofiwch Dryweryn' (Remember Tryweryn).[1] Little did I think at the time that I too would later take part in that gnomic writing, inscribing public surfaces with such sentiments as 'Dim Arwisgo' (No Investiture).

Poetry is, in some ways, a special language within a language, and I moved within that inner language. Poetry gave me answers to a world I did not understand, and gave me riches and values that made me at peace with myself. As the Chilean poet Pablo Neruda said,

> . . . something started in my soul,
> fever or forgotten wings,
> and I made my own way,
> deciphering
> that fire,
> and I wrote the first faint line . . .
>
> (Neruda 1975, 14)

His poem speaks of seeing 'the heavens/unfastened/and open' as he begins to write. Writing was, and still is, for me also, akin to a spiritual experience.

The writer within me started her journey as a private writer who needed none the less to communicate with the world at large. The need to feel and be vulnerable is, I hope, still fundamental in my writing, along with the need to raise my voice against the silence of indifference and apathy wherever it may lurk:

> From birth till death I fear living
> A being with no convictions, lost causes, not believing!
>
> (Elfyn 1978, 17, my translation)

I have, however, tried to distance my writing from all political causes. I prefer to join marches and demonstrations for a cause rather than write didactic work. In past years I took this to extremes. I have written very little verse that is about Wales or the language, rebelling in so doing against the armchair protest verses written during the seventies and eighties. A self-righteous attitude of course, but although I later came to see how blinkered it was I still tend to refrain from any heroic verse. In the late seventies, however, my husband's imprisonment for six months led to poems written in a different vein, poems like 'Wedi'r achos' (After the court case):

> While you were in prison
> the banks of the Teifi froze
> in civil disobedience,
> and the salmon died of broken hearts.
>
> While you were in prison
> all the birds of creation
> migrated in unwelcome
> and the stray cats of the parish
> had an attack of existential insecurity.
> (Elfyn 1990, 46, trans. Elin ap Hywel)

As a poet and protester, my aim was not only to change the status of a language but to change society as well, and by doing so create a more equal system. I sided firmly with those socialists who were behind the barricades in France and in the civil rights movements in many countries. Their non-violent acts of disobedience encited me to dream of a new dawn, a new social order. Most creative people are, at one time or another, dreamers. A law-breaking dreamer, I eventually went to prison myself as a language activist, but came out a feminist. Imprisonment brought home to me the existence of another silenced war, waged this time against women. But here there was no slogan painting. No visible, clear-cut answers to this campaign. No breaking of the symbols of oppression. I remember pontificating in prison about language and injustice to women who were themselves bereft of language, that is, of a language expressive of the female condition.

The poet too grapples with language and is an eternal learner, renaming words and experiences as she tries to voice herself. In my early twenties I wanted so much to be a poet like T. Gwynn Jones or R. Williams Parry, two great male classics of the Welsh tradition. But experience taught me that I could not be like them. When I found myself in hospital losing a child, I clung once again to writing, as the only medium that could save me from despair. I realized soon afterwards that my whole being was very different from that of the poets I had admired. I had come across a voice within me whose existence I had not previously guessed at: I was burying life as I had known it. It is difficult now to believe that it was 1977 before the common experience of miscarriage made its first appearance as a subject in Welsh poetry. This was touching on a human experience which had been kept private; now my writing began to voice specifically female experiences:

> Expecting and losing
> is a woman's lot;
> Expecting is to lose
> selfishness;
> When a new head pushes itself out
> to claim your palms.
> (Elfyn 1990, 26, trans. Harri Pritchard Jones, in Meyrick 1989, 43)

The joy of eventually succeeding in becoming a mother of two children brought with it also the difficulties of combining writing with motherhood. People are sometimes surprised when I talk of the roles of a poet and mother as necessitating similar responses. One cannot allow the wailing of a poem inside the head to go unheeded any more than one can ignore a child's cries. The work of poets like Ann Sexton and Sylvia Plath became for a while a fixation with me. Both failed to dovetail life as poets and mothers, but their lonely devastations led to a new poetic voice:

> Out of the living woman, language alive
> to riddle the revolution of the poem.
> (Elfyn 1990, 43, trans. Elin ap Hywel, in Meyrick 1989, 51)

Yet, through reading other women poets, I came to see that I myself did not share the same isolating obsessions as those which plagued Plath and Sexton; perhaps it was my Welsh Nonconformist background refusing me the indulgence of solipsism. I have always belonged to those women who want to 'tell and connect and see oneself among the many, and the many reflected in oneself. To commune with others in this truth telling.' Susan Griffin, who wrote those words, also made me understand other feelings when she said,

> When we preserve a culture, we acknowledge its value; we acknowledge the value of those who made that culture, and most important, we give to the daily acts and thoughts and lives of that people signification . . . To preserve a culture is to assert the right to culture at all.
>
> (Griffin, 1982, 189)

Through writers, poets, world famous or unknown, I came to understand one of the most important aspects of writing, namely celebrating life in its complexity. The power of poetry as celebration cannot be overestimated; it is a driving force which sustains and salvages people.

If my own voice has changed over the years, it is an inevitable consequence of the self-questioning necessary to any writer. John Berger said that:

> To be a writer was to be able to see to the horizon where . . .
> nothing is ever very distinct and all questions are open.
>
> (Berger 1993, 48)

Searching for wholeness in a world that marginalizes and divides one into Welsh, woman, poet, requires a great deal of questioning and contemplation. Those who speak Welsh and have tried to live their lives through their mother tongue will perhaps be able to recognize how similar their situation is to that of 'woman'. Both groups are relegated to second-class citizenship, yet both are now struggling to transform the system which tries to disempower them.

One of my recent poems, about Welshness and the experience of linguistic dispossession, was written while seeing the Kurds being driven out of their land. The voicelessness and powerlessness that one feels as a Welsh person is equivalent to the powerlessness of being female. But being a poet gives one a great opportunity to redress that void.

> 'Ga i rif yng Nghaerdydd os gwelwch . . . '
> 'Speak up'
> 'GA I RIF YNG NGHAER-'
> 'Speak up – you'll have to speak up.'
> 'Speak up' is of course
> the command to speak English.
> I sentence myself to a lifetime
> of sentences that make no sense.
> No pronunciation, no annunciation
> inflection? I am infected
> with dumbness, I can neither lampoon,
> sing in tune; much less can I intone. My grace-notes
> are neither music nor mumble.
> I am not heard at Evening Prayer

nor at triumphant Matins;
nor am I that voice in the dusk
that is husky but vibrant.

An impediment then? No. No thick tongue,
no chip on my shoulder, a compulsion to please.
And if I am without speech,
what of the fluency of my people?
We are mutes, Trappists,
conspirators in a corner.
The usurper's language pierces
to the very centre of our being,
a minister of darkness before whose tread
our civility must give ground.
From the safety of my television
I see nations forced into a hole,
possessors of nothing but their dispossession,
mufflers over their mouths,
their captive craft under curfew.
There is an injunction against their speech,
and I perceive it is Y GYMRAEG that is between us.

So the next time I am commanded
to 'speak up'
deferring to the courtesy
that is our convention,
with like courtesy I will require the operator
to 'pipe down';
and like 'sounding brass'
I will suggest the superfluousness of barbed wire,
since our language has berylled wares.
I will sing and make contact
in cynghanedd, as the small nations do,
a people in counterpoint
to the leit-motif, dominant
though its pitch be,
ending each time on the same
obstinate monotone
with the same passionate concern,
though mortally muted our metrics.

'A nawr, a ga i -
y rhif yna yng Nghaerdydd?'
                    (Elfyn 1982, trans. R. S. Thomas, 139)

Note

[1] In 1956–9 the flooding of the valley of Tryweryn by Liverpool water authority, and the uprooting of its Welsh-speaking village community, aroused much anger in Wales.

References

Berger, John (1993). *Keeping a Rendezvous* (London, Granta).
Elfyn, Menna (1977). *Stafelloedd Aros* (Waiting Rooms) (Llandysul, Gomer).
—— (1982). 'Song of a Voiceless Person to British Telecom', trans. R. S. Thomas, *Chapman Magazine*.
—— (1990). *Aderyn bach mewn llaw* (A Bird in Hand) (Llandysul, Gomer).
Griffin, Susan (1982). *Made from this Earth: An Anthology of Writings* (London, The Women's Press).
Meyrick, Ceri (ed.) (1989). *The Bloodstream* (Bridgend, Seren Books).
Neruda, Pablo (1975). *Selected Poems*, ed. Nathaniel Tarn (Harmondsworth, Penguin).

19

Beginning with Bendigeidfran

GILLIAN CLARKE

It seems to have begun with Bendigeidfran, his rhythmic syllables, the imprint of his huge foot on the shore, and the rocking stone on the headland that had been the apple in the giant's pocket.

A hundred yards from the door of the farm that had belonged to my grandmother from before I was born until I was almost grown-up, there lies a small cove between cliffs that extend parallel arms north-westward into Cardigan Bay. Its black shingle, the grey Atlantic seals that swam in its translucent green waters, the strangely hollowed, foot-shaped pool in a rock at the foot of the cliffs close to the bay, and the story my father taught me to associate with it, have haunted me longer than almost any memory. According to my father, the giant Bendigeidfran set off from the beach in such a terrible rage to wade the Irish Sea to rescue his sister Branwen from the Irish court, that his foot had printed a hollow into a black slab fallen from the cliffs. Those rocks lying broken on the shore and jutting jaggedly from the sea still have an air of turmoil about them for me. They loom out of dark times for which I have no certain explanation, but which cast up old tales of war and shipwreck and bear messages that seem to be coded or in languages I could not understand.

Seamus Heaney has said that his poetic imagination is rooted in childhood fear. When pressed, he added that every poem he had ever written began in the sharp emotions of childhood. Most poets would recognize that poetry is rooted in the deepest experiences, in memory kept too far down to name, stored in the senses rather than in the filing-system of the conscious mind. It is those feelings and experiences at the edge of language, where words are new-born, that the poet needs to draw upon. No wonder Keats said,

'O for a life of sensations rather than of thoughts.' I would further argue that this rich source of poetry is especially available to women. The girl-child often has an early advantage in language skills, is likely to talk earlier, to learn to read sooner than a boy, and to prefer imaginative literature. Words store memory, 'Nothing is until it has a word' ('Llŷr', Clarke 1982, 27). Women oftener record memories of babyhood than men and thus draw more deeply on the first physical, animal sensations of infancy, where body and mind are single, fact and imagination indivisible. It is not that men never share this characteristic, as Heaney proves, but that it is rarer in men, and might even be said to be common-place in women.

For me poetry is a rhythmic way of thinking, but it is a thought informed by the heart, informed by the body, informed by the whole self and the whole life lived, so that being a woman and being Welsh are inescapably expressed in the art of poetry. I tire of the old, critical debate, the tired question: 'Is there an Anglo-Welsh literature?' The term 'Anglo-Welsh' has rightly been abandoned for the clumsier but more accurate 'Welsh writing in English'. Our writers in both languages are connected by the relative classless-ness of Wales. Our place-names and our English speech are haunted by Welsh, as the ends of the streets in our towns and cities are haunted by hills and far blue mountain landscapes. We share history, ancestral connections with farming, Nonconformism, heavy industry, and an enduring respect for and ambition for edu-cation. There are striking biographical connections between the writers of Wales. It is a small country, a real place, whose writers tend to say 'we', rather than 'I', but we write in as many ways as do the writers of more confident and powerful nations.

My parents were, in their different ways, both word people, despite the impoverished formal education available in their youth. Both were English-speaking and from families with their root and culture in an old, rural Wales, my father from Carmarthenshire, my mother from Denbighshire. My paternal grandfather farmed and worked on the Great Western Railway. His forbears were Baptist ministers, farmers and preachers. My mother's father farmed and milled corn, as had most of her known ancestors. My sister and I were the first members of the tribe to be brought up with English as mother tongue. By the time I was born, my father had joined the BBC in Cardiff as an outside broadcast engineer, and my early childhood in that time of war was spent partly in Cardiff, then Barry, and partly at 'home' in Pembrokeshire at the farm to which my grandmother had moved from her native Carmarthenshire. Both parents valued words, literature, books. Both thought education the way forward for their daughters. My father treasured both his languages, but for my mother the way up and out of hardship was to speak and teach her children English only. A child of a tenant farmer, she noted that her father's landlords were rich, privileged and English, and she made up her mind in bitterness to escape her own heritage. She went to one of those insidiously anti-Welsh grammar schools that destroyed the self-confidence of so many of her generation, trained as a nurse, and gave it up to marry. Determined that her daughters would be educated, she spoke nothing but English from the day I was born, taught me to read before I went to school, and allowed Welsh a grudged place in my father's life. I knew that he spoke it everywhere except at home, so for me, too, Welsh took on the nature of a forbidden tongue, a language of secrets from which I at first felt merely excluded, and later learned to value as something stored away for my future by my father, against my mother's wishes. It is a history very like that of many writers of my generation.

My mother left the tall tales to my father too. The myth of Branwen and Bendigeidfran is not associated with Pembrokeshire, but, though the imagination thrills to name the stones, rivers, caves, islands or mountains as the grave or the birthplace of Branwen, Grainne or Europa, the geography of myth lies in the mind. The family version of the tale gave me possession of what was rightly mine, and should belong to all children. It offered me a place in the myth, and gave myth and naming a place in my imagination. By the time I first saw *King Lear* when I was ten, I already knew the sad story of Branwen, the beautiful daughter of Llŷr. My first bookcase was full of folk and fairy tale and the mythologies of several cultures, and my head full not only of Enid Blyton but also of the Mabinogion. I recall no real book of the latter, no illustrated collection specially for children, only a version of some of the stories told to keep me occupied in the car on the frequent journeys from Cardiff, to keep up my pace on a walk, or to get me to sleep at night. In fact they kept me awake. I heard the giant Bendigeidfran breathe, cough, stamp and rage in the waterfalls, tide, winds and storms at Fforest, and in the rumours of war on the radio or in the headlines of newspapers. The fact that literature, from nursery rhyme and fairy story onwards, was so closely associated with the natural world, has played a strong part in making me a country person, not an urban one, even during the long years of my life spent in the city. Literature hallowed the natural with the supernatural. It made the stones sing. It populated the countryside with animals, seen and unseen. It made natural phenomena reverberate with mythological meaning, turned a rocking stone to a giant's apple, a rock pool to a footprint.

Childhood in the 1940s was also dominated by a world war which even a child happily evacuated to the loving care of a grandmother, in what still seems like paradise, could not escape, and my earliest memories of Fforest coincide with the war years. To a child it was a legendary war, a giant's war of stormy seas, shipwreck, armies that crossed rivers on the body of their commander, bombs that fell from the sky. There was a monstrous enemy leader, and could we but kill him we would all be saved. Bendigeidfran was on our side, but I was not at all convinced that he was a sensible friend. I was not keen on his policy of revenge under those black skies of the early 1940s. Like most children, I found the quarrels of adults painful and bewildering, and what was going on up there and out there was all too raw a re-enactment of the unease in my own parents' marriage, symbolized by their difference over which language they should speak to their children. From all this turbulence Fforest was a refuge that felt, and indeed was, far safer than a bomb shelter under the stairs in a house in a south Wales port. In my grandmother's house and yard, Welsh and English, birth and death, the real and the imagined, were all equally natural and elemental and as necessary to each other's definition as the sea is to the land.

That poetry is for me both a creative and a thinking process is illustrated by the very slowness of the thought-journey towards an understanding of these things that has taken place since I began to take poetry seriously twenty years ago. From first publication in *Poetry Wales* in 1971, I began to give poetry due attention, in days of intense work between months of devotion to other things, such as rearing children, and earning a living. At first it was the live moment and its present tense that informed the poetry, and the present was made up in those early days almost entirely of familial matters and domestic relationships, which were the subject of the first book, *The Sundial* (Clarke 1979). My later books have explored the subject of ancestry, first the women's story in *Letter from a Far Country* (Clarke 1982), then the men's in 'Cofiant' in *Letting in the Rumour* (Clarke 1989), in an attempt to find the meaning of the present in the past. Now, among a tangled personal mythology of literature and reality, of real childhood memory and story memory, of legendary and real war, of father country, mother country and the rich turned ground between, new subjects are clamouring for attention. They seem objective and external, but they take their source and root from a lived past.

The first of these new interests is the world made intimate by the media and by travel. My generation's first journeys were made by radio in the time of war, when wireless 'let in the rumour, grief on the radio' (Clarke 1989, 7). Insights into the mysterious adult world, awareness of the movements of history as it happened, glimpses of great emotions that would otherwise have been beyond the experience of a child, came as the family listened to news bulletins, and some came from radio drama, especially serialized novels. I associate *Jane Eyre* with Sunday evenings in winter, my father absent, away at work in the reserved occupation of broadcasting, which exempted him from war service. About thirty years later, when I had become a published poet, came the first real visits to other countries, literary festivals, poetry exchanges with communist regimes keen to demonstrate their enthusiasm for the arts, and American universities supplementing their creative writing resources with visiting writers from the land of Dylan Thomas.

The second new subject I will call the new nature. It no longer seems merely the sentimental concern of what used, until quite recently, to be called 'nature poets' to protest at the spoliation of the earth. Reviews of my first collection, which appeared in 1978, spoke somewhat patronizingly of my concern for domestic issues and the natural world, and I and those who shared my concern were regarded as writing about marginal matters, away from the centre. Many of the writers most concerned with these matters were women, made alert to the danger and concerned for the future of an increasingly sick earth by motherhood, and a passionate desire for a good and wholesome tomorrow for their children. It was once seen as sentimental nonsense to fear nuclear war. It seems strange now to recall that the notion of the deterrent was popular, in the form of the school cane as well as the bomb.

I left education largely in ignorance of science, but I acknowledge now that the excitement of the facts of physics, biology, mathematics, were begun on those westward journeys with my father when, between the stories, he taught me about electricity, how radio worked, how he sent messages in morse code during his years at sea as a wireless engineer, where the weather came from, what stars were. An interest in natural phenomena and the living world arises directly from our night watches for otter or badger, listening for curlew, or spotting a kingfisher, hunting for a rabbit or a trout to supplement wartime rations. New nature poems are scientific rather than lyrical, concerned but not romantic. They aim to match the precision of metaphor and word-patterns to the clarity of the fact. They relish the patterning of things, the connections between the worlds of nature and ideas. They are hard at work redeeming the new jargon and making use of every fresh discovery in search of an imagery to match the times we live in. As Eavan Boland writes in 'The Journey', 'odes on/ the flower of the raw sloe for fever' are all very well, but we must make poems to antibiotics too, lest 'every day the language gets less/ for the task and we are less with the language' (Boland 1987, 39). R. S. Thomas, more than any poet in the English language in Britain, has consistently written of science and the new nature, warning of the calamity the earth faced long before it was fashionable to do so. 'Over the creeds/ And masterpieces', he has said, 'our wheels go' (Thomas 1972, 7). Pauline Stainer and Helen Dunmore in England, Christine Evans, Jean Earle and the American Anne Stevenson in Wales, are among many women poets who have used the themes and imagery of science.

We need Bendigeidfran too. He embodies the strangeness within natural phenomena and provides us with the myth we need to explain it all to ourselves. Giants 'are the metaphors that shift the world':

> Tonight, as Concorde folds her tern-wings back
> to take the Atlantic,
> I hear a giant foot stamp twice.
> You can still see the mark he made,
> a black space in the stars.

> (Clarke 1993, 9)

References

Boland, Eavan (1987). *The Journey and other poems* (Manchester, Carcanet).
Clarke, Gillian (1979). *The Sundial* (Llandysul, Gomer).
—— (1982). *Letter from a far country* (Manchester, Carcanet).
—— (1989). *Letting in the Rumour* (Manchester, Carcanet).
—— (1993), *The King of Britain's Daughter* (Manchester, Carcanet).
Thomas, R.S. (1972). *H'm* (London, Macmillan).

20

Welsh lesbian feminist: a contradiction in terms?

RONI CRWYDREN

Wales is my home. I was born, and have spent most of my life, in one small area about which I feel deeply and passionately. I feel comfortable and at home in its woods, on its hills, moors and cliffs. Coming, however, from an 'alternative' background before this was fashionable, and from a family of English-speaking outsiders in what was still a very Welsh area, I have not, in the past, been accustomed to feeling at home amongst Welsh people to the same extent.

Being an outsider was, therefore, such a natural part of me that choosing to become a lesbian did not mean risking rejection from society, friends, colleagues and acquaintances, or leaving my home area, as it does for so many lesbians. On the contrary, for the first time in my life I felt I'd found a people with whom I belonged. For me, feminism and becoming a dyke came hand in hand and introduced me to a world that made sense. This came about through a woman, who had been involved for years with feminist and lesbian issues, befriending me and introducing me to her world. Through her network of friends and acquaintances I learnt the value of loving and supportive friendship, both personally and through learning about the lives of different women. We spent hours discussing almost every issue imaginable, and I read much of her fascinating and wide-ranging library of feminist and lesbian books. I heard of, and read about, so many brave and strong women throughout the ages and cultures; my joy at finding them was diminished only by my sorrow at how hidden from others this wealth of her-story remained. I read stories and analyses written by and for women from different countries and cultures all over the

world – about their own lives and about the different manifestations of patriarchy. I learned something of the mechanisms by
which patriarchy oppresses us, suppresses our knowledge, and dis-
torts the few facts it allows to filter through for its own purposes.
Many things that had confused me started to become clearer, and
this in turn allowed me to feel somewhat stronger in myself, and to
start to ask more questions.

One of the threads I followed in my thinking was that of the
parallels which, it seemed, could be drawn between men's colonization of women's bodies, labour and knowledge, and European
colonization of other lands and peoples: just as women have something fundamentally important of their own to contribute, so do
these colonised people.

'Think global; act local.' Where did Wales and Welsh – people,
culture, language – figure in all this: oppressors or oppressed? And
where did I fit in with the picture? It was no problem for me to see
the patriarchal nature of society around me, the sexism and heterosexism, and I wanted to live my life according to my new-found
feminist beliefs and principles. I knew, however, that I came from a
middle-class, English and Anglicized Welsh background, from
which I was not automatically freed by becoming a feminist. I
needed to put my personal experience into a wider political framework. At the time, I felt it was easy for me, as a woman, to
appreciate what it was to be the victim of patriarchal oppression,
but not so easy to find out what part I was or could be playing as
perpetrator of English colonial oppression in Wales. In wishing to
play my part in changing society, I wanted to be sure I knew my
immediate society as it actually was, and was not inaccurately
interpreting it from the standpoint of a different culture.

It felt crucial, therefore, for me to learn to speak and read
Welsh, for both political and personal reasons (I believe that the
two cannot be separated). I felt anger at an education system that
had taught me Welsh from the age of four-and-a-half to sixteen (I
even have a Welsh 'O' Level), while not giving me the ability to
speak it, or any knowledge of its cultural or historical contexts,
dialects, literature – nothing. As a teenager I'd also received the
impression from the *Cymry Cymraeg* (that is, the Welsh-speakers)
around me that they did not want me to speak the language, both
because it was one of the few aspects of Welsh life relatively uncol-
onized and because, since I was learning a different, academic

Welsh, I might think theirs was inferior, for they had had it impressed on them by their schooling that their speech was not 'proper' Welsh. I have since learnt, as an adult, from other *Cymry Cymraeg* that it is important for everyone/anyone who lives in Wales to learn the language (though I've still not resolved the dilemma of which language to speak when *Cymry Cymraeg* choose to address me in English.)

It was through learning Welsh again that I learned how much of a stranger I was to most aspects of Welsh life, and how totally separate were the different worlds in that one small area in which I lived. The lesbians I knew were all incomers: they formed one group, one world, in which I could be at home. I was also accepted somewhere on the edge of the 'alternative' world, composed almost entirely of incomers or first-generation locals like me, but as, on the whole, this world seemed ignorant of, and uninterested in, both feminist and Welsh issues, we soon parted company.

I found it very difficult to integrate Welsh with my life, or to fit my life into a Welsh context or environment. As my feminist learning had been handed to me on a plate, without my having to search for it (though I had searched in all sorts of places before I found feminism), and as I had no strong attachments to my previous way of life but had readily left it behind, I had no prior experience of the struggle to integrate being a feminist lesbian with an another already existing lifestyle. Following previous experience, I looked for a friend who could lead me into all aspects of Welsh life and issues, and offer feminist interpretations – but I had no Welsh feminist friends. My learning of Welsh was considerably hampered by this lack: I was not able to discuss in Welsh with anyone the issues about which I felt strongly, and, therefore, was not building up any sort of Welsh context that felt relevant. I remember that this revealed itself in my vocabulary, and in my confusions and conflicts about issues such as the sexism inherent in the language. It took me ages to discover the words for 'lesbian' and 'feminist': there was no word for 'lesbian' in my Welsh dictionary (*Y Geiriadur Mawr*), and I guessed that the term for feminist was not one in daily use. I couldn't even decide which word to use for 'woman': should it be *merch* which also means 'girl' and 'daughter'; or *gwraig* which also means 'wife'; or *dynes* which has no plural; or *menyw* which is not used in north Wales? I was accustomed to having control over my use of words, choosing them with a certain amount of care, avoiding words or phrases with sexist, racist or other derogatory connotations, and being aware of how the language of an individual or society reflects and perpetuates its prejudices. I wished to learn as much as possible from the language itself – grammar, roots of words, original meanings and how they had changed, nuances and double-meanings. I wanted to know why it had been so necessary for the English and the Anglicized Welsh to suppress the Welsh language so consistently over hundreds of years. Was there a parallel between the oppression of lesbians and the oppression of the Welsh through language? To what degree is one weakened if such an integral part of one's life and identity is devalued or not acknowledged? And what happens when you feel that two separate yet equally integral parts of yourself are simultaneously being oppressed – and when the oppressors of the one part include groups you identify with by virtue of the other? I had hoped, had expected even, that these questions I was asking from my starting point would be matched by corresponding questioning coming from a Welsh perspective, and had looked forward to exploring these issues further.

It felt essential that I should explore these issues through the Welsh language itself. Through feminism, I had learnt that differences in cultural context, and in one's sense of one's audience, make for fundamentally different perspectives: that a woman writing for other women, for example, will have a very different viewpoint from that which she would have had were she writing with a male audience in mind. So not only did I feel it vital to learn about Welsh issues from a Welsh perspective, but also, in order to get to the 'true' essence, I felt I had to do this learning in Welsh. I feel now, however, that this perspective does not adequately take into account the experiences of the *Cymry Di-Gymraeg*, the non-Welsh-speaking Welsh.

With high expectations and hopes, a Welsh that was totally inadequate for making discerning judgements, and no friend on whose experience I could rely, I was tying myself up in knots and had to find a compromise. Rather than question a society which I did not yet feel sufficiently part of to have a right to interrogate, I questioned myself. Was I experiencing problems because I was only able to look from my own Anglicized perspective, so that the feminism could be there under my nose but I would be unable to see it, since I only recognized it in one particular shape or form?

Self-doubt came easily: if I was not part of the society could it not be because of my own inflexibility, exclusiveness and intolerance? Whilst I recognized that there were some compromises too large to be made (a neighbouring farmer had told me, quite accurately, that the best way to learn Welsh was to marry a local boy) I was aware that my life situation – a single woman relating to other single women, both lesbian and heterosexual – was not conducive to integration within the community as a whole.

I started living a double life. For the most part, my relating was in English, in intense and caring friendships. But when I was on my own, I thought in Welsh (which, given my deficient knowledge of the language, kept my analytical ability at an extremely low level), and listened to Radio Cymru. Occasionally I would be immersed in a Welsh environment, the Eisteddfod, for example, or Gwyl Werin y Cnapan (a Welsh Celtic folk festival). On such occasions, a part of me that I'd never known was in me, and that was starving, was fed by that culture which had always been a part of my life yet to which I'd never felt that I belonged. I was deeply moved to be greeted in Welsh, to be made to feel at home amongst the people as well as the landscape, rather than feeling an outsider and colonizer. That it was almost invariably men who spoke to me was a fact not lost on me, but I did little more than note it and store it away. Then I would go home, straight back into an English-speaking environment, feeling sad and guilty about dropping out of that atmosphere, yet also relieved, reaffirmed and joyful to be back again amongst friends who shared the values that made my life, including the Welsh part of it, meaningful. A vicious circle was created, which impoverished my Welsh, for it wasn't being practised and stretched in any meaningful way. When I did find an opportunity to use it, my self-confidence in my language and opinions would decrease at an accelerating rate throughout the conversation. My guilt would increase in proportion, since I felt my inadequacy was all my own fault, because I kept returning to my English environment. I felt that I could not keep on subjecting people to my halting, inaccurate, badly-accented Welsh if I was not 'truly', that is, completely, serious in my commitment. But, within Welsh culture, my needs as a woman-identified woman frequently did not seem to be recognized, let alone met. Or, when they were recognized, the response was negative, for they were deemed to be divisive in the face of more important issues concerning the future of Wales and its language.

It was therefore a very exciting day for me when I heard that, for the first time, a Welsh-language lesbian and gay group was being formed: CYLCH (Cymdeithas y Lesbiaid a Hoywon Cymraeg eu Hiaith), based at Aberystwyth (P. O. Box 23), had been established. At last I would have the opportunity and the environment to combine my lesbian and Welsh identities, to begin to explore the issues specifically related to being lesbian or gay in Wales. As a learner, I felt also that it would be an opportunity to learn words and concepts in Welsh which were already familiar to me in English as a lesbian feminist. There was talk within the group of building a 'network of connections', of being a 'minority within a minority', and acknowledgement that lesbians are further oppressed by sexism. Although I had previously not seen much in common between lesbians and gay men, I was now prepared to put aside my doubts, both for selfish reasons, as I needed something from this group, and also because there seemed to be awareness of many relevant issues, including sexism.

Since its beginnings, the group has largely concentrated on outward-looking public actions, aiming to bring about changes in Welsh society through challenging its homophobia and heterosexism. I myself have wished for more emphasis on building up a network of connections between what must frequently be very isolated gay and lesbian Welsh people, scattered throughout a largely rural land. Also, I've wanted us to spend more time discussing the similarities and differences which exist within the group, differences between lesbians and gays, for example, or between those who are *Cymry Cymraeg* and those of us who've learnt Welsh as a second language. I wanted an atmosphere in which we could grow and feel strong, and feel integrated within the Welsh community as lesbians and gays; this, I felt, would encourage more people to join us, and find themselves strengthened and nurtured by being part of a cultural group which was affirming its ties with its society, rather than feeling isolated within it, or rejected by it. This seemed to me so very necessary because I knew how vital it had been for me, in becoming a dyke, to have other dykes around me, and to know of so many more through the support systems which do exist in English-language culture, both in the form of positive representations of lesbian lives and of women's networks (like, for example, the group Border Women/Merched y Ffin, based at Ludlow, P.O. Box 42). But by now, through the recent establishment of our newsletter, this possibility is becoming a reality for the group; communication and participation in the group's activities can now take place even when it is difficult for people to meet up with one another face to face. This is, of course, especially important for the many who cannot afford to attend distant meetings, or may be unable to do so because of family commitments, or, indeed, because they are not 'out', or are 'out' only in a very selective context, a state of affairs still vital to the survival of many.

There have always been far more men than women involved in the group, perhaps for some of the above reasons, or perhaps because lesbians do not want to join a mixed group; more men have expressed an interest whereas lesbian involvement has declined. This makes me reconsider the question of how much we do have in common. Do we have shareable aims, or will lesbians once again find themselves helping gay men in their fight against homophobia, while gay men do not reciprocate by joining in the struggle against the fundamentals of patriarchy and sexism, in order to enable a change to come about in the situation of lesbians? Whereas gay men serve as useful scapegoats in patriarchal society, and as examples of the ostracism which occurs if men do not conform to prescribed role models, lesbians pose a threat of a totally different magnitude and nature, as the entire structure and fundamental basis of patriarchy is challenged by our very existence.

The more isolated and hidden we are as lesbians, from society and from one another, the less we can effect change, and the less we can support each other and affirm our reality: this I feel to be still, by and large, the situation in Wales today. The difficulties involved in integrating different aspects of our lives with our lesbianism, and in gaining recognition and validity, contribute to this isolation.

21

The highest honour

ELIZABETH J. MUIR

I have been told that if the construction of a bumble bee is analysed in the context of the environment in which it operates, it becomes apparent that, according to the laws of aerodynamics, it is impossible for the bee to fly. It seems, however, that no one has yet informed the bee of this, and so it continues to fly, in happy oblivion of the fact that it is breaking all the rules.

When I look back upon my career as a business woman in Wales, I see my 'flights' also as having been undertaken in a condition of blissful, and necessary, ignorance similar to that of the bumble bee. Would I have taken the steps I did had I been fully aware beforehand of the unwritten rules which govern business success, I wonder? Only gradually did I become aware of the factors – so apparently superficial and yet so vital – by which influence is acquired: the complex assumptions as to the appropriate appearance, weight distribution, educational standing, perceived technical competence, necessary for success. The values by which women are judged within this sphere have evolved within a culture which is recognizably masculine in ethos. Notions of the parts women can play, and the contributions it is deemed suitable for us to make, have been constructed by men. The male is the norm: the female is abnormal. Foreign. Other. A perpetual guest, there on sufferance. A breaker of the unspoken rules.

Walking down a street one sunny day, the well-known chairman of a public authority in Wales was chatting to me. We were reflecting on the fact that for the past two years I had been the only woman member on the board of that authority. He was greeted by a business acquaintance, who cast a dismissive glance, covered by a superficial smile, in my direction, and said to the chairman: 'I see you've got a nice new little secretary!' It would take some imagination to describe me as petite: on this occasion I was a good head taller than my companion. But the words were not of course intended as a straightforward compliment to me: rather they constituted an attempt to construct the situation according to conventional gender role stereotypes. I was stung by the notion that as a woman, obviously about to attend a business meeting with a man of some influence, my only perceived role had to be that of his secretary. Before I could protest, however, the chairman himself set the record straight, and told his acquaintance, 'You are behind the times. Let me introduce you to my colleague and fellow board member . . .' But no male member of the board would ever have been so misidentified in the first place: no man in the same situation would have been subjected to an assumption so potentially undermining of his confidence and authority.

Similar deeply ingrained assumptions as to the limitations of the feminine role operate on many different levels within the business world, and a woman has to be perpetually vigilant to guard herself against them. All too often, men appear to believe that they hold sole right of access to certain fields of knowledge. Science, engineering and technology are still areas in which few women have as yet been recognized as authorities. Much of my work involves products and services that are within these fields. I have had to listen carefully to the nuances of men's voices when they ask such apparently innocuous questions as, for example, 'I don't know whether you know anything about thermal efficiency?', in order to discern whether the query is a genuine attempt to determine my personal knowledge of the subject or whether it is a disguised put-down, the questioner having already assumed that I, as a woman, must be ignorant of such technicalities. In responding to such a question, I have to make a quick decision as to whether the most appropriate strategy would be simply to say enough to convey confidence in the level of my expertise in the area, or whether unspoken assumptions also need to be challenged and my gender recognized as an irrelevance in this context. The topic of such an exchange is as likely to be computers, mathematics, or diagnostics as thermal dynamics: the subject is irrelevant except in so far as it lies within an area of knowledge stereotypically designated as 'male'.

The memory is still with me of one encounter with the senior executive of a Welsh engineering company. My objective for the meeting was to introduce myself and induce sufficient confidence in my clients' work to initiate further meetings between their engineers and those of the company I was visiting. The appointment had been made by telephone, and, as business courtesy requires, confirmed by letter. For many years now I have adopted the practice of always including my first name in full in correspondence, and putting 'Miss' in brackets after my name, so as to ensure that there can be no confusion as to my gender. On this occasion I was kept waiting for some ten minutes before eventually being admitted into the executive's inner sanctum. His huge office, with its massive and ornately carved desk, its draped brocade curtains, luxurious pile carpets, and overpowering odour of expensive cigars, was clearly designed to convey an intimidating impression of the man's stature and power. Behind the desk, a diminutive figure, dwarfed by his surroundings, was busy with a pipe and pipe cleaner. I stared in some amazement, and growing bad humour, as it dawned on me what activity had preoccupied him to such an extent that I had been kept waiting until well after the agreed meeting time. At last he looked up, his jaw dropped, and he exclaimed: 'But you're a woman!' Had this man reached his position of power by dint of accurate observation? Or was he simply using some textbook technique which says that in the art of negotiating one should start by putting forward notions on which both parties can agree? Or was he momentarily so shocked out of his blinkered assumptions that he spoke those inane words before he could stop himself?

How many more times must the business world be shocked out of its blind sexism before it is ready to afford women genuinely equal opportunities with men? I have worked hard, and for the most part enjoyed my career. Motivated by the desire both to take control of my own life and to contribute usefully to my society, I have succeeded in starting my own business, and been privileged to have been appointed as a non-executive member to a number of public and private bodies; by now I have gained a broad experience of work in Wales. But the sense of perpetually fighting against a tide of unspoken prejudice still persists. Often I find myself in the position of being the 'token' woman, the sole female member of a company's board. Being in such a position requires the expenditure of an incredible amount of energy, for we are forever working across cultural boundaries. A man takes his place on such a board knowing that he has been selected above others in the running, that he has achieved a success within his own competitive world. A woman's place may also be hers by right, but her position is still perceived as a different one: she has been specially invited into a world not her own, into a male world. She may be very visible around the board table by virtue of her difference, but she still has to be heard. The female pitch of voice may gain attention because of its singularity, but the fact that she is speaking does not necessarily mean that she is heard, that her words are accredited weight and significance. Males and females alike have to learn the rules of engagement in board room discussion or management meetings, but the style of such engagements is predominantly masculine. The woman has to learn another language and another culture as surely as if she were in a foreign land. She has to decide whether or not to take on a cloak of masculinity and adopt the dominant style, knowing that by doing so she is risking being seen as aggressive, or domineering, or simply as acting a part. For the same characteristics are perceived differently in a woman than in a man, and judged by differing notions of acceptability. Should she decide to resist the pressure to conform with the masculine style, and respond, rather, in accordance with more female values, then she risks losing credibility; her standards are not necessarily valid within the male culture. Or she is called upon to speak on behalf of all women, simply because she is the only representative of her sex in the room: 'As a woman, what do you think?'

And yet she too is in the process of being judged and assessed on her individual performance as relentlessly as are her male colleagues. Her future also lies in her personal reputation: she too is only as good as her last project. Credibility and track record are as important to her as they are to her male competitors; during every new business encounter, and on each separate board, she has to make herself acknowledged as a force to be reckoned with before her contribution is accorded weight. Being framed 'as a woman' will always handicap her in this struggle, for she has to operate within a context in which the recognized voice of power is that of men. Do not think that I intend deliberately to denigrate men as individuals, for I am well aware that they are as much a product of social construction as women. But as members of the dominant culture, they do not have the same motivation as the 'second sex'

to understand, and work to undermine, the inequalities of the hierarchical gender system. It is in their interest simply to retain the
status quo. Rarely, in my experience, do men overtly subjugate
women in the context of a board meeting, yet even before a woman
enters the room, certain processes will have been set in train which
will serve to distinguish her from the rest of the group. A woman
can safely be relegated to the status of 'Otherness' merely by the
way in which the seating arrangements around a board table are
designated. Within the formal structures of British institutional
boards, members are still referred to by their titles and surnames
rather than their first names. Men's name cards, however, will generally identify members by their initials and surnames alone,
though the name may occasionally be preceded by a special title
highlighting status or other office – a 'Sir', perhaps, or a 'Cllr'. The
assumption is clear: there is no need to use the usual title 'Mr', for
of course all these names refer to men: who else but a 'Mr' is likely
to be a board member? But in the event of a breakthrough, when
the board actually acquires a female member, her anomalous
status cannot be allowed to go unmarked. She has to be labelled as
other than the norm; her name-card must serve to highlight her
gender difference, and also to mark her marital status, or record
her resistance to being labelled according to that status: invariably,
in my experience, her card records her as a 'Mrs', 'Miss', or 'Ms'.
Furthermore, the polite chairman's typical opening address –
'Lady and gentlemen', with subtle emphasis on the first word –
also sets the scene, and serves to draw attention to the 'Otherness'
of the 'token woman'.

Thus framed from the outset as a woman, a thing apart, the
female board member finds attributed to her the general characteristics of her sex, as they are stereotypically perceived, whether or
not they be relevant to her as an individual. For all the 'Miss' on
my name-card, I am generally expected to know all about such
womanly experiences as raising a family, and frequently have to
spell out the fact that as a single person, without children and
working full-time, I cannot speak for mothers. It should be
obvious that, when it comes to family matters, the life experiences
of any fathers on the board are likely to be of more relevance than
mine. But male experience within the home is not acknowledged
in business decision-making processes, as if it would demean

businessmen to associate them in their public working capacity with their private domestic roles.

Within such a context it is impossible for a woman to relax, for even when she holds the floor and believes, in herself, that she is making a valid point or a relevant contribution, all too often her voice will be ignored. I'm still smarting from the memory of my second meeting with one Welsh health authority in which I was thrice disadvantaged: I was outside the norm not only as a woman but also as a non-medic and the youngest by some years. A topic on the agenda held particular interest for me, and I listened carefully to the comments made upon it by various speakers around the table. Gaining the chairman's eye, I claimed my right to speak. Summing up the previous views, I added to them my own prepared contribution, concluded with a proposal for follow-up action, and sat back, anticipating at least some questions and further discussion of my suggestions. To my horror, the chairman smiled at me, then looked down at his papers as he said, 'Well, thank you for that contribution. Now we'll move on to the next item on the agenda.' I felt invisible. It was as though I did not exist – had not been heard. The chairman was already introducing the next topic, but self-respect, and an instinct for survival, forced me to interrupt him, though I had to concentrate on keeping my voice even. It would never do to betray emotion at such a juncture: to do so would be to be heard as typically female, prone to over-reaction, if not hysteria. 'Excuse me, Mr Chairman', I said – supplicating words of subordination! I immediately corrected my style of presentation and increased the volume of my voice: 'Do I take that to mean that everyone is in agreement? Are we going to take such action? Is that what we will make public?' By thus changing my emphasis, from the presentation of the proposal as an individual's suggestion and framing it, rather, as one with which *we* as an organization should be concerned, and by using enveloping hand gestures in my body language to draw in other board members, I managed to get them involved in what I was saying. My proposals were then discussed.

Like an actress, a woman in business life must use different voices for the various parts she has to play. And when in role she must also learn to hear others differently, and be alert to catch the least nuance of tone which betrays an intention, be it conscious or perhaps unconscious, to place her in a subordinate position. Apparently insignificant incidents can have an insidious effect upon the way in which she will be perceived. I have learnt, for example, that when refreshment is brought in to meetings, and a male colleague says 'Coffee?' in a certain tone whilst cocking his eye in my direction, he may well be implying 'Why aren't you, as a woman, pouring the coffee?' My response is an enthusiastic 'Oh yes, please. Black, no sugar.' I refuse to be subtly pressurized into accepting a predetermined feminine role, knowing that my resistance represents a stand, on however minute a scale, not only for my own self-respect but for that of women generally, and in particular for other women struggling to make their way up the business ladder. There can be no room for complacency: a woman must be ever vigilant. Only recently I attended a board meeting of an organization with which I have been involved for many years, and in which I am confident of having a valid voice, despite being still the only woman on the board. While presenting a section of the business plan, the chief executive described in most revealing terms the way in which he desired the organization to be viewed by certain sectors of the business community: 'We wish,' he said, 'to be seen as the bride and not the shark.' His male colleagues nodded in agreement and acquiescence. For all their nominal support for gender equality, these men's basic assumptions with regard to women and marriage, and their acceptance of the polarization of sex roles, were exposed in this one sentence. Needless to say, I did not let it pass without comment, and argued successfully to have the wording changed.

Otherness. Invisibility. For how long must women still have to work twice as hard in order to be considered half as good as their male colleagues? It is not that we are different so much as that we are judged by a different set of values. The business culture is decidedly masculine, and women are expected to aspire complicitly to standards set according to male norms. Consequently, even when we make it, the accolade of success can be a bitter pill. I truly believe that the following words were uttered without animosity, and were genuinely intended as a compliment: 'You are the only woman in our midst, but that makes no difference. The highest honour we can bestow upon you is to say that you are one of us. One of the boys.'

INDEX

abortion 210

accounts, as task of farm women 127–8

Acker, S., on gender and career plans 143

Afshar, H., on nationalism and reproduction 253

ageing
  gender differences in 61–2, 83; and loneliness 62; *see also* elderly people

agriculture
  cuts in farm income support 136; diversification of economic activities 124, 137; labour of farm women 127–30; recognition of wife's contribution 128; *see also* farm women

'alternative' lifestyles 233, 296, 299

Anglican Church 11, 268
  attitudes to Nonconformity 186; role of deacons 269–70; and women priests 11, 269–70

Arber, S. and Ginn, J., on division of domestic labour 44

Arnot, M., on equal opportunities in school 167

artists
  and colonization 275–6; difficulties of in Wales 11–12, 275–6; future for in Wales 278–9

Asen Adda (ed. Ruth Stephens) 194

Attfield, J. and Kirkham, P., on women as patrons 231

Atwood, Margaret, *Survival* 275–6, 277

Bangor Women's Aid 51–2, 54

banking industry 99, 101

Barrett, M., on exclusion of women from heavy industry 48

Beagan, Glenda, 'Scream, Scream' 196–7

Beddoe, D.
  on female identity rooted in

domesticity 31; on representation of Welsh women 1

Bendigeidfran (giant) 287, 289, 290, 292

Beneria, L., on concepts of work 123, 128

Berger, John, on writing and questioning 284

Betts, C., on Welsh language 253

Bidgood, Ruth 196

birth-rates 20

black community in Wales 4, 26

Boland, Eavan, 'The Journey' 292

Border Women/Merched y Ffin (support group) 300

Bott, E., on segregation of labour 31

Bouquet, M., on women in agriculture 123

Bourdieu, Pierre, on material culture 229

Bradley, H., on women in agriculture 123

Brannen, J. and Moss, P., on division of domestic labour 32, 44, 45

Breakwell, G., on women in top management 104

Brennan, T., Cooney, E. and Pollins, H., on segregation of labour 31

Brigley, Jude (ed.), *Exchanges* 194

Bristow, Alice 144
  on further education teaching 144, 148, 149, 153, 154, 155–6, 157, 158

British Social Attitudes Survey 45

Buck, L. and Dodd, P., on financial value 238

Buhler, on goal-setting and change 118

'bundling' 185–6, 235

Bush, D. M. and Simmons, R. G., on attitudes to motherhood 111

business
  and male norms 307; non-recognition of women 7; role of 'token' woman in 303–4; status of women in in Wales 13, 301–7; women on company boards 304–7;